Author's N

The first part of my book shows a tiny fragment of what life was like for my father during his childhood, and his subsequent life in the British Army. It was the Victorian/Edwardian era and in the 1860's and into the early 1900's labourers received the sum of three shillings and nine pence a week with no stipulation as to how many hours were to be worked daily!

Assuming they did a 51-week year, (no paid holidays then) that makes it the princely sum of £9.11s.3d per year!

squirrels in the jaffrey

Memories of a childhood
spent in India
during the Raj years

A Fisher Publication

Fisher Publications
fisher.publications@tiscali.co.uk

A catalogue record for this book is available from the British Library.

ISBN 978-0-9555576-0-6

Artwork and typesetting by
Impact Design & Print
St Leonards on Sea
12-14 Wainwright Close
East Sussex TN38 9PP
Tel: 01424 855558
sales@impact-ltd.com

Printed and bound by CPI Antony Rowe, Eastbourne.

ACKNOWLEDGEMENTS

'Squirrels in the Jaffrey' was written for my children and grandchildren. To give them a peek into the past where there were no televisions, computers, Game-boys or iPods, and children had to make up their own games sometimes.

Many thanks to the 'Cosmos' for the help I received when the words just wouldn't flow. Everyone should try it. It really does work.

Thanks to tutelage from my son John, I too know how to use a computer, without which this book might never have been written. Although I often think he wishes he'd never got me started, especially when I interrupt his evenings with my many queries and pleas for help.

Special thanks go to my husband Bill for encouraging me to continue when I had all but given up. Then, with the help of my daughter Melanie (who, it must be said, found most of the mistakes) also proof-read the book.

Thanks to my daughters Joy and Melanie for encouraging me to put down on paper the many stories I told them about my life in India. Again, without their continued efforts to keep me 'at it' I might have given it up as a bad job.

Thanks go to my sister Hazel for some help in 'remembering' events that happened so long ago.

Thanks to my granddaughter Sarah for her original cover design, and to Kevin for all his help with the PDF. Simon for all his sterling work and Stacey for being so patient and helpful.

Last but not least, all the people who encouraged me along the way.

My parents Teresa and Arthur Fisher.

Map of India showing Ajmer.

CHAPTER ONE

1931 - Little Monkey

It is believed by some that an infant chooses his or her parents before conception. The spirit part that is, I think the DNA, genes and other stuff kick in later, as in the nine month period of feasting and fasting, and believe me, I know all about fasting! It's bad enough having water dropped on you from a great height... but red hot curries! One minute you're lying there all warm and snug, and the next, this weight of stuff comes plummeting down all over you. You taste a bit - your mouth puckers up... it's on fire!

Then where's the water when you really need it?

But you don't want me bothering you with small details of my life before life, do you?

It's a well known fact that if you are choosing somewhere to live, it has to be location, location, location. And I was looking for a nice, warm, exotic, location. You know... balmy breezes... that sort of thing. So the parents I chose just happened to live in Ajmer in the state of Rajputana, India, now called Rajasthan.

Ajmer was founded by one Ajaipal Chauhan, sometime during the seventh century. The Chauhan Dynasty ruled until around 1193 A.D. Later on it was ruled by Shah Jahan, remember him? He was one of the Mugal Emperors - he of The Peacock Throne - who had the Taj Mahal built in memory of his beloved wife Mumtaz Mahal.

How cool was that?

Anyway, if it was good enough for all those Mugals, Maharajas and Princes in the past, it would suit me just fine.

Rajputana is also one of the largest states in India, its capital, Jaipur, being known as the 'Pink City' because of its beautiful pink painted buildings; these having been painted pink on the orders of Maharaja Man Singh II, in honour of the visit from the Prince of Wales, Edward VII in 1876. Jairpur is just a short drive from Ajmer, and has many beautiful palaces and temples, like the beautiful Hawa Mahal, or 'Palace of the Winds'.

The temple at Galta - one of many situated another short ride away from Jaipur - is dedicated to 'Surya' the Sun God. Built on one

1

of the highest peaks overlooking Jaipur, it can only be reached by foot or by rickshaw. The beautiful buildings themselves are reward enough after your long journey, but then you have the added attraction of large numbers of red-faced monkeys - who can be seen roaming around the ancient buildings.

The Jantar Mantar is one of five observatories built by Sawai Jai Singh II, the leading astronomer of his time and a contemporary of the emperor Aurangzeb. The Jantar Mantar is one of the best preserved observatories - completed in 1734 - and constructed mainly of masonry. The instruments continue to provide accurate information today.

The Rathambhor National Park, where tigers roam freely, is situated in eastern Rajasthan.

The Aravalli Range of hills runs through the state for about three hundred and fifty miles, from the southwest to the southeast of the region. Most of the hills are between one thousand and three thousand feet high and six to sixty miles wide, passing right through Ajmer.

Some hills!

From Taragarh Fort, high up on in the Aravallies, a panoramic view of Ajmer can be seen. The land filled with deep gorges and nullahs (watercourses) where monsoon rains sweeping down from these hills had carved a path through the sandy soil hundreds of years ago.

The fort stood like some sentinel high above, watching over everything in the valley below; surrounded by thick stone walls, with six massive gates, the main gate surmounted with some wonderfully carved stone elephants. It was built by the Mugals as a site for military activities and turned into a hospital and sanatorium by the British Army during their occupation of India.

The Thar Desert lies towards the west of the region. Sandstorms and high winds carry sand from the desert across the land for miles, to reach Ajmer and beyond, covering everything in a fine dusting of red sand which gets absolutely everywhere!

When we lived in Ajmer, we could see the red dust clouds coming, blotting out the sun as the sand was borne high in the sky and no matter how careful we were to cover and protect our possessions, the sand got into everything, so for days afterwards we could see it and taste it too.

Delhi and the Punjab lie to the north of Ajmer, Haryana in the northeast, Madhya Pradesh to the southeast, and Gujarat to the south. Ajmer has many beautiful places of interest, like the Tomb of the Sufi Saint, Khwaja Moinuddin Chisti. He was a Sufi Saint of the 'Chistiyya' order said to be a direct descendant of the Prophet Muhammad. After his death a beautiful Dargah (shrine) was built over his grave; and every year hundreds of thousands of Muslims, Hindus and others flock from the sub-continent and assemble at his tomb on the occasion of his 'Urs' (death anniversary).

Kishangarh Fort is famous for its wonderful eighteenth century miniature paintings, and Akbar's Palace - constructed in 1570 A.D. - for Emperor Akbar, was built to serve as a home for the Emperor during his visits to Ajmer. The Palace was used by the British during their occupation in India as a munitions house, and the Britishers nicknamed it the 'Rajputana arsenal'.

Pushkar, another place of immense interest, lies just eleven kilometres from Ajmer, and according to Hindu mythology, the town is a creation to Lord Brahma. Thousands of people flock there to worship, attend the Mela, (fair) and take a dip in the sacred lake.

There are other lakes too, like the man-made Ana Sagar Lake in Ajmer, which was created by damming part of the river Luni. This artificial lake is surrounded by hills, and on its banks there were once lovely parks, full of the most beautiful flower gardens called the 'Daulat Bagh Gardens' where royal ladies of kings and princes once strolled. White marble pavilions of exquisite beauty were built by Shah Jahan at a later date, and these pavilions sit in magnificent splendour, although the gardens are no more, alas! But who knows, perhaps one day someone will restore them to their former glory?

All the surrounding hills are reflected in the deep waters of the lake, a wonderful quiet place for relaxation and meditation, except for high days and holidays of course, when holidaymakers throng there in their thousands.

The large Carriage & Wagon Workshops in Ajmer - one of the biggest employers in the area - stretch for miles. Work setting up the Ajmer workshops was begun in 1877 by the Rajputana-Malwa State Railway, when the refitting of carriages already in use and the making of new ones was carried out. Next to it are the workshops

3

making the massive locomotives.

The people of Rajasthan are a proud and haughty race, gregarious, friendly and happy, respectful of all the different castes, religions and creeds living amongst them; all living together in harmony. The women dress in wonderful colourful costumes of bright reds, golds, and greens, with long, fully-gathered skirts reaching right down to their feet; tight bodices that leave their midriffs bare and brilliantly-coloured saris covering their heads. They carry their wealth about their person; thick silver bangles adorning hands, arms, heads and ankles, with even more jewellery worn around their necks and ears. Rajasthani men are content to let their wives dress up, while they wear a comfortable white cotton dhoti (loin-cloth) and shirt; their only concession to fashion being a large turban of red, saffron or white. But they can look equally elegant in their best clothes; a long embroidered tunic-coat/shirt, buttoned down the front and worn with pantaloons.

Many festivals and holy days are celebrated in Rajasthan, with Hindus, Muslims, Christians and dozens of other ethnic groups joining in; all celebrating as one; the air alive with the sounds of flutes, tambourines, drums and songs.

In February and March, Holi is celebrated; an exuberant Hindu festival marking the end of winter. People throw coloured water or gulal, a coloured powder, over one another. White clothes are worn especially for the occasion and these become more and more multi-coloured as the day wears on. It is believed the more colours one receives; the luckier one will be for the rest of the year.

In March and April Hindu temples all over India celebrate the birth of Rama and more 'special days' throughout the year are also celebrated, with sisters tying Rakhis (wristbands) onto their brothers right wrists for good luck and as protection against evil.

Ganesh the 'Elephant God' of wisdom and prosperity is worshipped too. Fireworks explode at all hours. Families buy clay images of the many-armed elephant which are kept in the homes to be worshipped before being taken ceremoniously down to a river, lake, sea or water tank into which they are immersed.

On the anniversary of the birth of Krishna - a national holiday in August/September - devotees fast all day until midnight. On this auspicious day, high caste Hindus replace the 'sacred' thread which they always wear looped over their left shoulder. All these colourful holidays and holy days culminate in the biggest celebration of all: Dussehra, the celebration of good over evil.

Men dressed in splendid costumes re-enact the fights of a bygone era. Dancing and prancing about as they circle the huge arena, sword in hand, to the delight of the hundreds of onlookers. Great swordfights and other tomfoolery abounds. Evil is eliminated, as with a fanfare of trumpets, the giant effigies - images of the demon king Ravana and his accomplices - are set alight. Fireworks, packed around the bodies, exploding with huge bangs, sometimes knocking the head off one of the giant figures, are met with great cheers from the watching crowds.

Then there is Divali, which must be the prettiest and happiest festival of all. This takes place in October and November, and for four or five nights countless oil lamps are lit and placed strategically to show 'Rama' (a very popular god) the way home from his period of exile. Almost every house is lit up with tiny oil lamps. These are small earthenware dishes about three inches round and an inch deep, which are filled with oil; a small cotton wick soaking in the oil rests on one edge, which when lit, burns brightly all evening, being topped up with a little oil when necessary. Every rooftop, step, and available space is lit up with these tiny lamps; the whole place taking on a magical quality.

Each day a different deity is honoured. The Goddess Kali, said to be the Source of Being, Krishna's victory over Narakasura. The friendly demon Bali and the Goddess Lakshmi. Food and sweetmeats are shared and enjoyed by young and old alike. Everyone wears their best clothes, visiting fairs and relations, with bonhomie spreading to all, no matter what their colour or creed.

So you can see why I wanted to be part of all the excitement.

There I was, patting myself on the back, thinking how clever of me to have chosen so wisely, poor misguided sap that I was! Well, how was I to know it got really hot during the summer months there. I was still learning!

The venue was a bungalow, courtesy of the Carriage & Wagon Workshops where my father worked; on a road called 'Five Bungalows Road', I kid you not! Of course, by the time we went to live there, more bungalows had been built on both sides of the road;

seven on each side to be exact. But the name still stuck!

Like most small places, everyone knew everything about everyone else, this was mainly through the servants, and of course the memsahib's (ladies) themselves who, with all their fine houses and many servants, didn't have much to do, except meet up at each others' homes for a good gossip over afternoon tea. The poor khansama (cook) having to interrupt his afternoon siesta to provide wafer-thin sandwiches, fancy cakes, biscuits and endless cups of tea for the gossiping memsahib's. Then he was left squatting behind the door, his head slowly dropping onto his chest as he rested, ready to jump up at the first ring of the bell for yet more tea.

The ayahs (nurse-maids) met up in the cool of the evening with their angrezi (English) charges bathed and dressed in their best clothes so they could be shown off. The ayahs were very loyal to the people they worked for, but it didn't stop them from talking about their employers; sitting in a circle - the better for a face-to-face gossip - on the cool green lawns of the 'Railway Institute' gardens, the children playing nearby.

The Railway Institute was the ultimate meeting place in those days. No ordinary places these 'Institutes', as the name might mistakenly imply, but huge, purpose-built, Victorian buildings that housed several well-stocked bars with drinks imported from 'Blighty' (slang term for England) behind which the Indian barmen - dressed in white with special red or black bands inserted in their turbans - dispensed drinks to the sahib's (masters) and their memsahib's (ladies).

There was a library and two or three lounges, all the rooms furnished to a very high standard with deep leather armchairs, elegant furnishings and polished wood everywhere, looked after by an army of servants.

The Europeans abroad always dressed up to the nines in those days, and in the evening could be seen in the Institute, parading through the various rooms, chatting or drinking in the bars, as they made full use of the facilities. Sometimes, if there wasn't a function on, the women watched their men play snooker at the brightly lit tables; the scores being kept on large wooden scoreboards lining the walls, along with pictures of the British Royal family.

The large ballroom - which doubled as a theatre, cinema and

venue for bridge playing and other occasions - had a polished wooden floor kept smooth by the application of powder. The first couples up on the dance floor slipping and sliding as they took their first steps in the foxtrot or waltz.

More slide than glide!

The band - from their vantage point in the pits - trying to do their best not to laugh at the poor couples, who were just about managing to stay upright on the slippery surface.

Beautifully appointed kitchens supplied food for the special occasions, while even more servants tended to the people enjoying other indoor sports facilities; like badminton, ping-pong, skittles and other games; always playing with the latest equipment.

There were other amenities too, like the ladies and gents toilets, kitchens, offices and store rooms. The administrators took great pains to provide a good service for the smooth running of the establishment, supplying everything that could possibly be required for the enjoyment of the English residents and their guests.

A large building in the grounds was given over to housing the most important items of all, English goods from Blighty, the NAAFI shop. This building and cafeteria must have been stocked with everything the British family abroad could want. Although the Indian shops stocked English goods, these were not always as fresh as the ones from the NAAFI. The intense heat and long periods of monsoon rain tended to wreak havoc with some food-stuffs: chocolate melted or turned white, with all forms of mildew getting through the stoutest containers to contaminate foodstuffs and clothing. The monsoon and its wet weather adding to the deterioration of articles like leather shoes. The NAAFI goods were quite a lot cheaper too.

By November the place would be bursting at the seams with children's toys, decorations, crackers, nuts, crates of drinks, tins of chocolates, biscuits and other delicacies too many to name. There was always a mad scramble by the English residents of Ajmer to get to the NAAFI when the shipment arrived. The store was busy throughout the year, selling everyday things like toothpaste, soap, letter paper and ordinary household items. But no matter how many items were stocked, there was always something that was craved from Blighty! Letters sent home begged for items urgently needed by the poor, hard done by British sahibs and memsahib's forced to live in India.

The buildings were surrounded by lovely gardens and beautifully-manicured lawns which were constantly being sprinkled to maintain their lush green freshness. There were velvet bowling greens, tennis courts and outdoor games areas offering more facilities for the already privileged.

But more about the Railway Institute later. Let me fill you in as to my arrival.

Having made the choice about parents and location, I then chose a fairly cool night, and at exactly eleven minutes to eleven on the eleventh of February, I made my '*Grande Entrance*' into the world as the fourth child of Mary Teresa and Arthur Thomas Fisher, both of whom happened to have been born on the same day, month and year.

My father, whose parents were English, was born in a small hamlet in Hampshire, England and my mother - of Portuguese extraction - was born on the other side of the world, in Pondicherry, Southern India.

Coincidence or fate?

Fate of course played her part to perfection.

Teresa, my mother, was a pretty, petite young woman of just thirty-four at the time of my birth. She had the softest brown eyes and curly brown hair, which she tried to keep tidy in a neat bun from which tiny wisps kept escaping to curl themselves around her face, the colour of caramel. She had a trim figure, and a mind as sharp as a needle.

It was no wonder my father fell head over heels for the pretty young nanny - which she was - when he first set eyes upon her.

She had been looking after twin boys; the children of Lord and Lady Somerville; and was quite an important member of their household, with several servants of her own to help out with washing the boys' clothes, cleaning of rooms etc. A nanny having a rather higher status than any of the other servants in the household.

She had given up the plush lifestyle; holidays in the Nilgiri Hills, and in some of the poshest places abroad, plus a great salary, everything in fact, to marry the man she loved - my father - who was in the British Army when they met. She was now a full-time mum, but without the perks, although she did have servants.

I'm told that every room in the bungalow was lit up on the night I was expected, perhaps to help the stork find its way? This was not so good for the poor moths and other insects who were hurling themselves at the window panes as they tried in vain to gain entry. Or for the poor servants who waited up anxiously, knowing that if the lights were on in the bungalow, they could still be summoned.

Lying in the double bed she normally shared with my father, my poor mother sweated profusely in between labour pains, and vowed this would be the very last time she would put up with the pain and discomfort. The electric fan on the ceiling whirred sluggishly overhead, its overheated engine clicking as the arms moved warm air about the room.

With most people asleep at that hour, the crickets in the shadows outside clicked their legs to give off their unmistakable chirping noises and in the distance jackals howled and hyenas laughed as they went in search of food. Waiting in the adjoining room was my father, chota peg (small measure of spirits) in hand, almost an old hand to the birthing process, this being his fourth time of waiting. He too was thirty-four years of age at the time of my birth; if you're keeping up with the story.

He was a tall chap, who stood nearly six feet in his socks; broad-shouldered, and powerfully built. A handsome man who made the ladie's hearts flutter although he only ever had eyes for his own pretty wife. He still had the ruddy cheeked complexion of his boyhood days, with a pair of the bluest eyes - which is probably why my mother had fallen for him - and a laid back manner that became even more laid back when he'd had a glass or two of the 'hard stuff'.

My parents had three other children: Ernest, a dark-haired, handsome, serious faced boy of seven: Hazel, a brown haired, elfin-faced, petite little girl aged five, who was prone to catching every illness going; and Billy (William) the baby; who had a beautiful face; a disposition to match, and was the youngest, aged three, and my mother's favourite.

Living at the same address, but in the servants' quarters, were a few of the servants: a methar (sweeper) and his family; a khansama (cook) without a family; and our ayah (nursemaid). The line of godowns - brick-built buildings used for storage and as servants quarters - were discreetly hidden behind the fruit trees growing in the back gardens, and consisted of an outside kitchen, and about four or five rooms; all lined up in a row with a long narrow veranda running along the length of them where the servants slept on hot nights.

The remainder of the servants came to work on a daily basis.

In attendance at the birth was Bridget Foley. Bridget was an attractive, big boned Irish lassie of about thirty-eight with an easy manner, a lovely lilting Irish accent, and laughing hazel eyes. She'd come out to India to be married to her soldier fiancé, but by the time her boat docked he'd died of cholera. Bridget was devastated, had cried, squared her shoulders and got on with her life. She'd worked as a midwife in the Railway Hospital for two years, before being sent out for this particular home delivery.

Helping Bridget was the ayah, who like my mother, had also been born in Madras. She was an indispensable addition to the family and had been looking after my younger brother Billy until I came along. Widowed for many years, with no family ties, she had gladly agreed to the move when my father's unit was transferred from Bangalore, although she missed the vibrant south Indian culture.

At forty she was still quite pretty, slim, and had a darkish complexion.

She also had the patience of a Saint!

Ayah wore her hair oiled and coiled into a bun at the nape of her neck and a spotless white sari with a blue border - her badge of office as a nanny - and a short white bodice that left her brown midriff bare. She always wore delicate chupplies, (sandals) which she took off before entering the house as a mark of respect; and a tiny jewel in her left nostril which glittered so much that I was always trying to snatch it off when I was a baby.

Her passion was paan (betel leaf), and she always kept a little brass box of the fresh leaves wrapped in a piece of wet cloth, plus several other accompaniments which she would add to the leaf; it was a ritual she enjoyed each evening after work.

Something similar to the glass of wine enjoyed after a hard days graft.

Taking great care, she would unwrap a single leaf, and add a creamy white paste over it, then other things like chopped beetle-nut pieces, and a sprinkling of this and that, before placing it into her mouth. She would then chew happily, eyes shut, for the first few precious moments. This was only ever done when she was off duty, as the beetle juice had to be spat out several times. Ayah being a dab hand at squirting the red liquid out from between her teeth, to hit a target several feet away! But tonight her ritual had been delayed by my arrival. So she wouldn't have been best pleased.

Bridget eased me into my new surroundings with efficiency and aplomb, pleased all had gone well, wiped me off, and turned with a flourish to present me to my mother.

Her job as a midwife was one she had thoroughly enjoyed - up to now!

What could be better than bringing a new life into the world?

She loved the way mothers looked when presented with their newborn child, they just glowed.

This was the part she loved the best!

Bridget couldn't wait to place this lovely child into its mother's arms.

"Here you are dear, a nice wee little girl," she said beaming proudly, about to place the precious bundle (me) into the arms of my mother.

Of course by this time I'd started bawling. My face, topped by a full head of black hair, was screwed up and red with rage, my gummy mouth wide open. My skinny legs and arms, covered in dark downy hair, flailing about as I fought off those invisible demons.

Taking a single horrified look my mother's next words were not what poor Bridget had expected at all.

"Get her away from me, that's not my child, she looks more like a monkey!" my mother cried.

Sure, I must have looked a wacky sight. But why did I have to cry? I mean... what was the protocol? They don't exactly give you printed instructions before making the journey, do they?

But she could think quickly, could our Bridget.

"How can you say that?" she countered, God bless her!

And I must have stopped crying, because she could see the colour of my eyes.

"Look at the poor wee thing, she's beautiful!" Holding me up but away from my angry mother as if fearing for my life, Bridget pleaded on my behalf.

"Aaah... will you look at the darlin' blue eyes she has on her, and the lovely dark hair. She's a true Irish Colleen, so she is."

"She ugly!" retorted my mother, turning her face to the wall. And no amount of coaxing made the slightest difference at that point.

You think I'm kidding? Well it was a fact; my mother recounted the tale to all and sundry, many times over the next few years. Luckily I was too young to understand what was going on or I might have done - what? Packed my bag and said, "Oh well, if I'm not wanted!"

What of himself listening in the adjoining room? What must my father be thinking? I mean, he hadn't even seen me yet. Was he wondering what sort of monster he'd fathered?

Funnily enough I never did ask him.

Oh, and wasn't it a good thing my siblings were staying away for the night. Imagine what they would have made of it all, but more about them later.

Just to show the kind Irish lady how much I appreciated all her efforts, I quietly peed all over her, a - nice - long - warm - pee. She didn't seem fazed by it either. This kind, sweet, warm-hearted midwife... What, can't I give praise where it's due? Listen, but for this wonderful woman, I might never be writing this story, might I?

The bath was nice and warm, so I peed in that too, and, I was reliably told, a serene look formed on my face as I shut my eyes contentedly. The warm water probably reminded me of that soft warm place I had occupied for the previous few months, a place where I had felt loved and wanted!

I was then dressed in a spotless white gown... had my mane brushed into some semblance of order... and was fast asleep when she put me up for my father's inspection. I must have looked okay to him though, because there was absolutely no rejection.

I don't think I could have taken two rejections in the same night!

Although I think his acceptance was something to do with all the chota pegs he'd consumed! Knowing my mother wasn't all that keen on me, he had obviously decided someone ought to care for the poor child whose lower lip was quivering even as she slept. Yes, I'd mastered the art from quite an early age, and must have looked pretty vulnerable, because he decided he'd take a bit more interest in his latest child.

In time mother grew to tolerate me, although she let ayah do most of the dirty work, like changing and washing nappies etc. She would have probably let ayah breastfeed me too, had the poor woman had any milk in her breasts. It was quite the done thing to employ a wet nurse then.

Most of my hair rubbed off within weeks, along with a big patch on the back of my head, which was caused by me continually trying to see what was going on around me. I was a nosey little beggar! But thankfully the hair grew back later.

My father, encouraged to choose a name for me, decided to name me after his mother Rose. Mum compromised, thought of a posher name, and called me Rosemary Grace. Talk about an inappropriate name! I mean with my dark hair and green eyes I looked nothing like a rose, but I was stuck with it!

CHAPTER TWO

1902 - Pigeon Stew

My father Arthur Fisher had been just five years old when he decided he was going to be 'kindness itself' to his own children when he grew up. No corporal punishment would be meted out to them - if and when he administered any.

The 'strap' would be so much scrap!

Covering his ears with both hands, he buried his face deeper into the sweet-smelling straw mattress, trying hard not to listen to the angry voices of his parents coming through the floorboards from the kitchen below.

Arthur had been born in the farmhouse, situated in a small hamlet in Hampshire, where his parents were jobbing farmers. His parents, Rose and Jesse, worked around the clock to keep the roof over their heads and earn enough money to support their family of five children: Arthur the youngest of the three boys, with Ernest thirteen, Sidney nearly nine, Cissie eleven, and Daisy seven.

With seven people to look after, Rose was kept busy from dawn to dusk, especially on a Monday, when she had to get the washing, cooking and her dairy work done. The rest of the week was marginally easier once all the ironing was done.

On bath nights, the old tin bath was brought in and put beside the hearth. Rose, having boiled up enough water in some of her bigger pots for the occasion would fill the bath, then by the light of candles, Jesse had the privilege of the clean water. Rose and the girls followed; and by the time Arthur, the youngest, stepped into the bath the water appeared quite a muddy colour. Hot water was added to the bath every so often, when required.

Most people had a 'privy' down at the bottom of the garden in those days and Arthur's family toilet was a makeshift shed which the wind whistled through on cold nights. A wooden box inside sat over a deep hole in the ground with a seat - hole in the middle - through which waste matter fell. The shed and seat were moved to a fresh site every so often, and the hole filled in with soil. Newspapers were cut into squares and threaded onto a string which hung on the inside of the door, and even these had to be used sparingly.

At night you had to be pretty desperate to want to use the toilet for anything more than a tinkle - a chamber pot under the bed was used for this - it meant having to creep down the stairs in the pitch-black darkness, with only a flickering candle to light your way to the outhouse at the end of the back garden, scared at every night sound - especially if the candle blew out.

Arthur took after his mother in looks. He had the same fresh-faced complexion, eyes the colour of forget-me-nots, and rosy red cheeks from all the fresh country air. His hair - blonde mousey in colour and quite thick - was cut by his father at least once a fortnight and kept really short.

The other boys in the village sported the same 'pudding-basin' look of home barbering unless their parents could afford the price of a proper haircut of course.

With all his features in the right proportions, and nicely spaced on his face, Arthur was quite a bonny child. Not that any of that bothered him in the least!

Like his father Jesse, he was sturdily built, which made him look older than his five years.

Normally a good-natured child, he'd inherited his father's stubborn streak, which often got him into a lot of trouble and like all small boys Arthur was always full of exuberance and curiosity; which landed him in one scrape after another, often being protected by his doting mother Rose, because he was the youngest of her brood of five.

Perhaps this time his mother wouldn't be able to cover up for him?

Arthur could hear his father shouting, and cringed. Their voices coming clearly to him as he lay trembling in the truckle-bed he shared with his brother Sid, who was still out bedding the farm animals with his older brother Ernie.

"You mollycoddle the boy," shouted his father, "Won't be good for nuthin' by the time he grows up."

And the softer tones of his mother, trying to pacify the angry man, yet again.

Arthur remembered the time when the kitchen downstairs echoed to the sounds of shouting and laughter. Then, his father would tickle him until he was helpless with laughter. But now, everyone tiptoed around the room quietly, trying not to attract their father's attention. Often, when they returned from school, his mother would give them a warning nod if he was in one of his bad moods. Everyone was on tenterhooks all the time, especially Sid, who had begun to look even more worried than he usually did!

Sid was the quiet one in the family, a serious looking boy with his head forever in books when he found the time. Sid loved making things with his hands, his long slender fingers always busy with something. His face, pale compared to his two brothers, never seemed to brown in the summer, it just freckled over his nose, cheekbones and along his arms.

His father's temper seemed to be getting worse every day, one or the other of the children being bawled out for some minor misdeed. Only that morning he'd shouted at poor Daisy, just because she said she didn't want her porridge.

"There's a lot would be more than happy to be sitting down to that, young woman," he'd pointed out forcibly. And poor Daisy, who hadn't been feeling well, had burst into tears. Their mother managed to stop Daisy crying by promising her she could help out with washing the eggs when she got back from school.

Arthur tried being extra nice to her on the way to school. "Look Daisy, how would you like a go at using my catapult?" he'd offered, but Daisy had declined.

Girls were funny, fancy not wanting to have a go at using his catapult, thought Arthur.

Daisy had been delicate from birth, always succumbing to colds and coughs, and no matter how much her mother tried to tempt her with morsels of food, she just didn't seem to put on any weight. Her pale face, the colour of alabaster, had a pinched look to it. She'd inherited her mother's bright blue eyes, which looked quite startling in her pale face, although her cheeks did pink up during the very cold winters. She had the makings of being a good looking lass, if only she'd put on a bit of weight.

Arthur withdrew his fingers from his ears which were now aching from the pressure he'd been using to keep the voices away, and tried to listen to what was going on downstairs.

Were his parents still arguing about him? Had his father found out about his latest escapade? If so, he would soon be coming... feet thumping up the stairs... any minute now, belt in hand.

He hadn't meant to break the window. It had been an accident.

His mind raced through all the events that could have been his undoing, thinking about the apples he'd been scrumping from Mr Tolley's garden?

He felt under his pillow for the catapult Sid had made for him for his birthday just a couple of weeks ago. He caressed the smooth, y-shaped bit of wood and the small leather thong made from the tongue from one of Sid's own boots which he'd hoped his father wouldn't notice was missing. Everything else had been easy enough to find. An old inner tube from a bicycle provided two lengths of rubber for the sling and a few thinner strips from the same tube were used to bind all the different parts together.

Yes, his brother Sid was a genius when it came to making things with his hands. He'd even managed to fix one of Arthur's boots with a piece of the inner tube once, marking the rubber out with a bit of pencil then cutting it carefully to fit, before nailing it on firmly. But without a proper last, some of the nails had penetrated through to dig into Arthur's toe, so Sid had been forced to pull the nails out again.

But the catapult was sturdy and strong, just about the right size to fit into his hand perfectly. He'd never had such a wonderful present before! Come to think of it, he'd never received a birthday present, ever! His parents couldn't afford such extravagances.

And as for Christmas, Jesse Fisher thought it was just a 'Pagan' celebration and not for the likes of him or his family. Although Rose had insisted on making a plum pudding last year, despite Jesse's displeasure... and very nice it had been too. Lovely plump raisins, flour, sugar and some suet; mixed and boiled up in a cloth. His mother had handed out huge helpings of the steaming hot pudding to the children, leaving his father out. But as the delicious smell permeated through the kitchen, Jesse had a change of heart, and accepted a portion for himself, which he'd thoroughly enjoyed even if he wouldn't admit it.

Arthur's mouth watered at the thought of Christmas pudding, nearly making him forget about the argument going on downstairs. His stomach then reminded him as it rumbled with hunger that he'd had no supper, having run upstairs when he'd heard his parents going 'at it' hammer and tongs when he'd slipped in earlier that evening.

Rubbing his fingers over the catapult, Arthur wondered how long it would be before his prized possession was taken away. Both Ernie and Sid had catapults and they were allowed to use them with their father's permission of course; mainly to keep vermin like pigeons, rabbits and rats from spoiling the farm crops. He'd been hoping to join them too, when he'd mastered the art of shooting straight, as if that would ever happen now!

If only that shot hadn't gone wrong!

His face was getting really hot pushed into the mattress, so he raised his head slightly, breathing in a little fresh air, and prayed for a miracle.

"Please, please, don't let it be about the broken window," he mouthed silently into the darkness of the room. His father always seemed to be angry these days! Bad-tempered and mean, flying off the handle at the least provocation and only last week he'd walloped Ernie for being late home from school.

"I'll - teach - you - to - be - late," his father had roared. Each shouted word accompanied by a resounding 'thwack', as the leather strap descended on his brother's bare buttocks. Being thirteen, Ernie had been mortified at being made to bend over the kitchen table - 'bare-arsed' - his trousers around his ankles and his eyes shut with pain. Not daring to make a sound as his father raised the belt again and again.

Ernie was a strongly built boy, his arms and legs hard with muscles from the heavy farm work he did before and after school. His hair was dark brown like his father's, along with his eyebrows and eyelashes, which grew thickly; shading the bright blue of the eyes he'd inherited from his mother. Although most of the time he kept his gaze fixed firmly on the ground, except when he was engrossed in his work. He couldn't quite believe it when the girls in the village made a fuss of him. Never for one moment believing himself to be handsome; even his constant scowl didn't seem to put them off him.

Straining against the urge to hit back at his father, Ernie took the vicious blows raining down on him. If it wasn't for his mother's sake, he would have been long gone because of his father's beatings and only stayed on because he knew that without his help; his mother would have had to work even harder than she already did.

Rose, their mother, had been down at the other end of the farm with his older sister Cissie, feeding the chickens, and hadn't heard about the beatings until later, and then only when she'd noticed Daisy crying; with Cissie doing her best to hush her younger sister up, had Rose twigged something was up. Demanding to know why Daisy had been crying - it being unusual for Daisy to cry for nothing.

Minutes later she was squaring up to Jesse and giving him both barrels.

"Proud of yourself are you?" she shouted.

"Whatever next, are you aiming to take the record for the meanest man around these parts?" And that was only for starters. Rose could be quite a tartar when roused.

The normally placid young woman could become quite a fearsome opponent, as Jesse knew only too well. Arms akimbo, sleeves rolled up, and still wearing her well-washed gunny-sack apron, with her red hair tumbling in curls around her face, she was getting well into her stride.

"That's it; I'll not have you lay another finger on any one of my kids from now on, or by..." And with the threat hanging like a dagger in the air, she flounced out of the room.

Outside she was 'all a tremble' as she realised she'd stood up to Jesse once again! Blue eyes blazing with the injustice of it all - the sight of poor Ernie's poor reddened bottom burned into her memory - angry tears welled in her eyes as she walked quickly round the farmhouse. The two dogs sensing her displeasure kept well out her way instead of gambolling around her legs which they normally did.

Later, a reluctant Ernie had to bare all again as his mother ministered to his wounds.

"Goodness Jesse, the child was only a few minutes late, look at what you've done," she scolded the now sorry man, gently applying a dollop of goose grease - thought to be an all-round remedy at that time - to Ernie's red, swollen backside, her pretty face still flushed by her previous outburst.

Everyone had tried to keep well out of the way of their father ever since, especially Arthur, who wondered who would be the next in line for a good hiding. Was it his turn now? Arthur could still hear the voices of his parents, but now they didn't appear quite so angry, and closing his eyes, he drifted off to sleep, still clutching his catapult.

Next morning his father was already busy tending the farm animals so Arthur - for once keen to get off to school without finding an excuse to stay home - swallowed his porridge in big gulps, because he'd woken up really hungry and wanted to be well away from his father.

Arthur loved the small quiet hamlet where he'd been born; the country lanes, bordered by hawthorn bushes bursting into bloom with thousands of small white flowers in the springtime; and the pink and white blossoms of the horse-chestnut tree promising lovely conkers afterwards. He loved the huge fields of corn waving like a golden sea in the breeze on a sunny day, and the sound of the bees buzzing as they gathered honey from the wild flowers.

He'd got used to the big gentle cows, not scared of taking short-cuts over the fields they occupied, although the cowpats were a bit of a hazard.

No matter what the weather, the birds sang in the trees overhead, trilling their little hearts out as they welcomed yet another day. He liked to hear the quiet sounds of the country; like the steady clip-clop of horses' hooves as they were being led off to plough the fields; following the farmer, who talked softly to them, as if they were human.

He often stopped to watch the cows in the fields, the big placid creatures calling to their frisky offspring with soft moos. The calves kicking up their hind legs as they lolloped about - never moving too far away - always ready to run back to the safety of their patient mothers; then small tails swishing about in ecstasy, they'd nuzzle the swollen udders for the sweet milk always on tap.

Arthur had his favourite places too. Like the clump of trees growing on a small hill behind his school. There, hidden from view, he and his friends would meet to climb trees, or just lark about. When they grew tired, they would lie down on the green grass, their faces turned up to the warmth of the sun, talking softly, or chewing sweet stalks of grass while they dreamed their dreams. He knew where all the sweetest apples were to be found too: almost always on someone else's farm; which made them all the sweeter. He knew the trees that produced the best conkers - which when hardened in the oven – would withstand any amount of bashing.

Yes, life could be really sweet if only his father would lighten up. He'd become such an old grouch lately.

Everyone in the small village had commented about the change in Jesse Fisher since his accident last year - when he'd been badly gored by a bull. This had left him with a terrible limp and a temper to match. The once-handsome man seemed only to scowl these days; his face dark with anger, lashing out at the slightest provocation.

He took longer and longer to do the simplest tasks, despite the help he received from his two older sons before and after school; Rose, Arthur's mother helping too, in spite of having so much to do herself.

She worked from dawn till dusk, milking the cows, before churning the milk into cream, cheese and butter for the market; looking after the poultry; feeding the chickens before gathering and washing the eggs; all this in addition of having to cook and sew for her own brood.

Cissie was a miniature version of Rose; a strong, handsome girl, with lots of pent up energy which she often used when beating the hearth rug on the line outside, sending clouds of dust flying everywhere. The rag rug - made by Rose as she sat by the fireside of a winters evening - used up the last bits of any old clothing the family had grown out of, and was the only floor-covering in the farmhouse.

Daisy, the frailest member of the family, being just seven years of age, wasn't allowed to do too many chores.

Rose kept a small kitchen garden where she grew a few flowers and vegetables for her family and in her spare time she gathered blackberries from the hedgerows, mixing them with a few apples, to make into the tastiest jam. She sold some at the local market to earn a few shillings. Treating her family to a few luxuries bought with the profit, but always kept back a big jar of the jam for her own family. The fresh jam spread over a chunk of homemade bread was to die for!

Arthur's mum was the best ever! She even managed to keep cheerful in spite of all the hard work.

Her face - as yet unlined - didn't need the benefit of rouge and glowed with health; her cheeks the colour of rosy apples. Her dark red hair grew luxuriantly down to her shoulders. Although since having had five children, Rose had put on a bit more weight than she would have liked, but it didn't worry her unduly.

On a Friday night, when they could afford it, she liked nothing better than a pint of ale down at the local pub. Then, cheeks glowing from the simple treat, she'd skip home; ready to take on the world once more.

Arthur loved Fridays; his parents seemed so much more cheerful after a visit to the local pub. His father would be smiling, and his mother, her ample bosom shaking with laughter, was as 'happy as a lark' as she picked him up and swung him round and round just for the hell of it.

His mum was a good cook too, and could turn fresh vegetables and a few bones into the most delicious broth. The bowls of soup accompanied by great chunks of homemade bread were always scraped as clean-as-a-whistle by the whole family. Meat was a luxury, eaten only on very rare occasions, Christmas being one of the 'special' days. Then, with permission from the farmer, Jesse would choose one of the old hens that had stopped laying and wring its neck with a quick turn of his hands. The poor chicken didn't even have time to know it was dead - shaking its wings, its legs treading air for a few seconds afterwards.

Arthur didn't much like seeing the hen killed, but it was quickly forgotten when the smell of the cooking bird set everyone's mouth watering. Then along with fresh vegetables, they'd tuck into the juicy, tender meat, wiping the last drop up off their plates with a piece of bread.

With money tight and his father's bad temper, his mother had more than enough to contend with.

Like all boys Arthur was a bundle of energy, getting into one scrape after another. Like the time when he was two years old, when he was determined to help his mother by feeding the chickens. But instead of corn, Arthur had taken handfuls of his mother's freshly churned butter to feed them, with the hungry birds pecking it off his hands and clothes as fast as they could. His poor mum had to lie, as she explained away the loss of half a pound of butter to a 'poor yield' from the cows that day.

Then there was the time he'd thrown stones at a wasp's nest he found in a derelict barn - lucky to have got away with his life, by running off in the nick of time. The wasps had finally abandoned their nest and flown off angrily - a mass of buzzing brown and yellow, fiercely intent on revenge - to attack a poor farmhand who had been returning from a hard days work.

Then, of course, there were the 'scrumpings'.

The list was endless.

The latest episode had happened just a few weeks ago, when he'd been sent by his mother to the butcher for 'three penny worth' of bones for the dogs. The dogs *would* get the bones eventually, but only after they'd been cooked up with vegetables to make a stew for the family.

It was a Saturday morning so there was no school. With the weather still warm, Arthur was dressed in just a shirt and breeches, as he helped his sisters with chores.

So he was more than pleased when his mother singled him out for an errand.

"Now then lad," his mother said to Arthur, "I've something I need." And taking a coin from her pocket, she held it out to him.

"Here's a sixpence," she said, showing him the tiny coin, "mind you take good care of it." Arthur nodded his head in agreement, so his mother continued. "You're to ask Mr Wardle the butcher for three penny worth of bones – for the dogs, mind you remember that." Then pressing the small coin into his hand, she reiterated; "three - penny - worth - of - bones - for - the - dogs, and mind you bring me back the change!"

"I will," Arthur promised, glad of a chance to get out of the chores, and feeling in the pocket of his breeches to make sure his catapult was still there, he started off for the shop.

"Don't be too long neither!" his mother shouted towards his retreating back.

"I won't!" he shouted back, glad to be off.

Holding the tiny coin tightly in his hand he set off, taking a short cut over the recently harvested fields.

The rich earth was still dry after the long summer, with the harvest safely in; lines of stubble stuck up in long straight rows along the ground, where once golden corn rustled and waved in the summer breezes. Red poppies, bright splashes of colour among the autumnal shades, grew wild amongst the yellowing stubble.

A low hedge separated him from a field of grazing cows, which were looked after by a big black bull, so Arthur decided to skirt around that field.

Feeding birds flew into the air with startled cries as he scrunched over the dry soil, startling him nearly as much as he had them. Patches of green grass, small bushes and wilted corn stalks still grew in some of the dips and hollows where the harvester had failed to reach; the abandoned heads of corn rustling and swaying in the morning breeze.

So when Arthur took short, he had just the spot where he could do his business; the small ditch just high enough to hide a small boy away from prying eyes.

Pulling his trousers down he squatted, quietly getting on with the job. Then because he needed to do something with his hands, he pulled his catapult out from his trouser pocket and pretended to fire away. But found the tiny coin he held in his hand impeded his movements, so he popped it into his mouth for safe keeping.

There was a nice warmth to the sun, and as Arthur sat quietly, there was a whirring of wings and two pigeons fluttered down to the ground nearby; their iridescent neck and wing feathers shining in the sun, barely yards away.

He wanted to laugh when he saw them strutting about and pecking at the ground; their little heads moving jerkily in time with their legs as they walked. Just as if they were connected by a string - their bodies plump with unlimited supply of corn left behind after the harvesting - stopping himself when he realised they were getting closer and closer to where he squatted, hidden by the bushes. They were so close; he could see the tiny white circles around their bright little eyes clearly as they pecked the corn on the ground, completely unaware of his presence.

Holding his breath lest he might scare them away, and expecting them to take flight at any moment, he sat as still as a mouse, watching them getting nearer and nearer.

Can I, he thought? It was a chance too good to miss.

With the catapult already in his hands he only needed a small stone... so with his free hand he searched in the loose soil for one, then slowly fitted it into the sling of his catapult. Then with trembling fingers, he raised the weapon, and taking careful aim, let the stone fly, and heard it whistle away... never for a moment thinking he really would hit anything.

There was a sudden flurry of feathers and startled cries as the birds flew off, tiny white feathers floating slowly back down to the ground... to where one of the birds now lay - its mate uttering a series of alarm calls as it flew off to safety.

Arthur couldn't believe his luck!

Leaping to his feet in triumph with a great shout of joy... he swallowed the tiny coin he'd been holding in his mouth. He gulped, his joy now tinged with horror, as he realised what he'd done! He tried coughing it up, putting his fingers down his throat, and even stood on his head, but it was all in vain.

The coin had gone!

A very worried Arthur had to return home minus the bones he'd been sent to buy, to face his mother and the music. Sheepishly holding out the limp dead body of the pigeon as a peace offering, instead of the bones she'd been expecting.

Again he missed punishment by the skin of his teeth, as Rose could hardly keep herself from laughing out loud, when she'd heard the whole story, trying to keep a straight face as she waved Arthur away.

She would often tell the story to anyone who'd listen, and never failed to go into fits of laughter as she recounted the tale in great detail.

With no bones for broth, she managed to produce a fine stew for supper that evening, flavoured with pigeon. Jesse thought Arthur unusually quiet that evening and wondered what was tickling Rose, but the stew was delicious so he just got stuck in.

For the next couple of days, unbeknown to Jesse, Rose could be seen going through Arthur's excrement - which he was made to do on the ground outside the toilet - with two sticks until the tiny sixpence finally presented itself once more.

CHAPTER THREE

School Time Again

Arthur hated school. The older children picked on the smaller ones calling them 'dunderheads', and so far the lessons hadn't been very enjoyable at all.

Their teacher Miss Savage had given them the letters of the alphabet to copy; which she'd written down on the right-hand side of the big blackboard behind her desk and was busy writing down the morning lessons for the older children - a line drawn down the middle to separate the two different lessons - they were called 'sums'. Not that Arthur knew much about 'sums' yet.

The school was a small one-roomed, purpose built, brick building with one large room for the classroom. Tables and chairs stood in neat rows on each side of a central aisle, which Miss Savage would walk up and down, in between writing on the blackboard, so she could see more closely what the children were writing.

Over towards the far side, the teacher's desk stood on a raised dais, with the big blackboard on the wall directly behind her. Above it the big school clock ticked away all day - its hands moving steadily with each monotonous tick - until it was time for the 'going home' bell. There was always a warning buzz of excitement and a great deal of activity just before the bell went off, which gave the younger children some idea of what time it was. Arthur being one of the younger children couldn't tell the time yet.

This morning the only sounds to be heard in the classroom were the ticking of the clock and the noise of chalk being pressed on slates as the younger ones laboured over their writing.

Glancing out from under his lashes Arthur could see Mary Drummond busily writing, and beyond her his best friend; Tommy Webster. The light from the two windows on either side of the room gave ample light to study, but were set just high enough so as not to distract pupils from any outside influences.

The scrubbed wooden floorboards had been left uncovered, except towards one corner; where the big metal stove stood, sitting on a square concrete base. Its long chimney reaching up through the roof to poke up outside with its cone-shaped metal 'hat' making it look like a giant firework ready to go off - especially if there was any smoke coming out of it.

The stove was only lit during the worst of the winter months, where it crackled away merrily, warming up the freezing classroom; although the wind still whistled through the gaps in the floorboards when the cold North wind blew across the land.

Outside the schoolhouse was a small playground surrounded by a wooden fence, beyond which a variety of bushes and trees grew in their natural habitat. While away on a small hill behind the school, hidden amongst a cluster of trees, was one of Arthur's favourite spots for playing. The pretty 'candles' of white flowers of the horse chestnut trees had now been replaced with hard brown nuts encased in their prickly casings, the requisite of every boy from five to fifty in the village. The nuts ready to fall with or without the aid of sticks and stones thrown up by eager boys in their quest for the biggest and best conkers. This was a yearly event that brought grazed knees from climbing, and bleeding knuckles from the overzealous boys as they 'batted' conker against conker until one or the other was cracked or smashed.

In the classroom, the screeching and scratching of chalk being pressed down too hard on the slates had got steadily worse, the irritating noise broken only by the occasional cough, or shuffling of feet until Miss Savage stopped what she was doing and turned to face the class.

"Will you please stop making those terrible sounds!" she shouted, her voice angry and sharp. Her face looked stern behind the glasses perched on the end of her nose. Her lips were pressed tightly together as she surveyed the children.

Immediately, the classroom stilled - all fidgeting halted.

Every child in the class was only too aware that her orders were not to be taken lightly. Miss Savage was strict but fair, without discipline she could not have taught all the children of mixed ages under her care.

She had a pale, well scrubbed complexion, her face being devoid of powder, and piercing greyish green eyes that seemed to read your every thought. Her light brown hair was kept short, neatly parted in the centre and held back on either side with hair grips.

Reaching for the small white handkerchief - which she was never without - she held it daintily up to her nose, before returning it to the little pocket in her dress.

Wonder why she never has a good old blow, thought Arthur. Whenever his nose ran, he was told to 'blow hard'. The piece of chalk was still hovering over his slate where he'd raised it as soon as the teacher had spoken, his mouth open in concentration. The only sound to be heard now was the ticking of the clock as the children gazed up with expectant faces, waiting for her next words.

"There is no need for all that scratching, write slowly and try not to PRESS DOWN TOO HARD," emphasising the last four words, she then looked around at the children, making sure that she'd been understood.

"Any child making those silly noises on their slates will be sent home with a note for their parents. Is that clear?"

The nodding heads of the children confirmed that they had all heard.

"Well, let me hear you say it," Miss Savage continued. And all the children quickly answered, "Yes Miss Savage."

"Right, now get on with your work." The younger children immediately bent forward to their task, trying desperately not to make any further noise with their chalks. The teacher's voice had carried clearly right through the classroom to the dozen or so children attending that day. Nearly a third of the children missing classes to stay at home and help their parents on the small farms and smallholdings scattered around the surrounding villages. A practise much frowned upon by Muriel Savage, but one she was forced to accept.

She always dressed in the same sort of clothes during the winter months; grey or brown plain dresses in a woollen mixture, rounded off with a small white collar. With them she wore sensible brown shoes, laced up the front, with thick woollen stockings, as the classroom could get very chilly. But during the summer months she wore nice flowered dresses, with the same kind of stout shoes - only these had a strap that crossed over the front of her foot and buttoned at the side. With these shoes she wore regular stockings.

"The older children can start their work now," she commanded, "QUIETLY!"

Once more the murmur in the classroom stopped abruptly, nobody wanted to take a note home, as they all knew what that would mean!

Miss Savage didn't believe in corporal punishment, letting the parents deal with the offender. This proved a blessing in disguise for her, but not for them. The respective parents often punishing their offspring with much more vigour than Muriel Savage ever would.

Bending down over his slate Arthur tried very hard to be quiet. But if he pressed down too gently the chalk hardly marked his slate at all and pressing a little harder would result in the offensive noises they'd just been told off about. Yes, he sure hated school. Looking up at the clock that still made no sense to him; he wished he knew how to tell the time. Sometimes he'd ask one of the older children but they just shook their heads and rolled their eyes, trying to make out he was dumb because he still didn't know how to tell the time. So he didn't bother asking them any more.

What was it with the older children? Why did they have to be so mean? If it wasn't for them, school wouldn't be half as bad.

Every morning Arthur woke wishing he had a sore throat or a really bad cold, so he'd be allowed to stay at home. But the trick hadn't worked too well after the second time he'd tried it on.

Getting dressed by the open fire on a cold winter's day was nice. His breeches and shirt were always lovely and warm from being beside the hearth all night, which was a bit of a bonus! His brothers and sisters having had to get dressed upstairs, before coming down to wash at the kitchen sink. But Arthur being the youngest had certain privileges, at least, for now.

His clothes were always well worn, having been handed down from his two brothers before him. The trousers and shirts being patched and re-patched so many times, that by the time Arthur finally got to wear them, you couldn't tell what colour the original material had been! Boots were handed down too, which was quite a problem if his feet hadn't grown, so he had to stuff paper into the toes to make them fit.

New boots, if you were lucky to get them, had to be worn with the laces tied together around your neck, on the journey to and from school. Stopping at the school gates to put them on, and reversing the process for the return journey home. 'The Old man', as Arthur and his brothers described their father, sometimes inspecting their boots for excess wear and tear when they arrived home. Then, 'woe betides' anyone if their boots had been scuffed!

The school was some two or three miles away, which was all right in good weather as you could cut across the fields. But in the winter or when it was wet, he had to go the long way round, which meant leaving home even earlier in the morning, the teacher being a stickler for punctuality.

Once at school Miss Savage would instruct the children to take off their wet things and place them near the old wood burning stove to dry. Clouds of steam rose throughout the day as boots, shoes and clothing dried slowly around the fire. At lunchtime, the children ate whatever they'd bought from home; mainly a big chunk of homemade bread and a bit of cheese, or jam if you were lucky, washed down with a drink of water from the tap in the school yard.

Like most children then, Arthur and his brothers and sisters were expected to do chores about the house and farm, before and after school. And everyone helped out at weekends before they were allowed out to play. The younger children were given lighter tasks according to their ages. But at harvest time everyone had to pitch in, with everyone working from dawn till well after dusk, when still covered in husks and stalks, they tumbled into bed exhausted.

School was often a respite for the older boys who were expected to toil alongside the men all day, and then on the way home they were made to sit and wait outside the pub while the older men slaked their thirst with a long cool glass of ale.

CHAPTER FOUR

Your Country Needs You!

The weather had been inclement for a few days which made the fields muddy and hard to traverse, so Arthur had been forced to go the long way round to school, leaving home in plenty of time to walk through the narrow winding lanes.

His mother had given him a nice bowl of warm bread and milk for breakfast that morning, then having given a final polish to his boots, tucked a clean hanky into his pocket, and told him to be a good boy.

And he fully intended to be just that.

Arthur was six, and had been attending the small school for a whole year; although he couldn't honestly say he liked it any better. There were always going to be the bullies around, but at least he'd managed to keep well out of their way. It had helped having his older brother Sid at school, as he was able to take the bullies on instead. But with his father still poorly, Sid had been helping on the farm with Ernie, his eldest brother.

Arthur felt full and happy as he set off for school, walking jauntily along between the high hedges bordering the road, until he came across an area that had been churned up by the hooves of cattle being driven from one field to another for fresh pasture. The holes had filled up with muddy water, so he'd been forced to negotiate the middle of the road trying to dodge the cow-pats, which were still steaming where they'd been dropped earlier by the cattle. Skipping over the dollops of greenish black muck that had been ejected like missiles to splatter the lanes and not judging his jumps too well he found himself ankle-deep in gloopy muck, making a right old mess of his boots.

The cow muck had enveloped his shiny boots and covered the tops of his socks too. Pulling up handfuls of grass Arthur tried to remove as much of the green grunge as he could, but just succeeded in spreading it around even more.

Giving it up as a bad idea Arthur made his way to school, knowing he was already late. The children were in the classroom when he got there, so he made his way over towards side of the schoolhouse where a tap was set against the school wall and holding out one booted foot under the tap he switched it on.

With a sudden swish the water shot out of the tap; spraying water over his boot, which not only moved the muck off, it also deposited it all over himself, the wall and the window above him... the cold water making Arthur gasp.

Turning the tap off, Arthur stared at the mess he'd created.

There was cow muck everywhere!

He'd managed to spread it around better than any muck spreader!

Somehow he'd just have to clean it up! So undoing his laces he took off both boots and his soaking socks, shivering in the cold as he desperately tried to clear up the mess, and was still busy when a familiar voice interrupted him.

"What are you doing boy?" Miss Savage's voice rose at the sight of the young barefooted boy; the soaking socks in his hands.

Arthur jumped - his face red with the exertion, and his feet blue with the cold, unable to speak as he stood transfixed to the ground. Then suddenly his whole body started to shiver uncontrollably.

It's true what they said about Miss Savage he thought. You could get nothing at all past her.

The teacher, who'd seen water and bits of dirt cascading over the window of her schoolroom, had come out to investigate, and Arthur, lost for words, could only look around at the mess he'd caused, his teeth chattering with fright and the cold.

Sizing up the situation, Muriel Savage saw before her a very wet, bedraggled and shivering child and decided explanations could wait until later.

"Stop whatever you're doing," she ordered Arthur, ushering him into the school room, where much to his surprise, a fire burned brightly in the stove that day. The schoolroom warm as toast for once.

Miss Savage gently nudged him in the direction of the heat.

"Stand by the fire and get yourself warm," she instructed the bare-footed shivering boy, "I wouldn't be at all surprised if you came down with pneumonia!"

For once, the rest of the class were silent, watching in awe as the teacher fetched a pair of well darned socks from a cupboard, and handed them to Arthur.

"Here, put these on," she instructed, her voice gentle for once as she spoke, realising the child was still shivering with cold and the shock of the sudden dousing he'd had.

The socks were a bit on the large size, coming right up to Arthur's knees, but he wasn't grumbling and soon his feet started to feel nice and warm.

When she was sure most of his clothes had dried, and Arthur had stopped shivering, the teacher sent him back to his seat, leaving his boots and socks gently steaming away by the stove; the other children, only then giggling at the sight of him in the long socks and no boots.

His ears, red as beetroot, were burning as he tried to look as inconspicuous as possible. Looking down at his still damp trousers, he noticed a large rip near to the knee and wondered how it had got there?

"All right, settle down now," ordered Miss Savage, quietening the class with one of her 'looks'. "Let's get on with some work, shall we?"

Coming home in a pair of someone else's socks, his own still very wet, had to be explained to his mother, making her bury her head in her hands once more.

"What am I going to do with you Arthur?" She moaned softly.

"Sorry mum," Arthur hung his head, wondering how on earth he'd managed to get into so much trouble.

And just for stepping into some cow muck.

"You wear out more breeches than both your brothers put together!" Arthur's mother exclaimed, but as usual, when she looked at his blue eyes gazing sorrowfully back at her, she was lost.

"Get yourself up and change your breeches, I'll see if I can put a patch on them tonight, ready for school tomorrow."

But the next day Arthur didn't have to pretend to be ill. He'd woken up with a very sore throat and a stuffy head. When his mother came to wake him for school, he could hardly answer. Rose soon realised this wasn't yet another one of Arthur's 'pretendings'. He was burning with a fever and looked really ill. Fetching some cold water in a basin, she sat down beside him to bathe his forehead with a lovely wet cloth, which felt ever so nice.

Arthur dropped off to sleep with the lovely gentle touch of his mother's hands, and during the next few days as he slipped in and out of consciousness, his mum was always there by his side, a worried look on her face.

She'd gone round to the school to thank Miss Savage for making Arthur put on warm dry socks after his shenanigans, taking the washed and dried socks back with her.

"You're very welcome," said Miss Savage in answer to Rose's thanks. "I do hope Arthur is back at school soon."

Afterwards at home, Rose said "She seems quite a nice young lass, does Miss Savage, 'tis a wonder some nice young chap hasn't snapped her up yet?"

Arthur didn't feel much like eating for several days, even when his mother tried to tempt him with some of her 'special' broths, or even with a freshly laid egg straight from the chicken coop. She knew he was very ill indeed, and fussed over him like a mother hen, making sure he was snug and warm with bricks heated up near the fire; nursing him back to health herself, with no doctor called in because they couldn't afford his services.

In time Arthur was up and about but feeling quite weak after his bout of pneumonia as predicted by Miss Savage, to find the winter had set in. The fields looked wet and miserable from his bedroom window as he gazed mournfully out, but Arthur was happy to keep his mother company in the warm kitchen until he was well enough to go outside and play. Digging out his catapult - which he could now operate reasonably well - he took pot shots at anything he could. But hitting one of the farm dogs was not a good idea! The dog had set up a fine old howl when the small stone caught it, instead of the pigeon he'd aimed at. So it was with much relief when he was finally deemed fit enough to attend school once more.

The years passed and with the help of Rose's cooking and the hard work on the farm helping to make Arthur and his brothers healthy and strong, the young boys grew into strong young men with stamina and muscles that were the envy of many an older man.

Over the years, there had been many changes to Arthur's family too. Ernie had finally left home to work elsewhere. He had met a young Irish lass, and was now courting. Cissie had married a young naval rating by the name of George and poor Daisy, who would have been nineteen, had died, at just sixteen years.

Which left Sid twenty, and seventeen year old Arthur at home to do most of the work on the farm.

Their father crippled with aches and pains brought on by his former injuries, still grumbled, but had begun to mellow somewhat! While Rose, relieved of much of the harder work, was at last able to put her feet up occasionally. Although she still cooked some fine meals for the three men still left in her life.

There was talk of war, with everyone whispering and speculating about what would happen, so when Arthur saw a poster of Lord Kitchener and his pointing finger, with the words '**YOUR COUNTRY NEEDS YOU!**' He decided to volunteer for the Army.

He was nearly six foot tall by then, broad-shouldered and powerfully built. After a very cursory examination, the Medical Officer, taking stock of Arthur's physique with a quick glance asked, "How old are you?"

"Eighteen, Sir," Arthur lied, trying to stand tall.

"You'll do," he was told, and he was signed up for a stint in the British Army.

Feeling quite proud of himself, he went back home to break the good news to his parents.

"What have you done?" his mother cried "You're not old enough."

"Leave the boy be," his father said gruffly, "I'd go me'self if I could."

So Rose turned on her husband instead, berating him for a solid half-hour, until Jesse took himself off to bed.

Arthur felt quite proud to be going off to fight for 'King and Country', little knowing exactly what lay in store but was quite surprised nevertheless when his usually grumpy father offered to take him to the local pub for a pint of beer!

"Here, get this down yer lad," his father said heartily, proudly patting Arthur on his back, as he told everyone in the pub his son was off to fight the 'stinking Huns'.

Arthur couldn't believe his luck!

CHAPTER FIVE

You're In the Army Now

Life in the barracks was tough, but buoyed with the thought that he'd be fighting for his King and Country Arthur knuckled down and worked hard. It felt strange being away from home. The only travelling he'd done in the past was an occasional trip into Portsmouth, for special occasions, and then only when he could afford it.

With so many young men volunteering for service in the British Army, space for all the new 'squaddies' was proving inadequate with petty fights breaking out as the men jostled for use of the limited facilities. The men slept on either side of long rooms, in beds that had to be made up to strict specifications every morning. Not an inch more or an inch less either side of the grey military issue blanket had to be folded under, so that the overall effect was exactly the same for each and every bed.

Small metal lockers standing by the top end of their beds held personal items such as toiletries etc. which were also inspected on a daily basis. Each soldier was expected to keep every inch of his space spick and span; the men having to stand to attention by the side of their beds as the officer in charge made his way slowly along first one and then the other side of the room, barking out reprimands as he inspected the area of each man's space.

The same recruits being bawled out repeatedly.

"I suppose yer mammy made yer bed for yer back home." This said sarcastically as the officer poked the offending unmade corners of the bed with his cane. "Well YOU'RE IN THE ARMY NOW, so you'll bloody well have to do it yer'self from now on, IS THAT UNDERSTOOD?" The last words shouted close-up and personal, spittle from the officer's mouth flying over the offenders shocked face, with the officer himself red in the face from his tirade.

"Strip that bed down and re-make it... PROPERLY next time."

"Yes Sir!" being the right answer to give. Anything else a sure-fire reason for the offender to be given extra drill duties, or be sent on a gruelling 'twenty runs' around the parade ground with a full pack, and carrying his rifle.

Sloppiness would not be tolerated!

The officers seemingly took great pleasure in making life as hard as they possibly could for the young men in their charge. Arthur quietly got on with whatever was thrown at him, used to roughing it much more than some of the others. None of the troublemakers fancied taking on the burly young country boy who looked more than capable of looking after himself, so he was left alone for most of the time, striking up an acquaintance with one or two other lads similar to himself.

All over the country, from large towns to the smallest villages of England, people were discussing the 'War in France'. Many believing it would be won and all over by Christmas at the latest. While in the barracks, the young men had begun to receive the training that would probably save some of their lives.

They were taught many things about fighting against the Germans, the best advice being, how not to underestimate their enemy.

They were made to charge - bayonets fixed - against swaying straw-filled bags that supposedly represented 'the enemy'. Sergeant Hawkins, or 'Shite-Hawk', as the men had nicknamed him, (because he'd threatened to 'shit' on them from a great height should any of them even try to mess about while under instruction from him) taking them through bayonet practise.

The cockney officer shouted at them constantly, making them even more nervous than they already were.

"That's a bloody knife yer've got stuck a'top of yer bloody rifle yer daft bugger," Sergeant Hawkins shouted at someone who was making a feeble attempt at stabbing the 'enemy' through the heart. The heart being a small square of paper pinned onto the straw dummies where the heart was supposed to be.

"I see none of yer knows where the 'eart is," bawled the Sergeant shaking his head mockingly at the sweating men. *"Yer all thinks it's in his bloody backside - am I right? Well yer WRONG. See them bits o' paper? That's where yer 'ave to stick yer bloody knife in!"*

Standing back, he shook his head sadly, before grabbing a bayonet from one of the soldiers, and then commenced to demonstrate just how it should be done. Jabbing at the straw figure, the point of the bayonet going right through the paper and straw, to come out at the other side, the Sergeant shouted at the top of his voice.

"*Frighten the bloody enemy an' then jest stick it to 'im. Stick the BLOODY THING IN!*"

"Wish I could stick it up his backside, that'd make the sod jump!" one of Arthur's mates whispered softly to him in an aside. Arthur managed to keep a straight face, aware that the Sergeant had very sharp hearing. But luckily he hadn't heard, being much too busy shouting out orders.

"*Yer not supposed to TICKLE them to death!*"

"*Get that damn bayonet in deep - remember if yer don't get 'im first, yer ain't goin' to get a second chance, 'cause 'eel 'ave yer. Inflict as much 'arm as yer can! Stick yer knife in, then give it a turn, before yer pulls it aht.*" The shouted orders always being accompanied by a few of the choicest swear words he could muster, to keep the chaps on their toes.

"*Spill his guts, that's what yer've gotta do. 'Cos if yer don't, it'll be you what's lying there. If none o' yer gets it right I'LL - KEEP - YER - AT - IT - All - BLOODY - DAY - IF - NEEDS - BE!*"

His shouted threats bringing groans from the tired men, who had already been practising for hours without a break.

By this time everyone had begun to really hate the ruthless Sergeant who made them demonstrate their skills again and again until they'd got it right.

But these were just sacks of straw. Could he do it to a human? Could he actually kill a man, thought Arthur, even if he was the enemy!

They were taught to understand their rifles properly, their lives depending on them. Having to take them to pieces again and again, and clean, and re-clean the barrels until they were 'passed muster' by the officer in charge.

Arthur loved target practise. It was a challenge to hit the target, which was a small speck away in the distance. First he'd wet the tip of his finger and apply it to the gun 'sight' to stop any glare, then squinting along the barrel; he'd get the target in his sight and press the trigger. Feeling the kick of the gun against his shoulder, and the anticipation of wondering how close he'd got to the bullseye.

The men tolerated but loathed the long hours spent on the parade ground as part and parcel of training, with drill, drill and more drill, until every soldier ached from their super-human efforts to work together 'as one'. The men, so tired by the time the bugle sounded for 'lights out', they would gladly have slept on a clothes line.

Memories of home were never far away from the men's thoughts. Speaking about home seemed to bring their loved ones closer, although Arthur found it difficult to talk about his own family at first. He missed his brothers and sisters - especially Daisy, whom he'd been close to - feeling sad because she'd died so young and before she'd had a real chance to enjoy her life.

He wondered how his mother was coping, also his father? Was he still as bad-tempered as always? He'd always taken his mum for granted and was surprised at just how much he was missing her and of course, her lovely stews. The army 'tucker' being adequate, but hardly what he'd call tasty. Arthur even thought longingly of his old school, which didn't seem at all bad in comparison with life in the barracks! If only they would let us get on with the fighting, he thought.

The weeks turned to months and all the soldiers wanted to do was get stuck in to some real arm to arm combat. The initial high of joining up to fight in the war now seemed like a distant dream.

Arthur always prone to getting into one scrape or another as a kid, seemed to be avoiding trouble and got on fairly well with a few of the other lads. Although he did get an awful lot of leg-pulling from them all, especially as he was constantly picked on by some of the instructors. His physique, height and fresh-faced 'country' appearance could be a bit of a disadvantage sometimes making him stand out like a sore thumb.

"I need a volunteer" one of the NCO's would request, then, noticing the 'big fellow' standing at the back, the officer would shout, pointing at Arthur.

"Are you any good at running boy?" Arthur could only stand tall and say "Yes Sir!"

"Okay, run down to the (wherever it was), and bring me back..." (whatever it was they wanted), he'd be told. More than once he'd been 'volunteered' for spud-bashing. He and a few others sitting beside a mound of potatoes which they had to peel ready for the cooks. But as it happened it turned out to be quite a cushy number, the head cook slipping them the odd bit of extra grub now and again. All the hard work of parades, drill and mock battles made them ravenous.

One day word got about that the officers were putting on a bit of a wrestling match, and Arthur was quick to put his hand up when the NCO shouted for volunteers.

"Any of you chaps got strong arm muscles?" he shouted, and a few of the braver ones decided to 'go for it'. A sea of hands shot up, but as usual Arthur was the one chosen; the officer's next words bringing more good-natured ribbing from the assembled men.

"Then get yourself a couple of strong buckets and clear out the latrines" he was ordered. Arthur had been 'had' yet again.

Orders for their departure to France came when the men least expected it. A parade was called and they were informed they would be moving out the very next day. Feelings were mixed and sleep was hard that night. The soldiers were keyed up and excited, but fearful at the same time about the prospects of what lay ahead! And long into the night they spoke in hushed tones.

"Wonder what it feels like to kill somebody?" A voice queried in the darkness, but was not answered; similar thoughts having occurred to most of them.

Next day, with their possessions packed into their kit bags, they were marched towards the army vehicles that took them to the station and the special trains waiting to transport them to the coast. The station was teeming with hundreds of troops milling about. The shouted orders of officers drowned out by the shrill whistles of trains, as first one and then another of the troop-filled trains departed from the crowded platforms. Guards strained to wave their flags high above the milling bustling throng. The soldiers themselves glad to be trading their cramped quarters of the previous months and excited to be on the move at last.

"Now listen up," Sergeant Hawkins shouted over the din and bustle of the station, when Arthur's unit managed to get onto the platform. "Remember yer in the King's Army now. I expect all of yer to do yer very best, AT ALL TIMES!" His last words practically drowned out by the noisy exuberance of the young soldiers waiting to board the train.

Amid train whistles and the babbling of voices from the hundreds of people thronging the platforms there was hardly enough space to move. Stowing their heavy kit-bags the soldiers 'bagged' whatever seats they could, before rejoining their sweethearts, family or friends on the crowded platforms.

Splashes of colour from the women's clothing and hats stood out from the sea of khaki uniforms; the male members who had come to send their sons and brothers off to war were more soberly dressed, in blacks, browns or greys.

Final sad goodbyes were said and with a long, loud whistle the train Arthur was on began to steam slowly out of the station; some of the soldiers having to jump into the moving carriages, before rushing to the doors and windows for the last glimpse of their loved ones.

Arthur, not expecting his parents to make the journey themselves was envious of some of the luckier ones who'd got girlfriends and parents waving them off. All caught up with the excitement of the day!

As the train moved out of the station amid cheers, waving, and raucous shouts, Arthur felt he would burst with pride.

We're really going to fight in the war, he thought.

Looking back, the departing soldiers craned their necks to wave at the crowded platform for as long as possible; watching tiny handkerchiefs being waved back from the hundreds of people for as long as possible and only when the train had rounded the bend to hide them from view, did they reluctantly withdraw back into the carriages.

Someone in Arthur's carriage produced a mouth organ and soon they were singing 'It's A Long Way To Tipperary' followed by other favourites like 'Pack Up Your Troubles In Your Old Kit Bag' and 'Goodbye Dolly I Must Leave You', which was sung with great gusto. Others songs followed, some with ruder variations to the words, before the boys were ready to settle down to play cards or swap stories. The main topic of conversation being what they would like to do to the enemy. All of them glad their stints at 'square bashing' were over and glad to be going to war at last.

The utter desolation of the battlefields came as a shock to Arthur.

There was a scene of total chaos for miles as far as the eye could see, with intermittent rain falling from grey skies. The ground was a quagmire, with the land bleak and dark with constant rain.

Soldiers returning from the front lines - bodies drooping with fatigue and wet uniforms - resembled scare-crows rather than fighting men as they stumbled back to the comparative safety of the shell-torn buildings where the new recruits waited. Caked in mud from head to foot, with their eyes blood-shot through lack of sleep, their only thought was for a good sleep, after a nice hot cup of tea.

These soldiers - many of them mere boys - told of the terrible conditions that prevailed; shocked and horrified by the loss of comrades who'd fallen - literally by their sides - cut down in the prime of their lives. While others who could barely walk themselves, led some of the other walking wounded; many of these suffering from shell-shock, or blinded by gas attacks. These were the 'lucky' ones, for although unable to see or do anything for themselves, at least they had survived the bloody battle - for now!

The badly injured had been rushed to make-shift medical stations. Where other battles were being fought by the surgeons and medical staff; as they tried to save the hundreds of wounded and dying men, the worst of the injured sent on to French hospitals, before being shipped back to Blighty.

Arthur and a few of the new intake found themselves delegated to filling sand bags, or carrying ammunition up towards the front line, and were given someone to show them where to go.

"Just remember to keep your bloody heads below the parapet and you'll be fine," they were told by the five foot nothing little runt, who could walk along quite upright in the trenches without the fear of having his head blown off. For Arthur and some of the taller ones – doubled over as they tried to traverse the boggy ground - it was sheer torture. And there was worse to come.

Nights were spent digging trenches, this being the best time to operate; some of the enemies heavier artillery stilled for now. Arthur found the heavy glutinous soil stuck to his shovel as he tried to toss it over the top, and trying to shake it loose meant he often got a shovel-full of it back in his face. All this while he tried to keep alert and keep his head down so he wouldn't get 'picked off' by the enemy.

Occasionally 'Fritz' would decide to let off a few shots wildly in the hope of hitting a target - just to keep them on their toes - making everyone dive for cover.

Before long Arthur found himself up at the front lines, and thick in the action! Shells whistled overhead and mortars from the howitzers arched through the skies over the stretch of barren land between him and the enemy; filled with craters of shells and barbed wire that had been dragged about in the mud; the tangled wire still holding bits of clothing and oddments in its vice-like grip.

Conditions for the fighting men were even more atrocious than he'd imagined. The trenches, just muddy water-filled holes in the ground; were difficult enough to manoeuvre in when dry, let alone awash with mud and water. There was hardly enough room to move, let alone discharge his weapon! Some of the trenches had duck-boards laid down to allow some freedom from the cloying mud; it wasn't long before that too was useless; the weight of the sticky mud oozing through to engulf legs and boots.

The soldiers were forced to walk knee-deep in wet sludge, their boots and feet constantly immersed in water for long periods, which caused discomfort and 'trench foot'- a kind of rotting of the feet. So orders were given for the men to change their socks two or three times a day! But within seconds, the water was back inside their wet boots, and they were no better off.

The weeks turned into months and Christmas arrived with still no sign to the end of hostilities; although both sides had called a sort of 'armistice' for a couple of days. Some of the Germans had even managed to obtain the odd Christmas tree, and proudly displayed them on top of their trenches. On Christmas morning Arthur had exchanged cigarettes with a young German soldier who was about the same age as himself. The two wary of one another, but pleased the war had been halted - if only for a couple of days. It was rumoured that some of the men had even managed a game of football with the enemy; bizarre events in a surreal setting of desolation that Arthur could not have thought possible even in his wildest dreams!

He thought nostalgically about home and the times he'd kicked a ball about with his brothers; wondering if his family had been sitting down to their Christmas dinner as he rolled a soggy cigarette between his fingers. Lucky devils!

After the Christmas truce it was harder than ever to fire a shot towards the enemy lines, but Arthur like all the others had a duty to his King and Country.

Hygiene became harder to maintain during the long months of combat, and all the men got lice, which proved to be more irritating than the shells constantly bursting overhead, showering them with shrapnel. Some of the men had scratched themselves so badly their wounds had festered, bringing more pain and discomfort.

Snipers picked off anyone foolish enough to put their heads above the parapet, so small mirrors attached to bayonets allowed them to 'keep tabs' on the enemy without getting their heads blown off. Then, when they were given orders to go over the top, the earth was so wet and slippery that they kept sliding back. The small ladders pushed against the steep sides were just as treacherous to use, as snipers could pick them off one by one as they ascended them.

The men made small dugouts cut into the sides of the trenches, which allowed them to rest away from the falling shrapnel in between the fighting. But even here, the rats scuttled over their bodies as they went hunting for food. Some of them bold as brass as they stole food right out of the pockets of sleeping soldiers; the rats growing bigger every day with their ample source of food; not discriminating between the dead bodies of the 'Bosch', British, or other nationalities.

Arthur hated those blasted rats, and wished he'd brought his catapult along. With much of the time spent waiting, he could have got a few of those stinking rats without wasting ammunition.

There was always some activity during the early hours or late at night. The enemy's field guns 'rat-a-tat-tatting' as if to remind them just how close the two sides were to one another, the British guns retaliating. Then, when they did go over the top into 'No Man's Land', they were cut down by the enemy; some of the injured having to be left behind until after dark. The luckier ones left feeling guilty because they'd had to leave comrades behind; the injured having to be rescued after dark by special teams.

Mustard and chlorine gas attacks made everyone scramble to get their gas mask on. The more fortunate were able to breathe with difficulty, while others, their eyes streaming and in agony as the gas burnt their lungs, coughed and retched as they slowly went blind.

Torrential rain turned the battlegrounds into a quagmire, then as night fell and the firing stopped, the men could hear dozens of frogs croaking all around them, and the sounds of rats scrambling about as they hunted for food.

Then just as he thought things couldn't get any worse, a mortar shell burst directly over the trench Arthur was in; killing several men in that section. Arthur was badly wounded, his face and legs a bloody mess. The stretcher bearers managed to get him and dozens of others to one of the field medical centres where orderlies tended to the wounded and dying as they waited to be seen by a Medical Officer.

After what seemed like ages, with Arthur slipping in and out of consciousness with the pain and weariness, he was seen by one of the medical doctors. The man nearly passing out with fatigue himself after dealing with hundreds of wounded and dying men that day. The tired M.O. finally made his way over to where Arthur lay - one blue eye visible in the swollen bloody mess that had once been his face – and after a thorough examination he stood back, looking down at the young soldier.

"Not good news I'm afraid," he pronounced.

Fearing the worst, and feeling like death, Arthur could only see a blurred image of the man standing near him.

This is it; he thought... my number is finally up!

"Too risky a job getting that piece of metal out of your cheekbone," the M.O said and Arthur couldn't believe his next words...

"Probably saved your life young man," the medical officer said, looking at some notes he held, while scribbling something down and turning to the orderly at his side, he barked, "unfit for further duty, get this man out of here." And he was gone!

"Are my legs that bad?" Arthur managed to mumble to the orderly, thinking his legs would have to be chopped off.

"Legs," the cockney spoke disdainfully, "twernt nuthin' to do wi' yer legs boyo, I've seen wors'n that... and the fella 'ad ter go back'n fight. Naw, 'tis that great chunk o' iron stuck in yer bloody cheekbone! Looks kinda nasty ter me," and he stuck a bit of paper onto Arthur's blanket.

"That's jest so's no one carts yer orf and tek's yer fer a corpse," he laughed.

"Nau how'd yer like a nice cuppa and a fag?"

Music to Arthur's ears!

All he'd been thinking of for the last couple of hours was having a fag. It was the ultimate language of the fighting soldier.

Arthur had often tried to fathom out the different dialects; the London cockney one being hard to follow; what with all the 'apples and pears' bits, but this message had come through loud and clear.

He was going to get that long awaited fag, and a cup of tea! AND he was going to live!

CHAPTER SIX

Onwards To India

After considerable medical care Arthur's wounds healed. The doctors in England had decided it would be dangerous to remove the piece of shrapnel embedded in his cheekbone; the skin healing over to leave just a small scar which was hardly noticeable, although Arthur did have a nagging ache in his cheek whenever the weather turned cold. The scars on his legs were permanent however; as were the scars inside his head; firmly etched into his memory!

Some of the patients injured in the battles raging across Northern France, and in the same hospital as Arthur, had come in with missing limbs, while the victims of 'gassing' had to be led around, bandages covering their scarred faces and unseeing eyes. But even this was not enough to keep the men and their fighting spirits down.

"Cor blimey mate, what happened to you?" The question posed to one bandage-covered walking wounded, was answered with a cheery, "got in a fight, didn't I, but you should see the other geezer!" While another wheel-chair casualty - missing both legs - confided to some of the assembled inmates, "I was always ashamed of my size twelve feet, bloody great clod-hoppers they were... perhaps now I can get shoes a couple of sizes smaller?"

The same good humour and banter they'd used in the trenches helped in getting them through their pain and misery. But at night - under cover of the darkness - the same men wept for lost friends and themselves.

With no visible signs of injury, some of the men who'd suffered shell shock sat around like zombies; unable to speak or interact with the others, nervous systems having shut down to blot out the sounds and scenes of carnage they'd been forced to witness. These men required full time care and the patience of good medical staff, but above all, the help of their friends and comrades. So when Arthur was able to get about, he and others on the mend were able to help out some of the more needy cases by feeding and washing some of those unable to manage for themselves and talking softly as they reassured the badly injured young men of better things to come.

"Just think, you'll be joining your family (or girlfriend) soon," with good natured joshing. "Good job you can't see mate! Your blood pressure would go sky-high with the sight of some of these pretty young nurses; you'd never get out of here!"

Returning home on leave after his stay in hospital Arthur felt restless and uneasy with feelings of guilt as to why he had survived. Constantly questioning himself about whether he could have prevented the deaths of some of his close comrades if he'd acted differently; playing out the nightmarish scenes of the war, night after night in his sleep, before waking drenched in sweat and shivering.

One dream constantly came back to haunt him. In it he saw the faces of friends and comrades who'd died; their bodies lying in mud and water; eyes unblinking as they stared up into the unrelenting rain. He wanted to run to them, and carry them back, but his feet refused to move no matter how hard he tried. He'd wake himself up with an anguished cry; which stayed with him for ages afterwards.

Many men had lost their lives trying in vain to rescue their comrades so orders had been issued that no soldier was to put himself at risk. Listening to the wounded out there in 'No Mans Land' begging for help had reduced grown men to tears, but orders had to be obeyed. Special teams were sent out under the cover of darkness to bring back the wounded and dead.

How many could I have saved? Could some of them have lived if they had received help sooner? Some of the questions many of the fighting men had asked themselves over and over again. But it would be many years before the doctors would find reasons for why so many survivors felt guilty that they had survived. Many, like Arthur, finding solace in a bottle, which only gave temporary relief.

Rose was delighted to have her young son 'back from the dead', as she succinctly put it. (Not knowing how close to the truth she really was!) Fussing over him as she plied him with the very best of her cooking; the only way she knew to show this new 'grown up' version of her son, how much she loved having him back home safely.

She was worried about his drinking too. Arthur spending most of his evenings down at the local, drinking so much he was incapable of walking home unaided.

"Sorry mum!" he'd say the next day, his face haggard from the previous night's bingeing; which was repeated night after night. He didn't seem at all happy about it himself either. So as any mother would do, Rose watched her son and worried what would become of him if he continued his downward spiral. She knew that there was something eating away at him, but as Arthur never spoke about his nightmares or the horrors of war, she was no nearer finding out what was troubling her son.

"He's not right," she confided to Jesse, "anyone with half an eye can see there's something bothering the lad!"

"Aye, he never were a drinker," Jesse sighed. "Give the lad time Rose, give the lad time, he'll come all right," and Rose had to content herself with hoping that time would heal whatever was ailing her boy.

If only he could meet a bonny young lass. Yes, that would be good, now he was at home maybe it was time for him to settle down. There was nothing like a good woman to settle a chap, Rose consoled herself.

But it was not to be. Arthur couldn't or wouldn't be bothered with the girls. Not even poor Mary Drummond whom he had been friendly with all through their school days. She was a pretty fair-haired lass and would make an ideal wife for Arthur, Rose decided.

Not long after rejoining his regiment Arthur learnt they were being sent to India, to a place called Madras in Southern India; where rioting in one of the coastal towns had to be brought under control.

This gave Rose even more to worry about! Weren't they all heathens out there? France was bad enough, but now her youngest son was going to move even further away! But Arthur had looked pleased about it, so perhaps it would be a good thing... if only to get him back on his feet again.

Arthur was pleased his old mate 'Chalkie' would be going out to India too. They had both come through the war in France fairly unscathed, Chalkie also having been injured by the same mortar shell as Arthur. Hopefully this new posting would be the very thing to help them turn both their lives around.

Arthur had filled out nicely since he'd come back from France and made quite an impressive sight in his new uniform. China blue eyes gazed out from under his Army cap; his strong handsome face – scar hardly showing – still had some of the 'country boy' look about it, but now there was an underlying seriousness that showed in his eyes. The carefree young boy who'd gone to fight in France had come back a troubled man. Although his face showed none of the turbulence churning away inside him; the flashbacks that played and re-played in his mind often left him feeling depressed.

Perhaps this new posting would be just what was needed.

He wondered what India would be like? It seemed such a long way off!

Most of the lads were looking forward to their new posting. Recounting tales they'd heard about the 'Mutiny at Lucknow', 'The Black Hole of Calcutta' and other gory stories, all doubly enhanced with the re-telling! Arthur hoped the rumours circulating around the barracks weren't all true. He couldn't believe some of the bizarre things being said. Like the conversation about food one night.

"Course they eats anything there," offered a know-all, "so stay away from those curries!"

Arthur had never even heard of a 'curry' let alone eaten one!

"What's a curry?" he'd enquired, and a dozen voices all spoke at once, only too happy to enlighten him with their views on curries. So Arthur turned to his mate Chalkie White who happened to be the nearest to him.

"Go on Chalkie," he urged, "do you know what a curry is?"

"Well I've never 'ad one me'self," Chalkie admitted, "but I have heard it's made with spices - hot and all - covers up the smell of the rotten meat!"

"Nah… 'E don't know what 'ees talking abaht Ar'fer," Sid Starkey ridiculed.

"I've tried a curry. Me ma's a dab 'and at makin' it. She 'as this tin o'curry powder what she sprinkles o'er the old mans stew." He gestured, using his hand to mime the action. "The old man loves it!"

"I know it's bloody hot!" another offered.

"Yeah, fair gives you the trots too!" yelled another.

"I know'd someone who said he really liked it;" Nobby Clarke spoke laconically from his bed where he'd been trying to read. "Course, he was a darkie his 'self" he said, laughing uproariously at his own joke, and a hail of missiles, from books to shoes was thrown

50

at the unfortunate man, with a rather large tome catching him squarely where it hurt the most. Leaping off his bed, Nobby made for the safety of the showers, holding onto the front of his pants in obvious pain as the rest of the men roared with laughter.

"I've heard the 'darkies' live in mud huts out there," someone else contributed. And there was more leg-pulling until 'lights out'. Lying back on his bed Arthur thought about the things he'd heard that night, smiling into the darkness at some of the more bizarre notions bandied about.

Won't do no harm to wait and see, he thought. Besides, what did they know? Most of this bunch hadn't been further than their local cinema, he decided drowsily.

Few of the young men in Arthur's group had ever been further than France before, unlike Sergeant Winter, who had already been to Mesopotamia and had done a stint in India which made him an authority on anything 'Indian'. This made him the obvious person to educate the soldiers under his care. Which he did when the occasion presented itself! Putting the men in the picture without mincing about with any of his words!

"*'Ot, bloody 'ot,*" Sergeant Winter, London born and proud of it, had roared, when someone brave enough had asked about conditions in India as the troops prepared to embark.

"*Yer could fry an egg on the piv'ment easy; it's so bloody 'ot. Yer'll want to drink gallons o' water too, but yer don't drink none o' the bloody water till it's bin boiled!*"

He looked around at the sea of faces to see if his message was getting across.

"*And another thing,*" he bellowed raising his voice even higher. "*And yer don't - bloody - well - fraternise with the bloody nig-nogs neither!*"

The officer had looked around the troops - standing stiffly to attention – as he stabbed his cane in the air to emphasise each word.

"*Hin - fact - yer - don't - bloody - well do - nuffink - till - yer checks - wi' - me - first. IS THAT UNDERSTOOD?*" He thundered.

Couldn't be any worse than the blooming Somme, thought Arthur.

"*All right you lot,*" ordered Sergeant Winter – well into his stride - *"Find yer'selves somewheres ta kip when yer climbs on board. We'll be orf first thing in the morning,' and GORD 'elp yer all when we gets there."*

"ATTENTION!" he shouted, seeing a higher ranking officer passing. And putting his swagger stick under his left arm, the Sergeant showed the men how to do the perfect salute; his back arching with the effort of 'standing tall' in front of his men until the officer had passed.

Reverting to his usual sarcastic self, he continued... *"Don't leave any 'o yer kit behind niver or yer'll 'ave ter pi' fer it, AND THAT MEANS - NUFFINK."*

"STAND EASY," he bellowed once more, and waited for the men to assume the position before shouting... *"DISSS...MISSS."*

The soldiers fell out before picking up their kit-bags to board the troopship waiting in the dock.

This time there was none of the pomp and ceremony that had been displayed at their departure to France. It had become commonplace for soldiers to be heading off to war and this was no exception, even though their new posting was on the other side of the world.

It had been a dull day with the skies over England grey and overcast, even though it was early September. Even the troopship looked grey and sombre in the fading light; with the huge gantries and chains on the docks silhouetted against the lowering sky. The air was beginning to feel damp, so everyone was anxious to get under cover.

With other battalions going out to India, the ship would be quite crowded. One of the decks was 'out of bounds' to the soldiers, being given over to 'officers and civilians only', the civilians being wives and relations making the trip out to visit family in India. So the 'other ranks' had to make do with whatever accommodation they could find.

Space was a problem 'below decks' and, even with hammocks slung close together, there was insufficient room to accommodate all the troops. So Arthur and a few others decided to 'rough' it up on deck, the spaces of warmth around the ships funnels quickly snapped up first.

Tired after a long day, most of the men retired early and were still abed as the ship sailed through the English Channel in the fog and drizzle that had set in. Arthur, Chalkie and a dozen or so other hardy individuals who'd sat around smoking and listening to the ships engines, before huddling down under their blankets and greatcoats for the night, were now able to watch the shores of England recede into the grey horizon before heading below for a hot drink.

By the following morning the ships rails were lined with young men looking 'green around the gills' and as the ship bucked and swayed in the Bay of Biscay, even more men joined them; the turn out for 'mess' down to about half the number of troops that day! Luckily Arthur hadn't succumbed to sea-sickness and was able to tuck into the more than adequate portions that were going begging!

Once the men found their 'sea legs' things were soon back to normal and the inevitable fights broke out amongst the men who'd been cooped up below for days on end when the weather got rough. Officers in charge made them clean their rifles again and again, taking them through various drills as a means of exercise. The cramped quarters on ship were not the best place to discipline the men or keep them occupied.

When things did get out of hand, the culprits were put in the hold or made to help out with the 'lesser' jobs, either scrubbing the decks or other never-ending tasks carefully calculated to tame even the most boisterous from any further trouble making.

The weather got warmer as they rounded Portugal and Spain and by the time they reached Gibraltar many more had opted to sleep 'under the stars'.

On Sundays there were Church Parades; the men being encouraged to follow their chosen religious beliefs, with Padres of different persuasions holding Mass or prayers.

With nothing to see and the weather blustery, even a game of cards on deck was no joy, so the men organised a couple of concerts which helped to keep them occupied. Then with the officers and civilians invited, a grand night was had by all, the entertainers earning themselves an extra ration of grog for all their hard work.

Arthur had been dressed up in a 'Buttons' sort of dress uniform and along with others, similarly clad, did a cheeky song and dance act that seemed to go down rather well. Although Arthur said afterwards that he'd felt like a right 'patsy' with his cheeks brightly rouged.

When they finally reached Port Said in Egypt, the tedium was broken by the sights and sounds of the new land and its inhabitants.

With the ship at anchor awaiting fresh water and supplies, the troops were treated to a display of diving. This was done by very young boys who jumped into the greasy oil-slicked waters to retrieve pennies thrown in by some of the troops. The boys dived deep into the murky waters time and time again; risking life and limb for very little reward and the rousing cheers of the soldiers.

"Brave little tykes, that's for sure," Chalkie said to Arthur as they watched the boys diving into the briny. "Don't think I'd like to chance going into that dirty soup me'self!"

"Wonder they can find anything with the water so blooming dirty."

"Aye, poor little buggers must be starving to dive for bleedin' pennies!"

From the crowded quayside vendors in small boats offered up goods for inspection as they urged the waiting men to buy.

"Lookie, lookie, velly cheap, velly cheap, you buy, you buy!" shouted several eager sellers as they tried to hawk their wares. Leather handbags, fresh fruit, local cigarettes and every manner of goods were sent up in baskets attached to ropes which had been hauled up to the decks of the ship. All watched by a variety of people packing the quay; mostly Arabs wearing the long white robes of the desert, with a smattering of other races, all dressed in colourful costume.

The scene was one of complete contrast to anything any of them had ever seen before and they were quite sorry when it was time to leave.

The journey through the Suez Canal was hot and dusty, with the ship passing huge sand dunes built up along the sides; dredged up when the canal was dug. And there was even more sand stretching for miles into the distance beyond! Sometimes, a group of men astride camels watched from up on the dunes, silent and ominous; their silhouettes etched against the sky.

When the ship entered the Arabian Sea the soldiers knew they were getting nearer their new destination and it was with great relief when land was finally sighted.

The weather was very warm and the sea sparkled in the glow of the bright orange sun beginning its ascent into a cloudless blue sky. The tall elegant buildings and green trees lining the coastal area around the docks at Bombay coming into focus as the ship got closer to the land which was now bathed in sunlight.

Although it was quite early the jetty was already bustling with crowds of people. The troops, eager to be off the ship, had been packed since well before dawn. Ablutions complete, fed and watered for the last time on board the ship that had carried them over, they now lined the decks to get a good view of their first sight of India; soldiers at the back craning their necks for a better view of the shenanigans down below.

Small tug-boats - looking completely inadequate - had come out to guide the troopship towards its berth; the vessel coming to rest, with a blast of the ship's whistle that resounded through the docks, to cheers from the delighted troops; glad their long journey was finally over.

As the ship swayed gently in the backwash after her long journey from England; the Union Jack flag was hoisted high on the masthead, where it fluttered proudly, helped by a brisk wind blowing across the Indian Ocean.

Everyone on board the troopship was quite unprepared for the welcome they were about to receive from the waiting crowds. The soldiers watching from their vantage point high above the docks were delighted by the glorious riot of colour and the bustling crowds thronging the dockside.

Military type bands dotted the quayside playing toe-tapping marching tunes, the Indian bandsmen dressed in matching uniforms of red, blue and white. Their brass instruments glinting in the morning sun as they played 'Colonel Bogey' and other popular tunes – badly – as they competed against each other.

"Will you look at that," breathed Chalkie as they looked down at the teeming, colourful mass of people, but Arthur didn't need telling. He was absolutely fascinated by the sights and sounds below.

Brown faces topped with turbans and assorted head gear mingled with pith-helmeted Europeans; some being accompanied by their ladies, who were resplendent in colourful dresses and wide-brimmed hats, holding tiny parasols aloft; Coolies carrying loads on their backs, fought to regain their balance as they pushed and shoved their way through the multifarious throng; while vendors of everything from 'chai' to leather goods shouted out their wares; each trying to outdo the other as they touted for business.

"Lookie Tommie, very cheap, very cheap," came from all sides as they vied with one another for the attention of the soldiers. Very similar to what they'd been treated to when they were at Port Said.

Licensed baggage handlers with small trolleys stood in the bright sunshine, waiting patiently for the mass exodus of passengers, the men dressed in white dhotis, red shirts and turbans, for easier identification.

The Indian Police in their khaki uniforms and starched turbans – with a high cocks-comb end of turban sitting proudly upright, insignia at its centre gleaming in the sunlight - carried long polished sticks under their arms as they patrolled haughtily through the crowds in an attempt to dissuade the usual pick-pockets and unlicensed peddlers from operating. Many sporting bristling moustaches that had been tapered and twirled high at either side of their top lips.

Indian women - faces hidden behind bright saris edged with gold borders - peered up at the white faced 'angrezi' (English) sahibs; who wolf-whistled and called out to the waiting crowds; the weeks of sea-sickness, rations and the close proximity of other sweaty bodies forgotten, as they witnessed their triumphant arrival into India; their future accommodation in the lap of the gods for now.

"Jesus, there must be bloody hundreds of them. Where did they all come from?" Chalkie wondered aloud.

But Arthur didn't really care where they'd come from. He was swamped by a myriad of feelings that he had never felt before! The air smelt of spices, and the sun was warm on his face. He felt good! After the cramped journey, where his companions wore the same dull khaki uniform as himself, the bright, cheerful colours down below were like the flowers in a beautiful garden. Inhaling deeply, he smelt the spice-laden air.

"Dunno mate," he murmured automatically.

CHAPTER SEVEN

The Tattoo

The sights, sounds and smells of India, were something Arthur could never have imagined in his wildest dreams. About how he felt, however, would take a little more time! If Sergeant Winter ever got off their backs!

"Right, get yer kit-bags on yer shoulders," roared Sergeant Winter, *"an try to look like yer bloody-well knows where yer goin'!"*

Sergeant Winter was addressing the assembled troops under his command prior to disembarkation. It was his job to make sure the troops conducted themselves with dignity and orderliness and he was going to make sure they did just that!

Indian bands lined the quayside at the port. The bandsmen, dressed in flamboyant uniforms of bright blues, reds and yellows - brass instruments glinting in the sun - had been doing their best to keep in tune all morning as they played all the well known marching tunes; the soldiers stepping off the gang-planks to rousing cheers and a rendition of one of their all-time favourites; the inevitable 'Colonel Bogey', with some of the soldiers singing their own naughty words to the popular song.

The people of India had become quite used to the 'British' presence after years of wars and counter wars under the British administration and things seemed to be running smoothly - on the surface at least! So as long as the soldiers kept out of trouble, paid due respect to the customs of the local community, and didn't cause too much trouble, everyone got on beautifully. Newcomers were greeted with great pomp and ceremony.

The latest batch of Army recruits being no exception.

"Eft - ite - eft - ite," Sergeant Winter called as he moved the men off smartly - cane tucked neatly under his arm - to more cheers from the onlookers. He looked every bit the soldier and the epitome of what the military was all about. Even the Indian Police Officers, who'd gathered to keep the crowd under control, joined in, standing to attention, and saluting smartly as the soldiers marched past. The unexpected honour bestowed upon the soldiers made them walk tall as they marched off, keeping perfect time, with a new spring to their step.

The band played on!

Although it was quite early in the morning the sun still shone with fierce intensity; the sea sparkling as the wind rippled over its surface. Fishing boats - their sails billowing in the wind - bobbed about in the swell as the fishermen brought in their morning catch; the land being marginally cooler here than it was inland. But not cool enough for the contingent of English soldiers, more used to the cool damp conditions of England; all of them sweating profusely from the exertion of just shouldering their heavy kitbags, let alone any extra movement.

Piling gratefully into the waiting transport, they were soon trundling down leafy roads towards the station. Glad they hadn't been made to march in the heat.

Arthur was impressed by the tall buildings and well kept roads, which he hadn't expected to see and especially the bustling throng of people going about their daily business. Gaily-dressed women, wearing flowers in their hair, balanced baskets of produce on their heads as they walked gracefully along, while the men, thin and wiry, walked quickly along under the weight of heavy sacks they carried on their backs; their knobbly knees protruding from under their white loose Indian pants - that someone explained were called 'dhoti's' - as they weaved their way through the traffic, making Arthur and some of the other soldiers - still dressed in full uniform - think that they too would like to be able to wear the loose-fitting garments themselves.

The traffic consisted mainly of small horse-drawn carriages, with a small brown man sitting behind the single horse which was harnessed between a pair of wooden shafts. These, Arthur learnt, were called 'tongas'. With a few army vehicles belching black smoke as they tried to manoeuvre their way through the traffic; the drivers shouting profanities and shaking their fists at the slower-moving traffic; generally a bullock cart, with a small, brown man sitting at the front of a fully-laden open cart. The brown skinned drivers completely unperturbed by all the horn blowing or other irate drivers forced to wait, or manoeuvre their own transport around the wide, low-lying cart.

Dozens of pedestrians seemed to be taking full advantage of the situation, glad of the chance to take a short-cut through the traffic, adding yet more chaos to the congested roads.

Smartly dressed policemen, in dark blue uniforms and white gloves, stood on small round platforms in the middle of the road, directing traffic; waving their arms about with exaggerated gestures; their faces impassive, looking for all the world like little wind-up toys as they spun around on their pedestals.

"Seems like everything here is under control," observed Chalkie sarcastically as they passed yet another junction where more chaos reigned. And Arthur, who'd been looking at the crowds of people milling about as they went about their daily business, nodded in agreement.

"Wonder where all the rioting is? Everything seems peaceful enough here," Arthur said, looking around.

"Place called Malibar, but yer've a long way ter go afore we get there!" Sergeant Winter's voice reminded them... and it was!

Even with transport the men were still expected to march part of the way, and it was another three days before they arrived at their destination in Southern India, thoroughly fed up and drenched in sweat from their long journey.

Their new barracks in Madras proved to be quite spacious, The 'Cantonment' offering a few extra comforts, like decent beds for one thing.

In common with most of India there were many beggars crying "baksheesh (alms) sahib, baksheesh," and, "you wanting good batman?" (servant) Their voices growing even louder if one of the soldiers put their hands into their pockets - even for a handkerchief; the din only ceasing when they were 'shooed off' by one of the Indian guards at the gates or Sergeant Winter, who once again took charge; drawing himself up, to bellow "Get yer'selves OUT of here, juldi, juldi" (quickly, quickly). Impressing his men no end by his mastery of the Indian language and scattering the beggars who had been pestering them for baksheesh; the little urchins scampering off in a cloud of dust.

The services of a 'batman' were quite normal in postings abroad. Most Army personnel above the rank of Corporal acquired a boy or man to 'help out' with anything from polishing buttons and boots to making the odd cup of 'chai'. The officers also availing themselves of this service, (although in their case it was one of the junior officers doing their running about) tried to look the other way when mere privates paid a few rupees for a young boy to help them 'blanco' his puttees, or fetch and carry, although it was frowned upon by some of the higher ranking officers in the garrison.

Later that week, and every time any of the soldiers left the cantonment, they were accosted by an assortment of beggars; some with missing limbs, begging for a few pice. (Indian money of very little value) One of the Indian armed guards usually shooing them off if they became too persistent.

One small boy however, had taken a shine to Arthur. This small, scruffy chap insisted on sticking like glue to the soldier who he'd singled out from the moment he'd first arrived.

"Salaam sahib, I am called Churi," he said, holding his hands together as if in prayer. "I am also speaking much English, oh yes indeed, I'm also working bloody hard, you bet!" he boasted. Some of his jargon obviously picked up from the soldiers stationed in Madras.

"I'm being very good batman sir, not much money, working bloody hard sir!"

Looking down, Arthur saw a small Indian boy, of indeterminate age - due to the dirt covering his face - with big brown eyes set in an elfin face. This dirty child was looking up at him from between and beneath a shock of dusty black curls tumbling down over his forehead, almost hiding the upper half of his face. Even, white teeth sparkled in the boy's face; in what Arthur thought was a maniacal grin; his quick appraisal taking in the ragged, torn, and dusty clothing, along with the boy's bare, calloused feet.

"But I don't need a batman," replied Arthur, trying to shake the boy off. "Go and help someone else!"

"Please sahib, I am being your chai-boy (tea-boy) sahib or doing anything sahib," the young boy begged Arthur. His brown eyes pleading as he held his hands respectfully together. "Letting me showing the sahib!" he implored.

Arthur, who could think of nothing worse than being served tea by this scruffy individual, turned away, hoping the boy would take the hint. He'd seen dozens of these same unkempt children on his way over from the ship and had felt truly sorry for their circumstances, but he couldn't tolerate dirt!

"Take no notice of them," he'd been warned, "they come out looking poor so they can get some baksheesh from you. Some of them even injure themselves, cutting off a limb to appear even more worthy of help!"

After having seen the many patients who'd been injured in the war, Arthur wondered how anyone could deliberately injure themselves in this way just to get a few pennies. Surely they must be very, very desperate.

"Please sahib," the voice at his side wheedled, "without working I am bookah (hungry)," the child said, rubbing his stomach to emphasise his words and giving Arthur a pitiful look.

Arthur understanding the universal gesture couldn't refuse. Taking a few coins from his pocket, he said, "here, now go and get yourself something to eat. And while you're at it, get yourself cleaned up too!" Not expecting to see the boy again.

But the little urchin was not to be deterred!

"Chai sahib?" a young voice broke through Arthur's sleep and opening his eyes next morning he saw a fairly smart young boy holding out a small tray, with a steaming mug of tea.

Rubbing the sleep from his eyes Arthur realised this was the young boy who'd offered to be his personal servant the day before. And he'd come back! This time, with his hair trimmed and brushed from his face he looked quite presentable. The boy had 'scrubbed up' really well too! And the clothes he now wore appeared to be clean.

But his nails still looked as if they held a bucketful of dirt, thought Arthur. "Take that tea away and get your blooming nails cleaned boy!" he ordered. "And don't come back until your nails are clean, understand?"

"Hai, (yes) I'm understanding sahib," Churi said quickly, "I'm cleaning the blooming nails."

Arthur realised he was stuck with the young boy who just didn't know when to take 'no' for an answer, but the boy was obviously willing to learn, and so Arthur struck a bargain with the youngster.

"But only on the condition that you clean your hands thoroughly before you make me another cup of tea!" Arthur threatened Churi.

"Atcha (all right) sahib," Churi stood straight and at attention to show he understood.

"What did you say your name was?"

"Please SAR, I'm being Churi."

"Well you look like a right 'Charlie' to me," laughed Arthur.

"Atcha sahib, Charlie I'm being from now!" Churi saluted the soldier and turning smartly, went off with the mug of tea to start his duties, returning in double-quick time with hot water for Arthur's shave.

Hmm... I could easily get used to this, thought Arthur.

Charlie, as the boy had now become, smartened himself up no end. His fingernails put up for inspection for Arthur every morning, until he was given the all-clear.

His "tik-hai (that's fine) Charlie, you'll do for now," bringing a beaming smile from the eager young boy, who would then walk away with a whistle and exaggerated swagger to show to any of the other young 'chokra' (boy servant) boys who may have been watching, that he was now officially a batman.

The bond between the soldier and the young boy grew daily as Charlie quickly made life more bearable for the young soldier in India. There was nothing the boy wouldn't do for his new master; Arthur's early morning tea, hot shaving water and polished boots were delivered punctually each day, and in time the small boy became indispensable to the English soldier.

With Arthur's help Charlie soon learnt some English, albeit interspersed with the odd swear-word he just couldn't seem to get shot of. In turn, teaching Arthur some Hindustani, and explaining something of his own Indian cultures and customs. He was always there if needed, no matter what time of the day or night, sometimes even putting Arthur to bed when the soldier had had too much to drink.

"Whereabouts do you live, Charlie?" Arthur asked the young Indian boy one day. "You seem to be here first thing in the morning and again very late at night? Don't your parents worry about you?" Charlie shook his head as he laughed. "I am libbing everywhere sahib, everywhere," the boy grinned, waving a hand that encompassed north, south, east and west. "No mother, no father."

Arthur learnt later that the boy slept rough just outside the barracks at night; along with dozens of others who got by on the meagre wages the soldiers were able to pay. Sleeping under the stars in the good weather, and squeezing themselves under whatever shelter they could find during the rainy season.

Most of the poor boys were from neighbouring villages where it was impossible for them to obtain work. More than three-quarters of the money received from their masters were sent back home, to help keep their families; the chokra boys themselves living on very little other than the food given to them by their 'masters', and whatever they could make 'on the side', whenever they got the chance. Converting anything their employers were able to give them - usually tinned food or cast-off clothing - into a few pice. The youngest boys smoked any 'cadged' cigarettes that they could, and the local 'beedies' (Indian cigarettes) too.

One afternoon, after Arthur and some of his mates had had one too many drinks, they foolishly entered a tattoo parlour. Nearly everyone went back with some small tattoo on their arms... except Arthur.

The tattoo he'd had done covering most of his chest!

It had taken hours to do and although it hadn't hurt at the time - Arthur being numbed by the effects of the alcohol - later on his whole chest felt as if it was on fire.

Charlie, as always, ministered to the soldier, buying and applying a lotion that could have gone either way, and although it did ease the pain marginally, for days afterwards Arthur couldn't bear the weight of clothes near his chest, having to sleep on his back as he waited for his skin to heal. Then in order to ease the pain, Arthur would drink a few beers each morning, and would be fast asleep in the afternoons.

Charlie, always ready to take advantage of any situation, came up with a real 'doozie' of an idea. He began sneaking a few of his mates in to see his brave sahib's tattoo. Holding out his hand for their few pice as they filed past the sleeping Englishman, who lay flat on his back, snoring loudly; the massive tattoo of a lion sitting guard over the Union Jack flag, still red-raw, on his exposed chest.

The lion seemed to be alive! Its mighty jaws moving with each breath the sleeping man took and expelled. The brilliantly coloured piece of art the biggest and the best they'd ever seen!

Although some marvelled at the poor 'pagli' (mad) sahib!

The verdict being... he must be absolutely 'bonkers' to have gone through so much pain. Charlie, pocketing the coins, happily agreed. His own chest swelling with pride as he bestowed many more accolades on his sleeping master, some real and some imagined.

Charlie the bat-boy would go far indeed!

Curries were sometimes cooked up by the military cooks, into which a variety of ingredients were added, including copious amounts of sugar. So when Arthur got his first taste of curry, he was sorely disappointed.

The mess hall had been too hot to eat in the day Arthur decided to try a curry, so he'd carried the plate of curry and rice back to the shade of a large tree in the cantonment, and was really looking forward to his meal. But the first spoonful had been enough to put him off curries for life! Pushing the plate aside, Arthur told the ever-present Charlie to finish it off; something he did quite regularly with the army food! The boy took the plate of food quickly, and squatting down on the ground nearby, took a mouthful, only to quickly spit it out again as he pulled a face.

"What's up, I thought you people liked curries?"

"Hai sahib, but that is not being curry," Charlie said sadly.

A few days later, Charlie appeared carrying a small dish, which was covered over with a fairly clean cloth.

"Please sahib, this is being curry," Charlie said proudly, a big smile lighting up his face.

Arthur, not wanting to appear rude, gave the contents a sniff and the aroma that went up his nose was unlike anything he'd ever smelt before! 'Won't kill me to try just a small taste,' he thought... Forgetting everything Sergeant Winter had told them. But as his ma often said…"You've got to eat a peck of dirt afore ye die!"

"Fetch me a spoon Charlie," he ordered, and dipping his finger into the now lukewarm food, he tentatively put it into his mouth. Charlie came rushing back, bubbling over with excitement to see his sahib doing the finger tasting.

"Its very good sahib, I'm buying it from a very well cooking lady" he babbled. Arthur filled the spoon with some of the mixture, lifting it to his mouth with some alacrity as his taste buds had already found it to be to his liking. Soon he'd finished off the plateful of curry; mainly vegetables, and certainly hot, but nothing like as hot as he'd been led to believe!

Charlie was over the moon about the fact his sahib had eaten the curry, and had obviously liked it! Telling Arthur he'd requested it from a very kind Indian lady who'd been pleased that Charlie was now in regular employment, and keeping himself so clean, wanted the kind sahib to try a proper curry.

"Wait till it goes through you boy!" one of the other men chortled, when Arthur told about his first real curry. "Bet your arse will be on fire!"

But the next day dawned sunny and clear, without any after effects from Arthur's moment of madness.

Then with his drinking out of hand, Arthur, who'd attained the rank of Corporal was 'busted' down to Private once more, losing pay and spending more time in the 'lock-up' for rowdy behaviour and earning himself yet more time 'spud-bashing'. Until one day the cookhouse found itself short of cooks and Arthur was 'volunteered' once more, this time coming into his own and finding he was a natural at this 'cooking lark'!

Remembering his mother's homemade soups and stews, Arthur added more ingredients – which his mother had been unable to afford – like chunks of meat, and suet dumplings, which had the men queuing up for second helpings. More broths, shepherds pie, and even the odd curry, added to his growing list of 'things' that were considered good enough for the hungry men.

The Catering Officer, whose job it was to make sure the soldiers were properly fed, was more than pleased with Arthur's proficiency and he was soon promoted within the cooking staff. The extra pay came in very handy too.

Recipes from cookery books were adapted for the troops, and Arthur went from strength to strength. His talents applauded and appreciated by the soldiers who were so far away from home.

Arthur had finally found his niche in life. He could cook!

CHAPTER EIGHT

The Cookhouse & Fate

Staff were often 'borrowed' from the army establishments by the Officers wives, especially any good cooks, to help out with the many 'soirees' that were given to entertain military dignitaries and important members of the upper echelons.

These parties were held in some of the more opulent houses, or large marquees; especially erected for the occasion, with additional servants hired to help out in the evening.

Everything had to be carefully planned, from the seating plan to the flowers decorating the tables, and of course, the food; which had to be 'just so' for these special occasions; with nothing left to chance, the person giving the 'bash' wanting above all to impress everyone with her ability to organise the event.

So the lady in charge of the party was often determined to have several courses of the worst possible things served at these events; having looked up various cookery books without having either cooked or tasted any of the recipes herself; which meant she went completely 'over the top' in her attempts to impress.

The menu, if presented in England, would have been impressive, but in a hot country like India, where temperatures soared in the summer months, the same food would be quite disastrous, spoiling any attempt at gastronomic excellence. Soufflés sank and meringues melted, while fish had to be filleted and consumed quickly in the hot weather of India; too many people had choked on fish-bones in the past, so Arthur would politely 'advise' the person giving the event to revise some of their over-ambitious plans, gently persuading them around to a good old fashioned roast for the main meal; maintaining it would be much more appreciated than the over-the-top dish that may have looked delicious on the colour-plate of a cookery book etc. But he was very tactful about it, so the lady in question invariably thought the menu eventually chosen had been her idea all along! His blue eyes, manly physique, and air of quiet calm winning them over much quickly than mere words could.

He did however give them 'carte blanche' when it came to the choice of hors d'oeuvres and desserts - so long as they left out the whipped cream!

Arthur had a 'light hand' with pastry, and turned out light and buttery, 'melt-in-the-mouth' biscuits for the petit-fours, garnishing them with tiny morsels of the tastiest bits and pieces. For the main course a few juicy, tender peacocks - considered holy and therefore illegal to shoot - could be supplied by the black market. If any awkward questions had been asked...Arthur was prepared to swear he thought they were just wild turkeys!

Meat could be bought plentifully, even though most Indians were vegetarians, and chickens although scrawny, could be fattened up in time for special occasions like Christmas. Wild boar, venison and other meats were available almost everywhere.

For the buffet events, the tables groaned under the weight of roast suckling pig, and huge glazed hams, as easy to carve as butter. With both English and Indian dishes, there were chicken legs, sausage rolls, plates of spiced meat, and other things too numerous to mention.

Bowls of fresh fruit and flowers decorated the trestle tables, and the food was always beautifully cooked and presented.

The extensive grounds and gardens were big enough for the large marquees, which comfortably held upwards of a hundred people. In the cool of the evening the elite came; women in their ball gowns and the men resplendent in their evening suits of white jackets and black ties, or regimental dress evening wear.

Soldiers from various military bands played a medley of popular tunes throughout the evening and everyone pretended they were back in 'Blighty' with the Indian servants quietly serving aperitifs and hors d'oeuvres - the only reminder that the assembled Europeans were far away from England.

So with ample good food, and plenty of drinks, the evening was generally a resounding success.

The compliments came rolling in for Arthur.

"That was a really lovely meal, thank you," the colonel's wife praised Arthur one evening, after yet another excellent dinner had gone well - and with the compliments of her guests still ringing in her ears. Buoyed up with the few glasses of 'bubbly' she'd had during dinner, she'd come to convey thanks to all the catering staff for all their efforts.

"Thank you ma'am."

"Have you been cooking for long?" The lady enquired, eyeing the tall good-looking sergeant in the smart white catering tunic before her. He really was quite a hunk, she decided... all those lovely muscles showing up under that white tunic! Very nice. She liked his open, honest face too... and those blue eyes.

The colonel's wife was quite good looking for her age, probably, 'fifty something' Arthur decided. But she had kept her figure, unlike a lot of the others and looked quite pretty with her face flushed the colour of her dress; blonde hair fluffed out around it, although Arthur himself preferred his girls younger, and darker haired.

"I don't think we met on the last occasion?" She queried.

"No ma'am," Arthur said, remembering the episode only too well.

He'd been extremely hot, and had had one or two - and maybe a few more drinks than he should have had, just to keep cool - and by the end of the evening wasn't in any state to 'see' anyone, least of all the wife of a Colonel! Thank goodness she hadn't seen him bunking off when he'd caught a glimpse of her bearing down on the marquee.

"Could you let my cook have a few of your recipes?" she gushed.

Any moment now she's going to ask me the dreaded question, he thought.

"Certainly ma'am," Arthur knew the signs too well, but knew his place even better. Here it comes, he thought.

"Would you care to attend my next gathering, only next time perhaps you can come as my guest?"

"Thank you ma'am," Arthur replied, secretly wondering what excuse he could give.

He was about to be invited to one of those 'Fishing Fleet' parties again!

With nothing much to do with their time in India, some of the memsahib's had become match makers. Any bachelor in India being fair game!

Many young women made the long journey out to India in the hope of finding a husband from the many officers stationed in India.

'The Fishing Fleet', as they were named, consisted of young ladies from England who were unable to find a husband there. So they undertook the perilous journey, facing malaria, dysentery and all manner of other ailments, in order to find a suitable partner to settle down with.

The men stationed in India, and still unmarried, were thought to be 'lonely' and fair game for the English women. With a few of the non-commissioned officers considered as quite eligible too.

The officer's wives put on 'special evenings' and invited the new arrivals along to meet some of the prospective officers or NCO's stationed in the area, who were unattached and available. Arthur was always being invited to some function or another. He didn't mind the cooking bit – but being quite shy didn't much care about mingling with his superiors. What if he made a fool of himself? So he always smiled politely, listened to what the officer's wives had to say about his cooking, while guessing correctly what really was cooking up in their fertile imaginations, before hightailing it back to the safety of the barracks.

Meanwhile, as he became accustomed to his new home, and the people, Arthur had begun to learn the 'lingo.' Charlie his young 'bat-boy' helping him with much of what he wanted to know. Most of the other men tried out their mastery of the Indian language too; the barracks echoing to the shouted commands given in an assortment of Indian words. "Juldi, juldi," (quickly, quickly) or "juldi karow," (do it quickly) followed by choice swear words, when provoking each other.

Arthur had taken a liking to the gentle Indian race, finding that if they were treated well, they reciprocated.

The Indian lady who'd made Arthur his first real curry, had been pleased that the sahib had liked her cooking and had extended an invitation for him to come around to their house for a meal at any time he liked. He'd gone gladly, partly to thank her for her kindness, but also out of curiosity.

The old lady and her husband made him feel completely at ease. Luckily the old gentleman knew a smattering of English, so between Arthur's shaky Hindi and the old man's odd English word here and there, they got by fairly adequately; even if they did seem to be at cross-purposes sometimes as the couple spoke in a mixture of Hindi and Tamil, but by asking them to speak slowly, Arthur was able to understand much of what was being said, thanks to Charlie's coaching.

The old lady wore fresh flowers in her hair, woven into a bun at the back of her head, her hair looking slick and very dark for a woman of her years! The husband, a wizened little fellow, had no hair at all; his face and head having the appearance of polished ebony. His bird-like eyes were always twinkling; either from pure merriment or faulty tear ducts.

The couple occupied just a one-roomed apartment, where they ate, slept and entertained; quite content with their lot.

The food was always fresh and good, even though it was vegetarian. Arthur enjoying the big plates of rice - each grain separate and fluffy - and the generous helpings of curry the lady ladled on. Remembering his first taste of chapattis they'd been placed in front of him. The beige round bread had looked strange to him, the old lady urged him to try, attempting to make him understand by saying, "khanna, khanna!" (food, food) Then, breaking off a small bit of the bread and wrapping it around a portion of food, she had held it to her mouth.

Then Arthur had tried it himself. Using his hand, he followed the woman's example; enjoying the bread's soft texture and flavour; tucking into his food with great gusto, much to the merriment of his hosts who were delighted the sahib could eat 'hot' dishes, although he'd noticed the woman never joined the men while they ate.

Charlie told him later that women in India always served the men and guests their food first. Eating only after they'd made sure the men had had enough. Arthur thought this a strange custom, but respected their ways. To compensate, he would take around something for the old lady whenever he visited. Sometimes a box of sweetmeats; which he knew she loved, or fresh mangoes - when in season - again on Charlie's instruction.

The woman's face lit up when she saw what he'd bought. She was like a child in her enjoyment!

"You don't have to bring gifts every time you come sahib" Amma would gently chide him, taking the mangoes, or other gifts he'd brought. Her delight just the simple pleasure of having someone else, other than her husband, enjoy her cooking. The old man ate quickly, burping once or twice to show his appreciation, his eyes watering from a different source than Arthur's when he bit into a large green chilli once.

God... that had been mighty hot!

Drinking gallons of water afterwards, Arthur had decided there were some things he just couldn't eat.

Always an early riser, Arthur went to the local markets to buy fresh fruit and vegetables for himself, and to check out the prices. Sometimes getting there almost before the vendors arrived. Buying himself a cup of hot 'chai' he would listen to the good-natured banter of the sellers as they stacked the mounds of plump red tomatoes alongside purple bringalls, red and green chillies, and fresh saag leaves.

The people in Madras dressed as colourfully as their vegetables. Their good-natured brown faces wreathed in smiles as they looked forward to another day of bartering. The flower sellers all wore fresh flowers in their hair; sometimes a bunch of sweet-smelling jasmine buds coiled around the bun at the nape of their neck, or a scarlet flower tucked behind an ear. Squatting on the ground, they displayed their flowers in big round wicker baskets; with braided garlands of flowers hung nearby, ready for the many 'offerings'.

Arthur learned that even the poorest people bought flowers nearly every day, placing them before their altars at home, or making 'poogas' (offerings) to their favourite gods and goddesses. The freshly cut blooms of white, sweet-scented jasmine, golden marigolds, roses and frangipani; mingling with the smell of delicious fruit, spices and freshly cooked snacks.

This was supposed to be a poor country, and yet they seemed to be far happier than many of his own countrymen and women, he thought.

He'd been amazed at the variety of fruit and vegetables available; from mangoes, that came in every size, shape and colour, to juicy oranges, that needed very little peeling, to huge bunches of bananas, complete with a massive stalk, with many more, as yet unidentified. Some of the vegetables looked quite weird, but by asking and being genuinely interested, he'd been told just how to prepare and cook even the most difficult ones. One particular wrinkly, green one fascinated him; it was called karela, Charlie had told him, but it was an acquired taste. But Arthur needed to know what it tasted like? And biting into one, he decided he'd give that one a miss. It was as bitter as gall, and made his mouth numb! Although there were many people who loved it, judging by the amount sold.

When Arthur's transfer to Bangalore came Charlie was heartbroken. He'd become attached to the young soldier whom he'd put to bed on many a night when the sahib had come back rolling drunk. As he thought back to the early days when the sahib got his lion tattoo, he felt his world just wouldn't be the same. These days, when he watched the soldier having a strip-wash he could see the immense work of art which covered the man's chest. And as the sahib's muscles rippled, the lion seemed to come to life!

So it was with a heavy heart that he bade his master goodbye... the many gifts the sahib had given him being little compensation for the poor boy who now had to find another master. The tears Charlie shed were genuine and Arthur too, had a lump in his throat.

Bangalore was much cooler than Madras had been and here too there were many beautiful gardens and sights to take his mind off thoughts of home. Arthur was now earning about twenty rupees a week, and was well into the catering. He also had more time on his hands.

One fine sunny day, he arrived at one of the houses to supervise the catering for a big party. The 'big dinner' was being given by a Lord and Lady Somerville, who lived in a large house overlooking a beautiful garden set in several acres of grounds.

The marquees had already been erected and the food preparation was going well, so Arthur popped out for a quiet smoke; standing in the shade of a lovely old neem tree, as he admired the beds of pretty flowers. He could hear the bees buzzing around lazily and if he closed his eyes, he could almost be back at home in England; the smell of the flowers reminding him of his mother's garden, before becoming aware of a voice calling - over and above the clattering, and chattering of voices in the marquee - and looking up, he saw what all the fuss was about.

Two very young boys, of about three or four, were giggling as they ran off across the beautifully manicured lawns. They wore identical sailor-suits, and were widening the distance between themselves and the young woman running after them.

"Clive, Peter, come back you rascals!" she called, but the youngsters just giggled all the more and made as if to run behind the marquee where Arthur stood.

"Whoa, whoa!" he said gently, putting a hand out to check their headlong flight. "I think you're wanted by someone." The two boys looked up at the huge figure of Arthur towering above them, and one of them immediately burst into tears, the other quickly following suit. He had two very tearful boys on his hands when the young lady finally caught up with them. She was out of breath, and could hardly speak.

"How could you be so naughty, and why did you run away from me?" she gasped.

"Sorry, nanny," the boys chorused, as their sobs subsided and allowed her to wipe away their tears.

Arthur could only look on in amazement.

Seeing the look on his face, she realised she still hadn't thanked the young man for stopping the children from running even further away from her. Brushing a few stray hairs away from her face with the back of her hand, she turned her attention to him and he found himself gazing into the loveliest pair of liquid brown eyes he'd ever seen.

"Thank you for stopping these two mischievous boys," she said and smiled up at Arthur, who stood, open-mouthed and bereft of speech.

"You cannot take your eyes off them for a minute."

Pausing for breath she continued, "I'm their nanny and this is Clive," she said, pushing a reluctant Clive forward, who solemnly shook hands with Arthur.

"And this other scamp is Peter."

Arthur shook hands with both boys, his huge fist enveloping their tiny hands, and answered their "how do you do sir?" with an "all the better for seeing you boys." Although his eyes were more on their nanny, than the two very subdued young gentlemen.

"Thank you again Sergeant," she said, noticing the stripes on his arm, and with a shy smile, ushered the boys back towards the house.

For Arthur, it had been love at first sight!

He wanted to shout after her, but could only watch her walk

away and out of his sight. Tonight, he thought, I might just get to see her after I've finished the catering... I mean... didn't the lady of the house always come to thank him? And then he'd ask casually after the two boys... and their nanny of course!

Arthur's imagination knew no bounds. All he knew was he just *had* to see her again. But although he managed to sneak a few looks inside the marquee after the meal, all he saw were couples dancing, and not a trace of the young lady he really wanted to see.

For days afterwards Arthur replayed the scene back to himself... thinking of all the things he could have said. But now it was too late. But at least he knew she was a nanny. And he had to see her again.

Until one day he had that 'eureka' feeling.

Just where did nannies take their charges on a nice warm day? Why, the park of course!

For days after that, whenever he was off duty, Arthur haunted all the parks near to where the boys lived, vowing never to give up until he'd actually spoken to her. But after a couple of weeks he began to lose heart.

Always a keen gardener - he'd helped his mother Rose in her kitchen garden when he was a small boy - Arthur now found he was beginning to enjoy the parks full of lovely flowers. Sitting on one of the park seats he gazed around at the well kept lawns and flowerbeds where he seemed to have spent much of his time recently. Noticing the different species of flowers, perhaps for the first time since he'd arrived in India, he suddenly realised the solution to all his problems was there... right in front of his eyes!

Flowers, he'd give her a bunch of flowers.

Why hadn't he thought of it before?

Next morning he was at the market bright and early and got one of the flower sellers to sell him a large bunch of mixed flowers, spending almost a day's pay on them.

Then, back at the barracks, he cadged a lift to the house, but his courage deserted him once more! He walked past the house several times, unable to pluck up the courage to actually try knocking on the door; much to his relief, he saw an old Indian man who looked like the gardener, coming out of a side gate of the house.

"Do you work at this house?" Arthur asked the man, who nodded in the affirmative, his eyes glued to the big sahib in uniform, holding tightly onto a bunch of flowers.

"Do you know the young memsahib who looks after the two boys?" And again the man nodded. "Could you take these flowers to her?" Arthur said, thrusting the flowers towards the man. But the man didn't take the flowers!

Again Arthur proffered the flowers, "for - the - young - memsahib - who - looks - after - the - two - young - boys" he spoke slowly and clearly so the man would understand. "Will - you - do - that?" And when the man still looked blankly at him, Arthur drew some coins from his pocket, offering them to the man. But when the man refused the money and the flowers Arthur thought he was going mad.

"Flowers - for - the - young - lady - who - looks - after - the - two - boys." He slowly articulated in his best effort to speak Hindi.

And a beatific smile broke over the old man's face, his head wobbled about as he slowly realised what the young sahib who kept thrusting flowers and coins at him, was talking about.

"But," he answered slowly, "there is nobodies being in the house."

"What do you mean nobody? Are they all out?"

"All going out... all going far away. The burra sahib, the burra memsahib, and the childrens..., all going too."

"Gone?" Arthur repeated stupidly, his heart diving into his army issue size ten boots. The conversation between him and the mali (gardener) might have gone on all day if someone hadn't come out of the house opposite, and seen Arthur with his bunch of flowers.

It was a nanny with a pram.

"If you're calling on Lord and Lady Somerville you're too late." she called from the other side of the road. "They've gone away for the summer."

Arthur crossed over the road to where the nanny stood, and asked politely, "any idea where they've gone?"

"Yes," the nanny replied, "they have gone to 'Ooty' for the summer."

She smiled as she walked off pushing a pram with her own charge down the road.

Arthur learnt that Ootacamund or 'Ooty' as it was known, was the very beautiful and popular hill-station in southern India, used by the 'upper crust' during the very worst of the summer months. So he had to take himself and his flowers off to bide his time, still wondering if he'd ever see the girl of his dreams again.

CHAPTER NINE

Flowers and Finger Bowls

The summer months seemed to go on forever. The shutters remaining closed at the Somerville residence whenever Arthur walked past.

Surely people didn't take this long on summer holidays thought Arthur. Perhaps it had all been a dream? What if there was someone else she was interested in? Was he really just wasting his time? It had been just the briefest of encounters after all. What if he was making a complete ass of himself? A girl like that wouldn't even consider someone like himself, would she? It wasn't as if she'd given him any indication that she was interested in him. All she'd done was smile nicely and thanked him for stopping the two boys from running off! Much better if he were to forget the whole thing, he reasoned.

As the weeks stretched into months, Arthur felt more and more despondent. Try as he might, he couldn't get those limpid brown eyes out of his thoughts. He stayed in, writing home more often, and generally mooching about. And he seemed to be forever losing his temper with everyone around him. The other cooks in the kitchens with whom he'd got on reasonably well before now avoided him.

"What's up with him?" They questioned behind his back, "never used to be this bloody grumpy!" And they would congregate in a huddle to have a quiet joke among themselves, leaving Arthur out.

He knew it was happening but was unable to be any different, reminding him of his father and his angry outbursts sometimes and he didn't want to turn out like his father, but he was.

"Call these bloody trays washed? You could feed an army with what's left behind on them!" he bellowed at the top of his voice one day, on seeing a couple of microscopic dots that had been left behind. "Get them bloody washed again, and do them PROPERLY this time!"

The two troopers who'd been assigned to scrubbing out the pans glanced at one another as if to say; 'Watch out, he's in one of his moods again.'

"He's doin' me 'ead in," whispered Bert Billings to one of the other men on washing up duties as they stood side by side in front of the big sinks, up to their elbows in soapy suds.

"Sorry Sarge," Bert called out, "I'll do 'em again!" and wiping his hands down the sides of his big apron, he walked briskly over to where Arthur stood; the trays in question not looking at all bad as far as Bert was concerned. And with a "Sorry Sarge" he carried them off to wash them out once again.

Arthur left them to it, and would have been quite offended if he'd heard their parodying of him when he was out of sight.

Even Chalkie was worried when Arthur continually refused to go out drinking with his mates.

"What? You've got to be pulling my leg," he accused Arthur. "You, refusing to come for a night on the tiles?"

"Just leave it be Chalkie," Arthur said. And no amount of persuasion could make him change his mind. There just wasn't anything worthwhile getting up for these days, apart from his work. And he had to get up for that.

"Must be in love," Chalkie confided to another. "For Arthur to give up on a couple of pints, he must be in love!" Lately his old 'mucker' had been acting peculiarly. Disappearing in the afternoons for no apparent reason! On the one occasion he'd followed him - from a discreet distance - he'd seen Arthur sitting in one of the municipal parks. So it stood to reason he was meeting someone, didn't it?

But Chalkie being diplomatic, had decided to leave it be for a bit.

With the regiment so far from home it had become imperative to keep the troops morale high. Christmas spent away from 'Blighty' being given great priority! With most of the food and drinks shipped out from England in plenty of time.

Arthur was getting things under way with the Christmas puddings; which he liked to get started at least six weeks before they were needed; this year he'd been asked to also do enough for the Officer's Mess. So towards the middle of November preparations began. Huge bowls of succulent dried fruits, suet, lashings of port and sherry along with dozens of eggs and other ingredients were mixed up; put into basins and pre-cooked. Then tied up in clean, white cloths, and hung up in the store room until needed; which still entailed at least another three or fours hours of steaming, before they were ready.

Arthur was pleased to get at least one job out of the way! There was ham to be salted, chutney and preserves to be laid down, along with huge quantities of pickled cabbage and pickled onions; the forces favourites. Then there were the special Christmas cakes to be cooked and decorated. The ingredients for mince-meat chopped up and left to soak in sherry, to make it even more acceptable for the 'lads', along with the everyday cooking of breakfast, lunch, and evening dinner to contend with. Getting through each day almost mechanically, he'd rise early and still be working in the kitchen till nearly midnight. But that was better than being left to mope alone.

Arthur worked almost like a robot now, his heart not really in his cooking these days.

And the complaints came rolling in.

The Mess Officer came round to see him about it.

"The chaps are complaining about the food Arthur. What the hell's being going on? I couldn't have tasted everything the other day. They say all the vegetables were unsalted? Not like you, what?"

The Mess Officer, being more used to giving praise about Arthur's cooking, hadn't been coming round as often as he should have to taste the food before it was given to the men; which was what he was supposed to do. His job was to make sure the kitchen was sending out food fit for the fighting men. Having to taste everything before the men were served, which up to now had seemed to be going swimmingly.

"Sorry Sir," Arthur said, standing straight and to attention, as he was being torn a strip off by his superior. Why was he getting all the blame? There were others involved with the catering. Surely he couldn't be held responsible for not salting the bloody vegetables? Then realising he was just feeling sorry for himself, he pulled himself together and replied; "won't happen again Sir."

"Very well Sergeant, make sure your mind is on your job in the future." Watching the officer walk off, Arthur made a resolution to forget about the young girl who was causing him so much distress, although sometimes he wondered if it would be a good thing if he was taken out of the kitchen. But, with peace reigning these days, it wasn't as if he would be sent out to do some real fighting.

The time spent in France was like a distant memory, although he still had the nightmares and flashbacks from time to time. And in his waking moments he often found himself thinking of some of the mates who'd perished in that bloody war.

The weather was still quite warm for November and as Arthur didn't drink quite so often, he enjoyed a stroll in one of the gardens or parks for a couple of hours every day. It was great to be out in the fresh air after the heat of the kitchens. He loved the riot of colour the flowers made against the lush green of the grass when he walked through the tree-lined pathways that led him from one pretty avenue to another. He couldn't get over the contrast of the coolness here to the heat of the city just a few hundred yards away, but maybe it was because of the constant water being sprayed over everything that kept the gardens cool.

The malis (gardeners) were always weeding, hoeing or dead-heading the flowers; their half-naked bodies glistening in the sun as they sweated for very little money. Yet they seemed happy enough.

The municipal gardens were kept open to the public all day, but very few of the locals took advantage of this wonderful facility preferring to be in places like the bazaars or Mela's, where the bucket-like seats of the hurdy-gurdies creaked and groaned their way round the central stem, to the shouts and screams of excited children. The crowds grew so dense there you could hardly move.

Out of sheer curiosity Arthur had visited one of these 'fairs' and had stayed for all of five minutes. The noise of the loud music - being played badly - was enough to put anyone off music. While the noise of the sweet-sellers shouting out their wares as they vied with one another to sell anything from clay figures of the gods, to ice-cream, and bottles of warm soft drinks. There were noisy toys too, like the little drums on sticks, called a 'dhol.' These being the noisiest things he'd ever had to put up with. The small hand-held hollow drums perched on sticks - had two short bits of string with bits of wood at either end - which when moved rapidly from side to side, would make contact with the skin on the drum, to cause a continuous loud rat, tat, tatting sound. As most of the children seemed to have one to play with, the noise was chaotic!

To add to the noise, children cried for the parents they'd been detached from, and frantic parents searched for their children, who'd become lost in the vast crowds of heaving humanity.

Fairs, Arthur decided, just weren't his cup of tea!

He much preferred the afternoons here in the pleasant gardens, when he often had the place all to himself. Nearly everyone else having opted for a quiet nap, as people did in most hot countries; even the malis disappeared during the heat of the afternoon having found a shady spot somewhere. So finding an empty bench in the shade of a tree, Arthur sat down to enjoy the peace and quiet. Lighting up a cigarette, he remembered the letter he'd received from home that morning.

Removing it from his breast pocket, he smoothed it out and read it carefully once more; this time in a more leisurely manner. Judging by the postmark, it had taken ages to get to him, his mother having written it during the summer months, and it was now November! She must have been writing her letter about the time as he'd first met... stopping himself Arthur realised he was thinking of that girl again. He really must stop dwelling on what might have been.

The weather would be cold back in England, he thought, looking round at the lovely blooms flowering around him. There had been others growing here all the summer, which Arthur had seen over the weeks. Brilliant Cannas; which reminded him of the Gladiolus back home, with bright yellow, red and mottled coloured flowers standing out against long curling leaves. Huge fragrant Lilies nodding in the gentle breeze, with bright orange Crocosmia, Antirrhinums - in colours he never knew existed - and the lovely Celosia or 'Cockscomb,' with their big velvety crested heads, so like the cock combs they were named after. There were dozens more, all flourishing in this wonderfully warm climate. The malis replaced the dead and faded blooms with astonishing speed, so there was always something blooming.

You'll love the flowers here, he'd written to his mother. There are so many colours, though they last but a short while because of the hot sun. I don't know the names of some, but there are others I recognised straight away. And the roses are just the same here too. I do believe they bloom even better in this climate and smell just as well as they did back home. There are corn flowers too, the same colour as used to grow wild in our fields and if you could only see the yellow flowers they call 'marigolds', their colours are so bright; yellows and deep orange; smelling unlike anything I ever smelt in England.

In her letter to Arthur, his mother had written back asking if he liked his new home in India, and how long it would be before he came home again.

It's not the same without you here, she wrote; making Arthur feel nostalgic for England and home.

Ernie is working in Southampton now. He came but for the day - such a long way to travel, for such a short time, she complained. Cissie now has two children and George is still away fighting. Of course Sid's wife Barbara, a right tartar, nags him day and night. I always thought she was a right flighty madam, but he's made his bed and he must lie in it.

The thought of Sid married, with a formidable wife, made Arthur laugh out loud. Poor Sid... first his father and now saddled with a nagging wife.

"I'm only glad you didn't do anything as foolish as to marry," Rose had continued. "When you come home you will have to find yourself a nice good-natured lass, for you won't be finding one out where you are, now will you? Most of those living in that country will be heathens I've no doubt?" To his mother, anyone living anywhere other than England had to be heathens! Arthur could just imagine his mother writing - with Jesse putting the odd word in here and there, and his mother snapping back... Just who is writing this letter, you or me? But she always ended up adding his little bits to her letters as well. Your father says young Mary Drummond is still single, and not yet courting! Although not for the want of being asked out I'm sure.

Arthur smiled, remembering his friend Mary, who'd surely find a nice chap in her own time. He'd been to school with her, since they were six or seven. But Mary had remained just that, a good friend. It was another dark-skinned lass he'd seen for that brief moment, whom he wanted to ask out. He wondered what his mother would think about her. Would she consider the swarthy skinned girl a heathen? Arthur sighed; perhaps it was just as well he thought.

Then continued to read... It's good to hear you are doing the cooking... better than feeding the chickens eh? Rose had gone on. The last being in reference to his younger days when he'd fed the chickens with Rose's best butter! The flowers sound lovely; perhaps you can send me a picture of them? Take good care of thyself son, and remember to change thy socks. (Rose often lapsed into her old fashioned country brogue when she was writing) and Arthur smiled, remembering how she still thought of him as her 'young' son. And mind you don't be drinking as much as you did when you were here on leave, for you had me that worried last time. You are a good lad son, so take care won't you? Mrs Webster from up the road was asking after you the other day. You remember her boy Tommy who was killed over in France? Poor soul, she'll never be the same again. But keep you well son, and mayhap we'll see you home in time for Christmas. Your loving mother.

P.S. Your father asks to be remembered.

She'd added three large crosses hurriedly on the bottom of the page, which she wouldn't have wanted Jesse to see. He'd only have laughed at her and called her a silly old woman.

Rose had kept much from her husband over the years, especially when it came to her children, and then she was like a mother lioness defending her cubs if she thought anyone else was criticising them.

The thought of all she'd done for him brought fresh tears to Arthur's eyes. Fat chance of being home for Christmas, he thought, folding the letter carefully before putting it safely back into his pocket once more. He'd have to buy himself a small camera so he could take some pictures of the flowers and other things to send home.

How Sid would have laughed to have seen Arthur with a servant of his own, even if he had been only a young Indian boy. He remembered the days they had both lain in bed together, making plans for the future. Sid had wanted to be an engineer. But Arthur had wanted to be a farmer and stay right where he was.

And now here he was... hundreds of miles away in a foreign land!

A few weeks later, Arthur was lending a hand at one of the gymkhanas that preceded Christmas. He'd just finished helping the laying of the tables for luncheon, ready for all the dignitaries in a large marquee, before donning his white cotton tunic and dark trousers, which made him look every inch the smart caterer. Although he still refused to be seen dead in those stupid hats they had issued.

With everything ready, he had slipped out for a quick smoke, and was just about to light up when... over towards the far end of the field he saw her.

There was no mistaking that slim figure anywhere! Throwing down the unlit cigarette, he started to make a bee-line for her when a voice spoke imperiously beside him.

"Can you tell me where I might get some cold drinks?"

Turning automatically towards the person Arthur saw a well-built elderly lady peering at him through an elegant lorgnette. And she didn't look as if she would brook any argument either!

"You'll find the refreshment tent at the other end of the field ma'am..." Arthur started to say, before he remembered just why he was there in the first place! So, standing smartly to attention, Arthur tried to smile, albeit a bit on the strained side, and, clearing his throat, he gallantly offered his services.

"Perhaps I can get something for you madam?" he asked, and was rewarded with a big smile.

"That is so kind of you," the lady gushed, seeing those blue eyes gazing down at her. "If you wouldn't mind, my grandson has just had his tonsils removed and needs constant cold fluids."

Arthur fetched a chair from the tent, and carried it out for the elderly lady; then marched purposefully across the well-tended lawns to fetch the lemonade; his eyes scanning the crowds as he walked over to the refreshment tent. Of all the bad luck! In normal circumstances Arthur wouldn't have minded fetching a thousand glasses of blooming lemonade. But not today... for once again, the young lady he glimpsed earlier had been swallowed up in the crowds.

Heading off to the refreshment tent, he gave his order over the counter, having to shout to be heard over the din of dozens of voices.

"Give us a glass of nice cool lemonade for a young chap wot's just had his tonsils out will ya Chalkie?" he shouted above the din. "And while you're at it get one for me, I'm blooming parched!"

Chalkie - rushed off his feet on this warm day - was only too happy to oblige.

"Here you are Arthur; get that down yer, plenty more where that came from," he said, placing the glasses down on the counter, before rushing off to serve someone else. The lemonade looked cool and inviting, and had bits of ice floating about on the surface too, so Arthur picked up his glass and was taking a good long chug, letting the cool drink ease his parched throat, when a voice at his elbow nearly made him choke!

"That's very kind of you Sergeant," a soft voice spoke softly at his side... and looking down Arthur nearly dropped his glass of lemonade!

It was the young girl he'd seen earlier!

And of course that bloody cat had got his tongue *again*!

So he could only grin inanely as he looked at the beautiful girl at his side. It was the girl with the brown eyes!

"You must be getting the drink for young Simon," she continued, "I hear he's just had a tonsillectomy? I do believe you are on a mission of mercy for Lady Montford, who told me a kind officer was getting some drinks for her. I'd better not keep you; the lady does not like to be kept waiting." And with a beautiful tinkling laugh she was gone once more!

It was as if she could appear and disappear at will, and there was nothing he could do about it?

"Cor... who the heck was she?" breathed Chalkie as he turned back to Arthur. "Bit of orl right I'd say."

"You keep your soddin' eyes off her," warned Arthur, looking daggers at his old mate. "And don't even think about chatting her up." Chalkie raised his eyebrows in astonishment. Who'd a thought a girl could get Arthur all riled up, he thought as he walked off. Narrowing his eyes, he watched Arthur take the glass of lemonade towards an elderly lady standing on the other side of the green; then rush off as if in search of something, or could it be someone? He thought... I was right all along... it's a bird Arthur's been moping about... but what a bird. Pursing his lips, Chalkie let out a long, low whistle.

Meanwhile, Arthur had thoroughly bewitched the elderly lady, who was now 'eating out of his hand'. When he offered to find her a seat in the shade somewhere, she was thoroughly charmed. Finding the lady a seat, and taking his leave, Arthur was off once more... determined this time to leave no stone unturned as it were... little knowing his good deed would stand him in very good stead in the days to come.

Hurrying off in search of the elusive young lady, Arthur was determined this time to at least find out what her name was...and it was his lucky day. It was she, who came to him! Albeit, with her employers, Lord and Lady Somerville, and their two sons. Arthur, being behind the scenes, busy cutting slices of ham for the diners, hadn't even known she was there! Sitting just a few yards away, as she and the other dignitaries tucked into the wonderful lunch he'd prepared. The elderly lady, who he'd been kind enough to fetch the lemonade for, was also there, sitting at a table with his Commanding Officer of all people. The table of elegantly dressed, upper crust personages had been tucking into his carefully prepared food.

Arthur only saw them after lunch had been served, and the plates cleared away, when he found time to take a quick peep into the marquee where he'd been 'gob-smacked' to see her. So when she left with the two children, it had been simple enough to follow her. Rushing out from around the back of the tent, Arthur 'pretended' to be strolling along – just as she came by - and feigning surprise, he was able to ask after her two young charges. They chatted for a short while, mainly about the holiday at 'Ooty', and Arthur got the distinct impression she could be interested in him. But what he didn't know then, was that Teresa had overheard all about Arthur's good deed, from none other than the old lady he'd helped earlier.

"Such a nice young man," Lady Montford had said loudly, regaling everyone at her table with the help she'd received from the 'gallant' young soldier earlier.

Impressed by what she'd heard about Arthur earlier in the refreshment tent, the young lady not only told him her name was Marie Teresa - such a lovely name - although everyone called her Teresa - she also told him she would be in the park at around nine o'clock the next morning.

Teresa had a nice ring to it, thought Arthur, and he would definitely be in the park next day, come hell or high water!

Hardly sleeping that night, he was up and showered by five a.m. He was also smiling in the 'mess' once more, much to the delight of his old chum Chalkie, whom Arthur had managed to wheedle into 'covering' for him. After another quick shower, because he felt quite sweaty with worry, and his heart pounding like a sledge-hammer, he was in the park long before nine.

Not knowing which gate she'd use, he walked quickly across to a bench by the main pathway, and right on the dot of nine, watched her trim figure; with her two charges, walking slowly towards him. Jumping up, he stood there, knowing he had a silly grin on his face... but unable to do anything about it.

While the two boys played with a ball, the two adults got to know each other. In between, the boys clamoured for Arthur's attention, but he was delighted at having got this far - played with the two boisterous lads, throwing them up into the air, until his arms ached. They'd loved it, and kept begging for him to do it again and again, until their nanny had intervened.

"Enough, enough!" Teresa cried, hoping the boys weren't going to be sick with all the man-handling just after they'd eaten their breakfast. "Let the poor man catch his breath!" she admonished them gently. "Arthur will play with you later."

And there were other days, and other meetings too, sometimes for the whole day, on one of Teresa's days off. It wasn't long before they found out that they had both been born on the fourth of August in 1897. Teresa thought Arthur was making it up at first, but when he produced evidence, she was flabbergasted. Especially to have found each other, having been born on opposite ends of the world!

It was as if fate had decided everything. The spark continued to grow. The two getting on like a house on fire. Until one day... out of the blue, Teresa invited Arthur to visit her at the house.

"My employers are giving a dinner on Saturday, would you like to come?" she asked. "They've often told me to invite any of my friends, but until now I never have."

"Me?" squeaked Arthur, "Me, come to dinner?" And she gave that lovely tinkling laugh of hers.

"Yes Arthur... you. I'd like you to be my guest. There are only going to be a few people coming, about twenty or so... you'll find them really friendly."

"How many? I thought you said a few, I'd only show you up," confessed Arthur. "I've never been to a grand dinner in me life!"

"I'm sure you won't. And anyway, I too had to get used to all these 'grand' people myself. They really are very nice once you get to know them." When she placed her hand on Arthur's arm, he knew he was undone! He admitted he wouldn't know the first thing about how to eat in front of 'posh' people, but Teresa just said he could follow her lead.

"All you do is work your way through your cutlery from the outside in, starting with the ones at the two outer sides of your plate, the rest is easy. I'll make sure I'm sitting right beside you, so I can tell you what to do." And like the fool that he was, Arthur agreed.

"What do I have to wear?" he asked. "I haven't anything suitable."

"Can't you borrow a Mess jacket from someone?" Get her, borrow a Mess jacket... like it was something he'd be likely to do, thought Arthur. But he knew somehow he'd be there on Saturday. With Arthur being quite tall and broad-shouldered, the next few days passed with a mad dash to obtain the right sort of dress for a 'nobs' dinner do.

Luckily, a durzi was able to alter a jacket, and with a pair of black trousers of his own, and a shiny new pair of patent leather shoes he'd had to purchase, Arthur was home and dry... almost!

"Clean underpants..." Chalkie ticked off the list...

"Yes," answered Arthur.

"Socks... vest... shirt... trousers... handkerchief..."

"Stop, stop, did you say handkerchief?" queried Arthur.

"Course you need a bloody hankie!" sneered Chalkie. "What if someone wants ter blow their nose?"

"Well, hopefully they'll have one of their own."

"Don't be daft man... didn't yer ma ever teach you to have a clean hankie by yer when you went out?" Arthur did remember his mother tucking a clean handkerchief into his pockets every day before he left for school.

"You are absolutely right Chalkie old boy," Arthur said, putting on an accent and strutting his stuff. "Fetch me a handkerchief my good man!"

"Fetch the bloody thing yerself, yer lazy bugger!" The light-hearted banter helped to keep Arthur from thinking about the evening ahead.

At last, he was ready. The durzi had done an excellent job on the jacket which fitted him like a glove, and Arthur's blue eyes gazed out from his pink, well scrubbed face, setting off the clothes to perfection!

This evening was going to be his make or break time.

He'd have to be on his very best behaviour too, promising himself he'd only sip at his wine, in case he made a complete ass of himself.

Then at the appointed time, he presented himself, along with a nice little posy of flowers for Teresa, and one for his hostess. He'd chosen violets for Teresa when he'd picked them up at the market and jasmine for Teresa's employer. But had worried all the way to the venue in case someone thought it was him smelling nice! Towering above the young girl, Arthur looked every inch as good as anybody else that evening. And Teresa felt very proud when she presented him to her employers, which she did very prettily as far as Arthur was concerned.

"Lord and Lady Somerville I'd like to introduce you to my friend Arthur," she'd said, and the elegant, smiling pair had given him the once-over; noting the well cut jacket and accessories in a single glance. He might only be a Sergeant, but with his bearing... he might well be from a decent background, going through their minds.

"Thank you for the posy that was most kind of you," Lady Somerville had said, impressed by the small action. Once again Chalkie had been right in his choice of flowers to take.

"So you're the young man my two boys are so keen to see every day," her eyes twinkled mischievously at him as they shook hands. "Please do enjoy your evening," and turning to Teresa, she said pointedly; "I know you'll see Arthur has a pleasant time Teresa." And she walked off to speak to some of her other guests.

"Nice to meet you young chap," the husband appraised Arthur. "What regiment are you from?" Arthur drew himself up to his full height, "Hamp's and Dorset sir," he said proudly. "Good, good, very good regiment the Dorset's," the Brigadier-General said gruffly, "hope you know we think very highly of young Teresa here," he said, bowing to the young lady at Arthur's side, "So none of your usual shenanigans eh, what?"

"Absolutely sir!" answered Arthur, breathing a sigh of relief to have got that introduction over!

"Please don't take too much notice of what Lord Somerville says," whispered Teresa, after they'd departed. "He's just an old sweetie really."

'I've heard everything now. A Brigadier-General called a 'sweetie', and she thinks everyone's nice' thought Arthur. 'Hope that includes me!'

"Who is that delicious young man?" breathed Hortense Southbury to Lady Somerville, her eyes taking in the fresh-faced sergeant.

"Really Hortense," Lady Somerville laughed. "But I think you're just a mite too late there. He's only got eyes for nanny I'm afraid. And if I'm not mistaken, I shall be losing the best nanny I've ever had. Shame, but who can blame her...," sighing softly, she continued, "It's been a very long time since someone looked at me like that. How I envy the young lady!"

It's going to be all right, thought Arthur as he was seated at the table. All I have to do is keep watching Teresa. It'll be all right. And it was. He sailed through the first course, drinking his soup without slurping even once! Bending his soup plate over towards the opposite end, and eating slowly - instead of the rate of knots he usually did. Nodding at whatever people said to him; glad the elderly lady on his left was a little hard of hearing... so if he had to speak to her, she wouldn't have known if he was saying the wrong thing.

Teresa was seated to his immediate right, and had smiled at him to put him at his ease; leaning over towards him, to ask if he was enjoying the meal. Although he was nearly undone then... her soft hair brushing against his cheek had made him blush bright red!

Then, they were served with the second course - which had to be asparagus! Arthur who'd never tasted it, let alone eaten it, watched carefully as Teresa took one small stalk of buttery asparagus in between two of her fingers, biting off the little flabby bit on the end, and finally laying the other end down on the side of her plate. And he'd followed suit. It didn't particularly taste of anything thought Arthur, chewing slowly, but the butter was delicious!

Clearing his plate with great confidence, he began to feel better.

Prematurely patting himself on the back... until the person on the other side of Teresa began talking to her, for what seemed like ages.

The empty plates were cleared rapidly off the table, and replaced with dainty little bowls of water with bits of lemon floating on the top. Teresa had now finished her conversation, and had turned back to Arthur... to see him lift the dainty bowl to his lips, and drink deeply...before she could stop him.

He'd drunk the water that he was meant to wash his fingers in after eating the asparagus!

Shaking her head slightly, she put her hand on the arm that was still holding the bowl, and got him to lower it to the table, her eyes going from his to her own bowl, then she proceeded to dip the ends of her fingers into the bowl in front of her, wiping them carefully in her napkin afterwards.

Arthur was mortified! How the hell was he to know you had to wash your blooming hands after using them to eat asparagus? He'd just licked them clean!

But luckily everyone was so busy talking to one another, it seemed no one had even noticed Arthur's gaffe. So he 'pretended' to wash his fingers and then carefully wipe them on his napkin, whispering a soft "sorry" to Teresa, who just smiled back mischievously, as she pretended to be wiping her mouth.

But the servant clearing the bowls must have wondered what had become of the nimbu-pani (lemon water) from the sahibs bowl!

CHAPTER TEN

Christmas in India

With Christmas on the horizon everyone seemed much happier, even the officers smiled occasionally.

Arthur was back to his original good humour, much to the relief of others in the 'mess' kitchens; possibly something to do with seeing Teresa on a regular basis, the pair sometimes spending whole days together, at least once a week, on her days off; when she took him to see the places of interest around Bangalore.

Like the Lal Bargh Botanical gardens; commissioned in 1760 by Haider Ali - the warrior king of Mysore, and finished later by his son Tipu Sultan. The area covered about two hundred and forty acres; so more than one visit was required to see everything properly. The name Lal Bagh (red garden) given to it because of the beautiful red roses that bloomed there throughout the year, and the beautiful 'flame-of-the forest' trees, whose blood-red blooms lit up the trees like a flame.

Apart from having some of the finest collection of trees and plants in the world, the garden also boasts some of the oldest. Like the huge banyan, with its roots pushed high above ground - said to be over a thousand years old. Other features, including the design of the lawns and flower beds, lotus pools and fountains, were a real joy to behold. Everything was kept beautifully maintained, and as where it has been ever since the gardens were first started, the famous 'Lal Bagh Rock' sat, one of the oldest rock formations on earth, dating back millions of years.

On other occasions, Teresa took Arthur to Mysore - a short journey away - to see the beautiful 'Mysore Palace'. The Palace was designed by Henry Irwin, a British architect, in 1897, the year Arthur and Teresa were born. It was so strange that everything kept repeating the year of their birth? The Palace was built for the fourth 'Wodeyar' Raja (King) of Mysore. On the site of an older wooden building that had been destroyed in a fire in 1897. With its domes, turrets, arches and colonnades, it was absolutely beautiful! The Palace was a treasure house of exquisite carvings and works of art from all over the world. Intricately carved doors opened onto luxuriously appointed rooms. The Durbar Hall with its ornate ceiling and many sculpted pillars, and the magnificent jewel-studded throne, took Arthur's breath away.

It was amazing to think that just one man had once owned all this!

Another visit had Arthur climbing up the thousand steps of the 'Chamundi Hill,' which was about three hundred and thirty five metres high, and left him out of puff. So he was glad of the halfway stop, where he saw an awesome four metre monolith of 'Nandi', Lord Shiva's bull. Then at the very top, there was a lovely twelfth century temple, dedicated to the Goddess Chamundeshwari, who was worshipped by the Wodeyars.

Legend said this Goddess killed the wicked buffalo-headed demon Mahisasura, and every year since then, at the festival of Dussera, good over evil, had been celebrated by the people of Mysore. Arthur was awestruck by all he saw, and pleased he had someone as lovely as Teresa to explain things to him.

He loved watching her face become animated as she described other places and things she'd been taken to see as a child. Everything about this new country - and the bewitching young lady accompanying him - was fascinating. The long arduous climb up the steep-sided hill was more than worthwhile, if only for the wonderful views from the summit. From there, the panoramic view took his breath away, as he gazed down on Mysore's lakes, parks and palaces.

The fact that Teresa had offered him her hand - to pull him up the last few steps to the top was joy enough. She wasn't to know his loss of breath was partly due to the joy of just holding her hand in his!

A visit to 'Brindavan Gardens', one of the best gardens in Southern India, spread over one hundred and fifty acres, was another fabulous experience. With its magnificent flowers and shady pathways it was a perfect place to stroll with the person you loved!

St Philomena's, a beautiful Cathedral, reminiscent of medieval architectural style, was one of the largest churches in the country, a really imposing structure, with stained glass windows, and lofty towers.

Arthur felt quite overwhelmed by the splendour and watched as Teresa bent a knee before crossing herself; her graceful movements in keeping with the wonderful sense of peace that prevailed there. They lit candles, and sat quietly on one of the benches for a few minutes; the coolness and quietness ethereal after the hustle and bustle of the outside world.

Arthur loved listening to Teresa as she quietly explained some of the myths and legends attached to nearly every place they'd visited. So when they visited the sacred Cauvery River, they went to see the 'Hogenakkal Falls' and bravely sailed in a coracle through the turbulent waters; the noise of the water roaring in their ears, as they were tossed about near the waterfall; the craft spinning like a top, round and round, making them quite giddy as it tossed them about; expecting to be thrown out at any minute; Teresa holding onto Arthur - much to his delight - as they laughed nervously.

Afterwards, when they'd returned to 'terra firma', damp from the spray, Arthur had had to relinquish Teresa's hands from his own as she explained the River Cauvery was sacred to the Hindus. The water that had sprayed over them was a sort of a blessing. In fact anything that came in contact with the holy waters - even the land it passed through - automatically became sacred as well.

Of course there was a legend attached to this too, which had been passed down over hundreds of years.

Teresa explained that a young earth-born girl, named Vishnu Maya, was really the daughter of Brahma, a great god, but her divine father had permitted her to be regarded as a child of a mortal. In order to obtain blessedness for her adoptive father she resolved to become a river, whose waters would purify all sin. Hence it is said, that even the holy Ganges resorts to go underground once in the year to the source of the Cauvery, so that she, the mighty Ganga (Ganges), might also purge herself from the pollution contracted from the crowd of sinners who have bathed in her waters.

Teresa had looked closely at Arthur's face as she told of the legend, and noted he didn't laugh, as many others often did. He also seemed to actually enjoy all the places and things she'd showed him, although some of them must have seemed strange to him, coming as it were, from a completely different culture. If only she could have known what really was going through his mind?

Wish I were back in that silly boat. Holding onto her was the most magical moment of my life. Never mind getting the blessings of the river. Wonder if she knows what effect those brown eyes have on me? Reminds me of the first chocolate I ate. No, that wasn't it... more like melting chocolate... yes... that's it! He was melting like chocolate!

Arthur tasted many new things with the help of Teresa. Like his first custard-apple; a delicious fruit that was green on the outside, but sweet and juicy on the inside - if it weren't for the big black pips that seemed to fill the fruit! He quite liked the pungent smelling guavas, and even the foul smelling jackfruit; once he'd learnt 'not' to breathe in, when he put a bit into his mouth. He had even tried one of the tiny sweet 'sucking' mangoes, which left him in a right old mess. Even after she'd showed him how to squeeze the tiny fruit round and round in his hands - before making a tiny hole at the very end - to suck out the lovely sweet juices, though he quite liked the bigger ones which could be cut up on a plate and eaten with a spoon.

Already in love with India, he was finding new things about this wonderful country; the food, culture, traditions and above all, the people, especially a young swarthy-skinned girl with brown eyes!

As the weeks turned to months Arthur knew he couldn't live without his dusky beauty. He loved the way she smiled demurely, lowering her face as she blushed.

Arthur had only known one or two girls before, but Teresa had never been out with other boys as she'd been brought up by strict parents. Her mother was a devout Roman Catholic, and her father had been of Portuguese extraction. Teresa's mother had remarried, and her stepfather was a hard man to get along with - so Teresa had decided to get work away from home, as a nanny. Although well educated, office jobs or other important positions were not offered to many young girls, but Teresa was truly happy working with children. Her employers treated her just like one of the family, especially Lord and Lady Somerville, who saw to it that Teresa got extra time off to go out with her new beau.

Arthur often wondered how fate had managed to bring the two of them together. Their mutual attraction for one another had been obvious from the start, but Arthur had deliberately kept their relationship light and friendly, not wanting to unduly worry the shy young girl who had had very little contact with the outside world, having been 'cocooned', as it were, by her position of nanny since she'd left school, at sixteen.

One afternoon, however, he couldn't help himself. They were sitting under a shady tree, and she had been telling him about yet another fascinating legend. Her face alive and animated as she spoke, he just couldn't help himself! She had looked so beautiful... so he bent forward and kissed her gently on her cheek.

Teresa put a hand up to where he'd kissed her, and looked both pleased but worried, her brown eyes searching his face, as if questioning his action.

"Don't tell me you didn't know I fancied you," he said.

"Nn-nooo, it's not that..." She hesitated.

"But you do like me, don't you?"

"Oh yes Arthur, I do..." Teresa said, wishing they weren't having this conversation. She had always been in full control of her emotions up to now, and couldn't get over the tumultuous feeling that was making her feel quite faint. "It's just..." But Arthur couldn't wait any longer. He quickly gathered her in his arms, and kissed her again, this time a long lingering kiss on her mouth, and to his delight, Teresa responded; kissing him warmly back. Her skin felt as soft and smooth as velvet under his lips, and her eyes looking back into his own made him want to hold her in his arms to protect her from the rest of the world.

The electricity between them could have lit up an entire garrison!

"Will you marry me Teresa?" he whispered, and as he held her trembling body, he knew she was the only girl in the world for him.

"But we've only known one another such a short time," she protested, not pulling away from him at all, "You haven't even met my parents!"

"Will they object to me?" he asked fearfully.

"I don't think so," she sighed. "Anyway, it's my step dad, I don't think my mother will mind, at least I'm not sure... Actually I'm not very sure of anything any more." Teresa was trying desperately to pull herself together, a myriad of thoughts running through her mind. She'd heard so many stories…

"So how soon..." he started, when she placed a small finger across his lips.

"Hush, hush," she said quietly, as if she were back in the nursery with her two small charges. "You are going much too quickly for me."

"Oh Teresa," he groaned, "can't you see we were made for one another? I'm making enough money to take care of you, and once my time is up here, we'll go to England..." Then Teresa *did* pull away from him.

So far he hadn't even mentioned the word 'love.' In all her fantasies people fell in love. Was that what she was feeling now? She needed time to think! She wanted him to go on kissing her forever... but didn't know if she could trust herself... and now this; who'd said anything about going to live in England?

"England? Who says I want to go to England?" she said, looking agitated. "I can't just up and leave my family. Why would I want to do that?"

"Well, if that's what you want, we'll stay in India... anything at all. Just name it. But at least please say you'll marry me."

But Teresa was not going to be rushed into anything. Besides, she'd heard about the soldiers who'd promised some of the local girls all sorts and then they'd been sent home, leaving the poor girl pregnant and penniless. That wasn't going to happen to her. Not if she could help it. She loved this big strong, but gentle man, and she had no doubt he meant everything he had said... at the moment.

Teresa replaced a few stray wisps of hair that had escaped their confines, then, smoothing back her hair, she stood up.

"It's getting late Arthur; please let's talk about this another time."

And Arthur was forced to follow.

"You still haven't answered my question," he chided her softly.

"Let me think about it Arthur." And he could see he had a fight on his hands. But he wasn't prepared to give up at that point.

"Have I offended you?" he asked.

"No, no of course not, how could anyone be offended by a proposal? I am honoured you asked me, but please, can we sleep on it?" her gentle eyes beseeched him to stop.

Arthur was gutted and understood that Teresa wanted time to think things over. If only he hadn't rushed things. But they had been going out for some time now... He would agree to anything at all, if only he could go on seeing her.

"You will see me again?" he asked anxiously and Teresa nodded, giving him a tiny smile, which gave him a little hope?

Back at the barracks, Chalkie looked gob-smacked when Arthur said he'd proposed to Teresa, especially when Arthur confided pathetically.

"She turned me down."

"Bloody hell!" was all Chalkie could manage.

"Bloody hell! Is that all you've got to say? I've just told you I can't get her to marry me and all you can say is Bloody hell!" Arthur stormed off.

"Bloody hell!" Chalkie managed for the second time. "Poor old Arthur, if you don't stand a chance, what about the rest of us?" This said to the empty room.

Chalkie was aware that the birds just fell over one another for a chance to chuck themselves at Arthur. So if Arthur didn't stand a chance with a bird... what chance had any of them? This girl Teresa hadn't seemed like a hard nut? They'd been seeing one another for a few months now, so she obviously liked him well enough? Fancy turning him down?

"Bloody hell!"

Much later, when Arthur had had time to cool down, Chalkie wanted to know what had gone wrong with the day, the conversation went something like this.

"Where did you go today?"

"Oh leave it be Chalkie, I thought she liked me or I wouldn't have proposed."

"You must have said or done something wrong!"

"Like what?"

"Well I wasn't there, was I?"

"Look," Arthur said testily, "we had a nice day, we were getting on like a house on fire and then I kissed her, okay?"

"What... no bloody preliminaries?"

"What bloody preliminaries? And what's that got to do with it anyway?"

"EVERY BLOODY THING... you stupid bugger!" Chalkie shouted. "When you woo a girl, you do things properly... Oh God, no, Don't tell me you tried it out on her?"

"Course I didn't, what do you take me for? I respect her, so I kissed her, and then, I asked her to marry me."

"Did you tell her you love her?"

"Well it stands to reason..." Arthur blustered. "I wouldn't have been kissing her otherwise, would I?"

"So you never told her you love her at all?" Chalkie persisted.

"No... I don't suppose I did," Arthur admitted sheepishly.

"You, poor... bloody... silly... sod. Every girl needs to know you love her!" Chalkie shouted back at Arthur. "Fancy asking a girl to marry you... yes, marry you... and not once telling her you love her!" Chalkie shook his head in disbelief... "NO BLOODY WONDER SHE TURNED YOU DOWN!"

CHAPTER ELEVEN

Truth and Consequences

Arthur didn't get much sleep that night, thinking about the events of the day, and whether Teresa would ever see him again.

He'd sent her a 'chitty' (note) the next day - dictated by Chalkie - to say he was sorry, and to apologise for acting so boorishly. Although Arthur hadn't wanted to put 'boorishly' down at all, but Chalkie had persuaded Arthur that he had acted quite insensitively and clumsy to boot, so the word would be sufficient for now. He'd squirmed at writing the words 'love' but had done it nonetheless.

"But I don't think I acted boorishly," insisted Arthur.

"Well what would you call 'forcing' yourself on an innocent young girl then?"

"Okay, I admit it was a bit insensitive of me, and maybe I was clumsy."

"Listen Arthur, you can take it from me, when it comes to grovelling, I'm your man," Chalkie said convincingly. So Arthur, grudgingly, sent off the note.

It had been much easier to write it down on paper, then actually admitting it to her. Looking at the words spelt out in black and white on the paper, he realised he did indeed love her very much.

How could he have been so bloody stupid? Of course women needed to know where they stood. No wonder she'd gotten all 'funny' with him! But they'd been getting on so well before then... or so he thought? Besides who could have resisted not kissing her? She'd looked so lovely... her face animated as she told him the story of the blessed sacred river! He hoped she would give him another chance?

Chalkie had talked to him like a blooming 'Dutch Uncle'. Going on and on about women this, and women that, and Arthur had switched off from listening to him in the end. Letting it all wash over him as he moped about getting himself ready to go out for a drink with the lads. Something he hadn't done for some time, as most of his spare time had been spent with Teresa.

"You do know you've quite a job on your hands, don't you?"

Chalkie was still rambling on and Arthur had to try and concentrate on what he was saying.

"Remember old Frankie Booker? He had quite a bit of trouble getting permission to marry his girl. Sent him back off to Blighty to think about it too."

"What were you saying Chalkie?"

"Bloody hell, don't tell me you haven't heard a word I was saying," Chalkie sighed. "Listen, I was just trying to tell you... remember when Frankie wanted to marry that bird he met up with in Madras? Well, he had to go in front of the C.O., didn't he? And he was refused permission to marry her, wasn't he? So maybe it's a bloody good job your Teresa did refuse to have anything to do with marriage."

"That's not exactly what she said," Arthur quickly reminded his mate. "She said she wanted time to think about it."

"Same difference," Chalkie snorted back, coming round to where Arthur was sitting.

"What if she had accepted and then you couldn't get the old 'Old Man' to give you the OK? You'd a looked like a right 'Charlie', an' no mistake."

"Christ Chalkie, I never even gave it a thought!" Arthur looked really worried remembering how they'd all thought Frankie was making the biggest mistake of his life. He'd only known the girl for a couple of weeks, and they were all surprised when he'd announced he'd asked her to be his wife. They'd all ragged him rotten, telling him he hadn't even had time to get to know her, let alone marry her. But Frankie had been certain the Anglo-Indian girl he'd been seeing was the right one for him, the fact that she already had a child - a light-skinned girl from another liaison with a British Tommy - making no difference to his feelings at that time. No amount of persuasion could shake him from wanting to marry the lady. It was only when word finally got around to Sergeant Winter that the dirt hit the fan.

"Are yer out of your tiny mind Booker?" he'd yelled. 'Wot makes yer think ye'll be allowed to marry the first bloody 'bint' that comes along? Have you forgotten everything I warned yer abart? 'as the sun gotten to yer bloody, soddin 'ead?"

Standing with his face inches away from Bookers face Sergeant

Winter had eye-balled the poor soldier: "Yer stands abart as much chance of getting permission to marry that poor bloody girl, as I've got of flying to the bloody moon."

By this time, his face was about an inch from the poor misguided trooper. When he had finished his tirade, he turned on his heel, marching out of the barrack room, stopping once more at the door.

"I don't want to hear any of yer even think about goin' wiv another Indian bird, let alone promising ter marry em! Is that bloody clear?"

The outcome of poor Frankie Bookers plans to get married quickly had evaporated as he was posted back home to Blighty, to 'think' about things for a bit.

"Wonder how Old Frankie is these days," pondered Chalkie, slyly watching Arthur's face. "Bet he's standing in a pub somewhere, chatting up an English bird or two eh? Lucky bleeding bugger."

Of course the thought of what he was going to say to Teresa about having to get special permission before he could marry a foreign girl made Arthur squirm. But he resolved to leave that till a later date.

At the weekend, Arthur took himself off to the park where he usually met up with Teresa and the two young boys, and was very relieved to see her enter the gates. She seemed much shyer with him, but Arthur was determined not to let any further actions on his part interfere with his relationship with her. He also knew he would have to explain about this special 'permission thing' with his C.O. Little knowing that Teresa had already had a word with her employer.

Lady Somerville had come into the nursery later that night to say goodnight to the boys, and had seen that Teresa was not her usual self.

"What's wrong nanny? You seem very far away tonight," she'd enquired. And, as the young girl hadn't got anyone else to turn to, she'd blurted out what had taken place earlier that day.

"Do you think his intentions are honourable?"

"Well, it did seem as if he meant it, although I told him I'd need time to think about it." Teresa looked at the older woman; "Did I do the right thing?"

"Absolutely... no young lady can make up her mind suddenly, you were quite right to tell him you needed time to think things over. Arthur seems quite a nice young man and I'm sure he means well. Do you know if he's asked permission from his commanding officer?"

"Permission? I don't understand." Teresa stopped folding up the children's clothes and faced Lady Somerville. "Does he need permission to marry me?"

"Well, it's all very complicated and I'm not sure I really know all the ramifications, but some years ago it was made necessary for the Officer commanding the battalions to give permission..." Lady Somerville didn't go on when she saw the look on Teresa's face. "Look, let me find out a bit more about all this. I could be making an awful mistake. I'll talk to Lord Somerville and find out just what the situation is, shall I?"

She didn't want to be the one to add more grief onto the young girl who was obviously finding it difficult enough to cope with her first ever proposal, let alone with any of the army red-tape.

"Please don't worry nanny, I'm sure your young man's intentions are quite honourable. I'm sure there can be nothing that could stop the two of you from getting married, if that's what you decide to do, that is," she hurriedly finished. "Now, let's leave ayah to keep an eye on the boys while we have dinner." Then, taking Teresa by the arm, she gently steered her towards the door.

So now Teresa had added problems to worry about. The first being... had Arthur really meant it when he'd proposed to her? Would he be able to obtain permission to be married? It was getting too complicated by far! Perhaps she should just forget about the whole episode? Teresa decided wisely to sleep on it!

Next morning, when she received Arthur's note, Teresa was delighted. She so wanted to believe him. They'd been friends for so many months now, she felt she knew him, and could trust him too. Besides, she'd already said she wanted time to think, so she was going to make maximum use of that time. Everything else could wait.

Seeing him in the park on Saturday, her heart gave a little jump; as she remembered how passionately he'd kissed her - and how she'd kissed him back.

"Arthur, Arthur!" her two charges clamoured as soon as they spotted the familiar figure walking quickly towards them. Running towards the tall young man, they hurled themselves at him, giving Teresa time to compose herself. She noticed how he'd quickly searched her face for any sign of rejection, and she smiled shyly at him.

"Morning nanny," Arthur greeted her, "lovely morning for a stroll in the park?" Turning to the boys, he ruffled their hair. "And what about you pair of scamps, ready for a push on the swings?"

The delighted cries of the boys were enough to answer Arthur's question, as they made their way towards the part of the park that was their favourite.

Conversation - when Arthur got his breath back - started off a bit strained, but soon they were back to the old familiar footing. Teresa felt something welling in her that she'd never felt before. In his note he'd mentioned he loved her... and now she knew without a doubt that she loved this big country boy. Because that's what he was really, just a big boy. Watching him run after the two smaller boys she knew everything would be all right. Later, when they were alone, she shyly let him take her hand.

"I really did mean what I said the other day you know. But I respect you enough to give you as much time as you think you need too. In fact, there's something I have to confess... no, no, I'm not going back on my proposal, you're not getting off as lightly as that young lady," he laughed. "It's just that I've found out it might take a bit of time to convince my Commanding Officer about a little matter of permission." Arthur looked closely at Teresa as he spoke, wondering if she thought he was backing out of what he'd said about wanting to be married as soon as possible.

"I know about the permission thing", she said softly.

"You do? But how...?" Arthur was relieved and worried at the same time. He'd wanted to convince her he meant every word he'd said before, and no one would stop him from marrying her. But she'd taken the wind out of his sails, good and proper!

"I spoke to Lady Somerville."

"You did?"

"Yes, I'm afraid I was a bit upset when I arrived home, so I confided in her, do you mind?" She placed her tiny hand on his sleeve. "I needed to talk to someone."

"Mind? Course I don't mind."

"Anyway, it's like you say, you have to get special permission from your Commanding Officer, am I right?" Arthur could only look at her in amazement. He'd always known there was more to this slip of a girl. Most other girls would have been crying their eyes out by now, but his Teresa was made of sterner stuff.

"So when I do get this permission, you'll marry me?"

"Hey, not so fast," she reprimanded him, but smiled up at him with those large brown eyes, and his heart leapt. "I'm still thinking about it. Besides I haven't even spoken to my mother about you yet."

"You mean you will, I mean... speak to your mother about me. Oh Teresa, I promise I'll never let you down. I, I love you so much." As Arthur stuttered out his love, Teresa knew he would be the only man for her.

Arthur had made an appointment to see his Commanding Officer, and as he waited nervously outside his office, he wondered just what all this would entail. He was soon to find out!

"So, you've met a young lady whom you feel you have to marry, do you sergeant," the Colonel asked. Arthur stretched himself up to his full height, and smartly answered, "Yes Sir."

"And what do you know about the young lady in question?"

"Well, she works as a nanny, sir."

"I see, she works as a nanny. So you think that's sufficient cause for you to marry, do you?"

"Not exactly sir. But we happen to love each other."

"Ah, love… that wonderful all-consuming passion you young men feel when you meet a young lady. Love, but can you be sure it's love sergeant?"

"I think so sir."

"You only think so? Yet you want to marry the girl, surely you either know or don't know whether you love her or not?" This was said sarcastically. "Let's see, how old are you sergeant?"

"Twenty-four sir."

"So do you think you are old enough to make up your mind about getting married?" And the stupid questions went on and on.

Chalkie was right, they'd grill him, try and make out he didn't

105

know his own mind, then ship him home to think about it for a few months... hoping he'd come to his senses. Well he wouldn't. His time in the army was nearly up. He'd find a job in India and still get married despite all the top brasses. See if he didn't!

"Well sergeant, I see you've been in a few scrapes in your time", the Commanding Officer said, looking down at some papers in front of him. "But it looks like you've steered clear for some time now?" Arthur continued to stand tall, even though the Colonel was immersed in reading. "Hmm, I see you've done quite a bit of service for such a young chap... served in France." He must have come to the part about Arthur's injury, because he looked up suddenly and closely scrutinised the young man standing before him. "Nothing wrong with your face now, is there?" he asked, noticing the smooth complexion and very slight scar.

"The doctor's decided the shrapnel was better left in my cheekbone, sir," Arthur said, realising that was what the Colonel was searching out.

"D'you know how big the bloody thing is?"

"Didn't get much of a chance to see it sir," Arthur answered truthfully.

Looking up, the C.O fixed an eye on Arthur, noting the well-honed physique.

"Hmm, I'd like to think about this for a while, so leave it with me, and come back in a day or two, unless," he paused, looking keenly at the young man's face before him, "unless there is an urgency about your getting married... you haven't got the young lady pregnant, have you?"

"Certainly not sir," Arthur replied quickly. "She's not at all like that sir?"

"Well, that surprises me somewhat." Arthur had to stop himself from hitting the stupid man.

"As I said, leave this with me. I'll let you know my decision later," and, with a flick of his hand, he dismissed Arthur.

By then Arthur was livid, but not wanting to antagonise his superior officer, he saluted smartly and marched out of the office. Afterwards, he told Chalkie he had almost decked the man for suggesting Teresa was in any way a 'loose woman'.

"I could'a really given him one Chalkie," he smouldered.

"Who in the hell does he think he is?"

"Your bleeding Commanding Officer, that's who, you silly bugger. If you'd touched a hair of his head you'd be in bloody big trouble. They'd have locked you up and thrown away the bloody key and then packed you bloody well home."

Chalkie looked at Arthur sadly, "Why couldn't you do the same as me, just love 'em and leave 'em, that's my motto; all this marriage lark is daft if you ask me!" ...then ducking just in time to miss the boot Arthur had thrown across the room at him!

CHAPTER TWELVE

Arthur loses it and Wins!

With the interview going so badly, Arthur decided to go out for a few 'bevvies' with some of his 'oppo's'. He was still mad about the colonel's insensitive remarks concerning Teresa. *I really should have decked him,* he thought. As the evening progressed, and with each glass of beer he drank, Arthur got more and more aggressive.

"I'll flatten him, that's what I'll do" he slurred. "Who the bloody hell does he think he is? As if my Teresa...," and trying to stand up, only managed to teeter sideways, until he ended up against a wall.

Chalkie, the worse for wear himself, tried to do his best to change the subject, but some of his other 'mates' had begun to goad the now drunk Arthur into doing something about it!

"You bloody-well-show-him A'fur," a well-sozzled comrade urged.

"Think they're so bloody 'igh and mighty, them bleeding of'cerrs, lot a tossers, that's what they are," another contributed, drunkenly slurring his words, as he lurched alongside his 'muckers', getting Arthur well and truly 'riled' up.

Returning somewhat worse for wear back to the cantonment, the inebriated party 'bumped' into another bunch of soldiers, who had also been 'out on the town' that night. And what started as friendly banter, erupted into a right old slanging match and finally into an all-out brawl; bringing the Military Police quickly to the scene. The troublemakers were quickly rounded up, and man-handled into the back of a truck.

On their arrival at the guardhouse, some of the men, including Arthur, were charged with being drunk and disorderly and thrown into the cells to cool off. Next morning the culprits were faced with hangovers and their commanding officers; the price for Arthur being particularly high as he was given twenty-eight days in solitary confinement and relieved of his stripes.

In the past, when his drinking had got him into trouble, he could take it in his stride, but now he realised it was a stupid, mindless thing to do. The stripes he'd worked so hard to achieve had also brought an enhanced wage packet. But now that he was back to being a mere private once again, how was he going to afford a wife? After all his promises to Teresa, he now had nothing at all to offer her. He was supposed to be seeing her in a few days, and needed to let her know he couldn't make it now. But with Chalkie and some of his other drinking mates also confined, how was he going to get news of his incarceration to her? This was just one of the things worrying him at the moment!

What was she going to think of him? How could he have been so stupid?

To throw away everything he'd worked so hard for too?

Arthur felt sick and mad at himself. What of Teresa? Would she now think there was no way she could marry a drunkard? He had to get word to her.

In desperation, he bribed one of the soldiers who brought them their meals, offering the man two packets of cigarettes to take a note to Teresa. In it, he explained his predicament, and why he would be unable to meet her as planned. Hoping she would let him explain more fully when he was finally released. He worried about how he could explain his stupid behaviour when he did finally see her, then worried even more in case the young 'squaddie' he'd entrusted with the note, had let him down.

As Arthur didn't receive a reply, he spent the rest of his time in the 'lock-up' in utter misery.

Soon after his release he made his way to their favourite park, where he usually met up with Teresa and the boys, but there was no sign of them. Other nannies came and went with their charges and he tried approaching one or two in case they knew where she could be. But he drew blanks. Eventually, he was forced to call at the house where she worked. Going round to the back door, he tried to question one of the servants as to the nannies whereabouts, but was devastated when he was told the nanny was not there.

"What do you mean," he asked the bearer who stood before him. "Has the nanny left this house for good?"

"Please sahib I am not knowing any reasons for why the chota-memsahib (junior lady) is not here. She is not being here for a long time now." The servant bowed low to Arthur as he closed the door, leaving Arthur with his heart in his boots.

Walking back to the barracks, he felt as if his whole world had collapsed!   I've really mucked things up big time now, he thought. Teresa had finished with him, and who could blame her?   She'd probably told the servant to say she wasn't there and they were just following orders.

If only he hadn't gone out for a drink!

But then perhaps it would have been something else?

It was as if everything was conspiring to keep them apart; just when things seemed to be going so well too.   She must have received his note - the young soldier had sworn he'd delivered it - even describing the house to Arthur.   So he had to face facts.   She had probably decided not to have anything more to do with him, what with him being such a lousy drunk and incapable of offering her the life he'd promised.

As day followed dismal day, Arthur sank into a fit of depression. Until Chalkie fed up with seeing Arthur's defeated look, decided to try and find out if Teresa had really finished with Arthur, by using some subtle bribery, receiving better news than he'd expected.

Teresa was on leave... her mother had taken ill... and the girl had had to rush off to be with her, but was due to return shortly.

"So yer see Arthur, yer've been beating yer'self up for no reason at all," Chalkie explained.   "I couldn't get a word out of any of the house servants, but yer know how they all love a gossip.   Anyway they said yer girl Teresa was on temporary leave only, apparently her mother's ill or something.   And yer owe me ten rupees, by the way. It's what I had to pay the syce (groom)."

Arthur's face lit up when he heard about the reason behind Teresa absence, although he hoped her mother would be well soon, and with the tiny crumbs of hope still there, he was able to kick himself out of the doldrums.   It had now been over a month since he'd seen Teresa and he'd decided he was going to throw himself at her feet and beg her forgiveness.   So, with this new resolve in mind, Arthur threw himself into whatever he had to do.   Determined, never to let her down again, but he knew he had a long way to go.

The second interview with his commanding officer regarding his permission to be married did not augur well!   The officer pointing out that Arthur did not seem ready to take on the responsibility of marriage if he continued to drink. Besides, now that Arthur had lost his status as sergeant, he could not even be considered for permission to marry.

Arthur was gutted, returning to his barracks with a very heavy heart. How the hell was he ever going to tell Teresa about this latest bomb-shell?

Then one day out of the blue, Arthur received a letter. Thinking it was from his mother, he quickly went forward to collect it. Good old mum! A letter from her always cheered him up. But the writing was unfamiliar? Opening it quickly, he scanned the unfamiliar writing; until he saw the signature; Teresa! He was over the moon! Finding a quiet place, he sat down to read his letter.

Dear Arthur, she'd written in nice neat handwriting, I was sorry to hear you had been in a spot of bother. Although I was surprised you had been locked away for it? I do hope the punishment you received was not too horrible? I know you will explain it all to me when we see each other. The reason I left in such a hurry was because my mother had taken ill and I was needed at home. But you will be pleased to hear she is now much better. I'm sorry I could not get word to you, there being no time and I was so worried. I only found out about your troubles because Lady Somerville forwarded on your note to me which, you will agree, was extremely kind of her. She also told me I was to take as much time off as I needed, which was nice of her. But I have no wish to abuse the privilege. If mother continues to make good progress, I will be able to return sometime next week. I will try and let you know by letter as soon as I return. Then she'd ended the letter with just her name: Teresa. There were no love or kisses, as his mother always added onto her letters, noted Arthur, but at least she'd written.

Finding Chalkie, he explained about the letter he'd received.

"Thought yer looked a lot chipper Arthur." Chalkie had said drolly. "Now all yer've gotta do is get yer bloody stripes back!" Which was easier said than done. He was now doing many of the menial tasks, like washing-up, and scrubbing down stoves etc. The sergeant in charge, made him slog away at mind-destroying jobs just for the hell of it! Arthur was now finding out how hard he'd pushed some of his own men at times.

His pay had also dropped to next to nothing now, the few rupees insufficient for himself, let alone for taking Teresa out when she finally returned. So there was only one way out; he was going to go A.W.O.L and try and get Teresa to go with him... to hell with the army!

"What d'ya thinks Chalkie?" He sounded out his idea on his best friend.

"Dunno Arf' me old cobber," Chalkie said, sucking his teeth. "Seems like a daft thing to do... besides where will yer go? T'ain't as if yer'll get far neither. Then, when the Military Police catch up with yer, yer'll be for the high-jump again! But if that's what yer want ter do...?"

"Thanks mate; I have given it a lot of thought. It all depends on Teresa agreeing... so I'll just have to wait and see."

Arthur was on tenterhooks waiting for word from Teresa. She'd not given a forwarding address; otherwise Arthur would have taken himself off to Pondicherry where he knew her mother lived! But again, he listened to the good advice offered by his best friend Chalkie.

"Best not Arthur," he'd said. "If she'd wanted yer to write she would have given you her mother's address. Besides, Pondicherry is a big place, yer wouldn't know where to start looking, would yer? No, best to wait... after all, who knows, she might even be making her way here as we speak."

It made sense to Arthur, so he decided to wait. And once again Chalkie seemed to have hit the nail on the head! A note from Teresa came within a few days of their conversation, telling him she was back with her employers and she could see him in the park the following day, if he was free? She would understand if he couldn't make it - because of his recent troubles - and had given an alternative day too. But Arthur knew he'd move heaven and earth to get to her on the appointed day and managed to wrangle a few hours off, saying he had toothache and needed to see the medical officer.

It was another lovely warm day, the sun shone down with a yellow glow through the leaves of the huge trees lining the pathways in the park, the brightly coloured flowers dancing in the slight breeze that prevailed. Everything looked perfect, thought Arthur. The moment he saw Teresa's slight figure walking with her two small charges towards him, Arthur thought his heart would jump right out of his body. It began to beat so loudly, he wondered if she might notice. As he hurried to meet her, he noticed she was actually smiling. She'd missed him just as much as he had missed her!

The two children pulled away from their nanny as soon as they sighted Arthur, running full-tilt into his strong arms and as he scooped the two excited children up, he gazed over their heads at her lovely face.

She seemed to be just as pleased to see him!

The sweet smile on her face was breathtaking, he noticed as he looked into her lovely eyes. It had seemed she'd been away for years, instead of just a few weeks.

"Hello Arthur," she greeted him softly, wanting to throw herself into his strong arms. With so many others in the park on this lovely morning she had to be content to walk quietly alongside him, until the boys wriggled down from his arms, to run over the manicured lawns. And then it was their turn.

"How is your mother?"

"She's as well as can be Arthur, thank you for asking. She had malaria." explained Teresa.

"I heard it makes you feel really bad?"

"Yes, you're quite right; my mother's is a recurring thing. She gets it every other year. At times it's worse than at others, this time she had quite a bad time with it."

"Is there no cure?"

"Well at the moment she has been prescribed quinine tablets, which seem to help... but time will tell."

"Is it contagious?" Arthur asked quickly, hoping Teresa hadn't been open to any infection.

"Oh no, not at all," Teresa laughed lightly. "I would never have come back to these two young scamps if there was any danger of them contacting the fever." She smiled, looking fondly at the two boys who were rolling about on the cool damp grass.

"Boys, boys," she called. "You'll get grass stains all over your clothes," and they came running back to where she stood with Arthur.

"Can we go to the swings now, Arthur? Can we go to the swings?" they chorused each trying to grab one of his huge hands in their tiny ones, to pull him along.

"What do you say nanny," asked Arthur, flashing a smile at Teresa.

"Do you think they deserve a swing?"

"Oh do please say yes nanny, please, please, please," they begged.

"Oh well," she pretended to be undecided... and the two youngsters looked up into her face. "We promise to be ever so good, don't we Clive," prompted Peter the more boisterous of the twins.

"What do think Arthur?" Teresa pretended to seek help from him.

"Oh yes please, we'll be ever so terribly good, won't we Peter?" echoed Clive. Teresa smiled.

"Oh, all right then, but only if Arthur doesn't mind," agreed Teresa.

And with whoops of joy from the twins Arthur allowed himself to be pulled along by the two young children towards the swings, both of them huffing and puffing as they tugged at the big man.

Then with the boys happily perched on swings - Arthur and Teresa pushing one each - he was able to broach the subject of her mother once more.

"Did you tell your mother about me?"

"Yes Arthur, I did. When she was better I told her all about you," Teresa smiled.

"And?" Arthur waited.

"And she said you sounded quite nice." Teresa teased, as Arthur hung onto every word.

"Does that mean she approves?"

"Well, what she actually said..." Teresa looked over towards Arthur who'd just given Clive a big push on the swing.

"What she said was 'Whatever makes you happy child!'" Teresa was now getting quite puffed out with chatting and pushing Peter on his swing. Stopping, she called out to the boys.

"That's enough for today children."

And as she walked back to the nearest bench she held out her hand to Arthur.

"Did you tell her I'd lost my sergeants stripes too," he asked tentatively, watching her face.

"No," confessed the girl, "I really thought one thing at time would be better, don't you?" she said, looking up at the big handsome man at her side.

"Anyway, you haven't told me all about your escapade, have you? But perhaps that had better wait until my day off?"

Although Arthur was dying to tell her what he'd decided - with her co-operation of course - he decided prudently to leave that for another day. For now, all he wanted to do was hold her lovely soft hand in his, and pretend they were already married... and the two little boys on the swings were theirs!

It seemed like an eternity until Teresa had her next day off, and they could be together to have a really good talk, and Arthur couldn't wait to tell Teresa of his plan.

"First of all, I want to tell you how much you mean to me," Arthur said, holding both of Teresa's hands in his own, and as she faced him, he continued... "It might be some time before I get my stripes back, but I would still like for us to be married." Stopping to look closely at Teresa's face, he took heart when she looked back at him without pulling her hands away.

"I know I promised you time to think things over, but I just can't go on without you in my life." He stopped to take a breath, and bent forward to kiss her gently on the lips, and then drew her towards him. Holding her tightly against his chest, he whispered, "Please, please marry me Teresa, I cannot go on without you." She could feel the beating of both their hearts.

"Yes." Arthur could hardly hear the softly spoken word, drawing back to look at Teresa in amazement. "Do-o do you mean 'yes' as in YES you'll ma... marry me," he stuttered. Teresa smiled at his dear face so close to hers.

"Yes, as in yes, I'll marry you," she laughed, and it was nearly her last breath, as he drew her back into his arms, kissing her passionately - oblivious to any others who happened to be passing - as he held her tightly. It was some time later, that he was able to continue any conversation.

"I must be the happiest bloke in the whole world," he whispered in Teresa's ear. "But you know I can't wait for any permission, don't you?" She gazed back at Arthur quizzically and waited for him to continue.

"Lets just get married privately, we're both twenty four, and we don't require any permission from anyone, do we? You pick a church, and I'll go along with anywhere you choose."

"But Arthur, we'll have to have the banns read out... and...?" Arthur stopped her with another kiss, before continuing.

"I'm not waiting for any damn colonel to give me permission to marry the girl of my choice, anyhow, who's going to let on?" He urged. "I've already told Chalkie my best friend and he's said he'll help."

"Wait! wait!" cried Teresa, 'what on earth are you talking about Arthur?" she said, pulling away from his embrace to look closely at him.

"Didn't I just say...?" Arthur looked worried now.

"What you were saying is that you want me to marry you, but you don't want to wait for permission from your commanding officer, right? So how do we get married then?"

"I'm asking you to elope with me," Arthur said, "I thought you knew?"

"No, no it wasn't clear what you wanted me to do. You were talking so quickly I could hardly keep up."

"Well, now that you do know, what do you think about it?"

"What I think is... Oh Arthur...what I really think is, you haven't thought about it very carefully, have you?"...Teresa sighed.

"If we eloped, you would be hunted by the army. I would have to leave my job. We would have no money, and nowhere to live. It's all just impossible. Have you thought what our lives would be like? Look, I admit I love you too, and I'll gladly wait for however long it takes for us to be married, but I'm not going to throw away all I've worked so hard for. So please, no more talk about eloping okay?"

Arthur looked crest-fallen, but realised he hadn't been thinking as far ahead as Teresa had.

"You mean you wouldn't mind waiting?"

"I really wouldn't mind waiting Arthur. Not if it means we can do things 'properly'. But only if you promise me you won't get drunk again and ruin any chances you may have for our future," she said, smiling to soften her words. "Besides, it will give us a chance to be engaged for a while, won't it?" She said, her eyes twinkling. Arthur knew he'd wait for her for however long it took! Marvelling at how easily Teresa had solved what had been bugging him for days.

Then fate stepped in - to give a helping hand.

A few days after he'd had to tell the young man he was refused permission to marry, Arthur's commanding officer had guests around for dinner. It was just an informal gathering - mostly family and close friends - so the conversation was of a casual nature.

"Did you see the dress Daphne wore to the party the other evening?" Somebody asked, and the ladies were off... They discussed what was 'a la mode', the price of clothes, and what was being worn in London now. Then, someone changed the subject to the food that had been served at the dinner party.

"Disgraceful," snorted Lady Montford.

"Oh mummy it wasn't all that bad," her daughter - the colonel's wife - said.

"Your mother's quite right Harriet," Patricia - the wife of an eminent visiting colonel - cut in... "The meat I had was quite unacceptable."

"I said disgraceful, and I meant disgraceful," the dowager Lady Montford repeated. "Nothing at all like some of the other dinners we've attended."

"Really Mama," Arthur's colonel said mildly to his mother-in-law. "Which one of the many are you referring to?"

"Well, I can name quite a few dinners I've had lately Bertie," this said as if she were reprimanding a child, instead of an officer commanding an entire battalion.

"I have, as you know, a very fine palate - as my recently dear-departed Timothy often told me - so I do know good from bad." Giving her son-in-law a withering look she went on... "Now that nice young sergeant who always comes up with the most delicious menus." She raised her hand as if trying to recall someone, or something.

"... The big good-looking boy who was so kind...?"

"Ah, I think I know who you might be referring to mother, could it be that nice blue-eyed sergeant who you were so taken with last year at the gymkhana?" Her daughter smiled, trying to ease the tension between her husband and her mother.

"Yes, yes... I do believe he's the one. Ever such a nice young man too. He really did everything he could for me that day," recalled Lady Montford. And looking haughtily over at her son-in-law, she continued... "Your Godson had just had his tonsils removed, and the young man was very helpful indeed, fetching cool drinks for Simon... and I'm told, the delicious lunch we had, was prepared by him too. Now that's what I call good food! The boy's a credit to the army!"

"Well I've bad news about him I'm afraid Mama," her son-in-law informed her. "He was one of my sergeants until a few weeks ago. Came to me for permission to marry... seems he'd found this nice young gel... and then he goes and gets drunk! Had to chuck him in the 'cooler' for a few days, and demote the damn fool to boot. No chance of getting permission to marry. Only given to NCO's and above, you know? There is certainly no chance of doing any catering for a bit either, anyway, why does he want to become entangled with one of the Indian girls? So many nice girls back in Blighty, what?"

"Are we talking about a young man named Arthur?" demanded Lady Montford.

"Why yes, I do believe that might have been his name as I recollect mama." The colonel seemed to be trying to recall the events. "Young chap, as I recall, used to be in the 'Hampshire's'... fought in the trenches too... shame, shame. Good old English name... Fisher... yes, Sergeant Fisher. Damn big fellow, looks as strong as an ox to me, but smitten by some wee Indian girl...," The colonel mused.

"Not Lady Somerville's young nanny?" One of the ladies present asked.

"What? Oh... you mean Lord and Lady Somerville from Redcliff Lodge, out on Richmond Road?"

And very soon it was established that it was of course the very same young lady who, indeed, looked after the Somerville twins. Many of those present had already met the young lady - on several occasions - and had taken a liking to the intelligent, quietly-spoken girl.

Arthur's fame as to the functions he'd been catering for had already become well known by most of the ladies around Bangalore cantonments too! In fact someone had actually seen Arthur as a guest of Lord and Lady Somerville once, along with their nanny. And if they approved?

"Not Indian at all, Portuguese extraction Lady Someville told me," someone said of the nanny. "Apparently had a marvellous education at one the better schools."

"Can't you do something Bertie?" Lady Montford demanded. Not many tried to thwart this dowager, especially her son-in-law Bertie, even though he was an officer, commanding hundreds of soldiers.

"Not much use being in charge if you can't do something! I've seen you listing to starboard many a time, haven't I? Chaps entitled to get rowdy occasionally; my Timothy liked a drink or two himself - didn't make him unsuitable to marry *me*."

A few days later - to Arthur's absolute amazement - he was sent for by his commanding officer.

What now, he thought I've nothing to lose this time!

Maybe now would be a good time to put the colonel right about Teresa? And as he stood waiting to be called in, Arthur decided he'd do just that – even though Chalkie had advised him to try and be diplomatic.

"Listen Arthur, Chalkie had said, yer'll probably make things a hundred times worse than it already is. Yer've already promised Teresa yer won't be getting into any more scrapes haven't yer? Well what on earth do yer think having a go at the 'Old Man' will do?"

Thinking about what Chalkie had said, Arthur had to agree with him after all. It was no good making a bad situation even worse! He'd just listen to whatever the colonel had to say - but if he tried to besmirch her name again.

Then was flabbergasted when he was announced in by the adjutant, to be greeted with...

"Come in, come right in sergeant." the colonel boomed out from behind his desk when Arthur was announced, a broad smile lighting up his face. Marching smartly in, Arthur saluted, and stood easy as directed by the colonel.

"Now look here sergeant..." the colonel began... something wrong here thought Arthur; he only took my stripes off me a few weeks ago, had he already forgotten? I'm not a sergeant any more.

"I might have been a trifle too harsh on you last time," his Commanding Officer proceeded.

"Seems you were not to blame for that little episode the other night, had one of the other chappies come forward, it seems you were in the clear. So I'm giving you back your stripes, and you will be on full pay as from today, is that clear?"

"Yes Sir," Arthur stood straight and tall, hardly believing what he'd heard! The colonel harrumphed then, clearing his throat, as he spoke. "About that permission thing... can you make out another chitty in a couple of days... I do think I was a bit hasty turning you down, probably be the making of you eh? There is nothing like a wife to make a man settle down!"

I'm bloody well hearing things, this just can't be happening, thought Arthur as he walked out, his head bursting with the last five minutes conversation, which was all it had taken to have his life turned upside down, he nearly bumped into the adjutant who was just going back into the colonel's office.

"Sir." Arthur swung his hand up to salute the officer, the young man gave him a quick flip of his cane, and a half-hearted salute back. But Arthur didn't care a damn. He was over the moon!

Chalkie didn't have to be told things had gone right for Arthur, the smile on his friends face was enough. Although, even though Arthur wanted to celebrate his new-found status - plus the extra money - he refused to go out drinking later that night.

'About that permission... Come back in a few days... I do think I was a bit hasty'... ringing in his ears. In a few days he would be able to ask Teresa to marry him, and this time he knew she wouldn't refuse him!

And the rest was history, as they say!

CHAPTER THIRTEEN

The Water Screens

Growing up as a child in India was pretty good. We lived in a nice three bedroomed bungalow, which had been built slightly off the ground - like most of the bungalows in India; as a deterrent to snakes, scorpions and other creepy-crawlies and of course the heavy monsoon rains. Although nothing really stopped a determined snake!

Our bungalow had two flat roofs - much like a two-tiered cake - the inner rooms taller than the rest of the building. With flat roofs as you'd expect, the surfaces were made slightly slanted, to allow any excess rainwater to run off via the gutters cut into the parapets at intervals.

Wide shallow steps led up to verandas at the front and back of the building, with more steps leading to the toilets, bathrooms, dressing rooms and bedrooms at either side of the bungalow; the main rooms in the middle of the property having much higher ceilings.

The big neem trees growing at the side of the bungalow gave shade to part of the building and the compound at one side - and access to the rooftops via the branches, which we used to climb as children. But we never climbed up onto the parapets for fear of falling. The view from the roof was marvellous! We could see the vegetable garden and the whole of the maidhan (field) at the back; and the front garden, with the rest of the bungalows on 'Five Bungalows Road' at the front. The numbers of trees growing along the road and in people's gardens hid nearly all the other buildings, affording just the occasional glimpse through the dense foliage.

Most of the buildings in India were white-washed; the theory being the white paint would refract the heat of the sun, keeping the inner rooms cool during the summer months. But laying in bed on a very hot summer's night you wondered if it really did work? The heat used to be intolerable; the inside of the bungalow felt like an oven, and without the help of the khuss-khuss tatty (porous roots) screens - there being no air conditioning then - sleep would have been impossible!

The sound of water trickling softly through the sweet-scented roots was comforting and soothing. The cool breeze bringing refreshing sleep as the water screens continued working throughout the hottest of nights. The soft 'clunk' of wood-on-wood as the tipper fell... releasing water with a sudden 'swishing' sound as it went cascading down the screen; soaking the porous roots as it went... down... down... down, until, with a soft trickle, it reached the wooden container at the bottom. A pump then sent the water back up to the top again - to continue the process over and over again; the hot air from the outside being cooled as it passed through the khuss-khuss roots. The sweet, slightly musky, earthy smell of the wet roots wafting through the bedroom - better than any perfume - drying sweat from your brow and sweaty limbs, the soothing coolness lulling you off to sleep at last! Such a simple contraption - but so very efficient!

The container of cold water at the bottom of the screen made an excellent cooling-box too - no fridges then - so everything placed above on the ice-cold water was kept lovely and cool. The large mangoes father loved or any other fruit tasted much better cooled, and bottles of milk left in the water kept longer and were lovely and cool to drink – especially in the lovely tall glasses of 'mango-fool' we enjoyed of an evening.

Sometimes on very hot nights my sister and I would get a few handfuls of the water to sprinkle over our sheets, and then lie back down on the wet sheets... sheer bliss! The state of ecstasy short-lived as the heat of our bodies soon dried up the wet patches within minutes.

We never told my mother about this though, as I don't think she would have approved! This of course is not recommended for arthritis sufferers!

There were some nights when even the cool khuss-khuss tatty screens didn't bring enough relief, and we would be forced to sleep alfresco; the servants carrying our beds and linen outside to the back compound.

We'd all play games of cards, draughts or guessing games, or get mother to tell us stories until it was dark, then we'd jump into bed and listen to the night sounds... the jackals always sounded so much nearer as they wee-a-waaaed their distinct calls to one another. We would draw the sheets up to cover our heads, only to find the heat under it suffocating... and if like me you had a vivid imagination, you thought the wild animals could get right underneath your bed!

The funny thing is we never were bothered by any creep-crawlies that might be about. Even though you could see tracks of 'something' that had gone over our footprints, that we'd made the previous night.

It was exciting lying out under the stars and looking up at the different constellations of stars. Even from quite an early age I could distinguish between 'The Plough' or the 'Great Bear' and 'Little Bear'. Mother knew them all, and would point them out as we lay looking up at them – recounting little tales about how they had come to be named. I loved it that the 'Milky Way' was called the 'Road of the Gods' because the stars making up the constellation were so brilliant. There seemed to be many more stars in the sky then, and we would watch them 'shooting' across the sky in their dozens; flashes of silver against a black velvet sky; they went so fast... leaving a trail of silver star-dust in their wake!

Mother told us how the sun travelled round the earth - and even now it would be shining brightly right on the other side of the world, as we in India were watching the stars at night. She had travelled extensively and would describe different countries, their people and traditions - leaving father to tell us about where he'd been born, and all about England and his life as a young boy; which was very different from our own lives in India. But of course at the time we all thought he was exaggerating somewhat!

I only found out about his war experiences as I got older - pestering him to tell me about what he'd done during the war. Although even then, so many years later he had been loath to tell me some of the horrible things he'd witnessed; but sometimes when he was 'in his cups' he would talk sadly about events in the trenches - a thing he couldn't do when sober! But what I do remember is that he never forgot! At every Remembrance Day service he would stand tall to honour all the fallen in both World Wars with tears in his eyes.

At night as we slept, the chokidar (night watch-man) would do his rounds, big lathi (metal-tipped stick) at the ready, as he 'patrolled' the grounds round the bungalow - keeping a discreet distance away as he walked. He always made sure we knew he was there - and awake - so would cough, clear his throat, or give a little stamp of his feet every so often. It was a nice feeling to know someone was there and awake to look after us as we slept outside under the stars.

The back veranda of our bungalow was covered in a 'jaffrey.' A sort of woven wooden screen to keep flies etc out, but of course they could always find their way in. So the 'flit' pump was always on standby. It was my father versus the flies as he 'stalked' them - flit pump in hand - but with their three-hundred-and-sixty-degree swivelling eyes and 'feelers' they could see him long before he got to within a couple of feet of aiming his 'gun' at them. So when he did get to spray them - they were long gone! The windows, mirrors and other surfaces getting a liberal puff of 'flit' that left a hazy glaze over them, but killed few flies... so it was back to the old fly-swat; a square of leather about four inches by four inches; held on a long-handled cane, to swat pesky flies. A disgusting habit, but you just had to keep the little beggars down! You had to be really quick too, as the wind - pushed by the descending swat - gave the little bug-eyed insects advance knowledge; they'd be long gone before that piece of leather got anywhere near them. I swear you could hear them laughing as my father chased them all over the house before they finally flew right back out of the holes they'd come in by.

The occasional centipede, scorpion and snake finding their way into people's homes too; to hide out in the most unlikely places - mostly the toe of a shoe or the folds of a damp towel - and anything you'd foolishly left on the floor. So it was always wise to shake out fresh clothing and shoes before getting dressed, just in case you'd got an unwelcome visitor!

When my eldest brother Ernest was a baby, my mother had left him sitting on a cotton dhurri (rug) on the floor; where he was playing happily with a few brightly-coloured streamers left over from the Christmas decorations. She had only gone into the next room to fetch something and had been no more than a minute but on her return she could hear Ernest 'talking' to someone, and to her horror saw a snake - its head poised to strike - as it swayed gently from side to side before her baby; seemingly fascinated by the coloured paper the child was holding out to it. She couldn't snatch the child up – which was her first reaction – knowing that any sudden movement would cause the snake to strike. So she withdrew quietly – one of the hardest thing she'd ever had to do in her life – and returned almost immediately with one of father's sticks. Then walking swiftly towards the baby; who was still babbling away saying 'pretty, pretty,' as he tried to offer the snake some of his coloured papers, she raised the stick in both hands... and whacked it against the snake with all her might... away from the baby...with one strong blow that sent the snake yards away, then scooping up Ernest, she ran from the room shouting 'naga! naga!' (snake! snake!)

My brother's screams and mother's shouts brought the servants running; everyone thinking the child had been bitten by the snake, but that wasn't the reason he was crying. Oh no! He'd just been annoyed that his 'game' with the pretty striped creature had been interrupted! Suffice to say, no other children were left on their own after that. But it hadn't stopped other little 'happenings'.

Ayah was with me the whole time when I received my comeuppance!

I too was a chubby baby at the time, many years later than my brother's encounter. Having just breakfasted on some fruit - which I'd managed to get all over my face - I was washed and put outside in the shade of the neem tree, to get some fresh air. It was a lovely sunny morning and I was quite content to sit on the rug, playing with my toys; ayah sitting quietly beside me and picking up the odd toy I decided to throw away... which I decided was a much better game. So I started to throw the toys further and further away; ayah patiently retrieving the thrown toys to bring back to me. So serve me right when she had to walk several yards away to fetch one of them back! A big black bully ant had quickly walked up over my toes, making them tickle, which was when I first became aware of him, until my eyes must have crossed as it perched atop my nose... and it tickled. So I raised my hand to scratch... and wham... that big bully sank his pincers into my nose, and bit down hard. And I mean hard!

I of course, let out a yell that brought not only ayah, but a whole platoon of servants running at the double. But ayah was the first to come to my aid, being on the scene so to speak... and she plucked that nasty old ant off me... quick as a flash. But as he was holding on so tightly, his body went... leaving his head and pincers still embedded in the tip of my nose.

That big bully ant wasn't going to give up too easily!

It really hurt, the formic acid from an ordinary ant bad enough, but times that by ten for a bite from a big black bully ant, then you'll know how hard - and how long - I screamed.

Of course, even after the hurt had subsided, I still made the most of the petting and fuss I received from everyone around me - which of course I deserved - and was told, at a much later date, that I was still sobbing long afterwards in my sleep. Poor ayah, convinced she'd neglected her little charge, kept blaming herself for not having washed the fruit juices off my face properly. Thinking that was what the ant had been attracted too. I was too small to explain it had all been my fault; I'd only wanted to play with it... and had intended only to scratch my nose, not antagonise the ant.

As they say, let sleeping dogs lie... and snakes... and bully ants!

After having looked after my brother Billy - a quiet, really good-natured little boy - ayah must have been driven out of her mind with me! I was the most contrary child. At four I was a squat little child, my hair still very dark, had been cut in a bob that reached just under my ears, and I had a fringe. My eyes were greeny/grey and my eyelashes and eyebrows very black. I'd inherited my dark looks from my mother, but had my father's stubborn streak; and would rather be smacked than back down if I thought I was right; even though I was nearly always wrong! I could cross my eyes quite easily whenever I wanted too - much to ayahs cries of 'nai, nai, missy baba' (no, no young miss).

Even my mother warned me that if the clock struck while I was doing it, I would stay boss-eyed forever!

No matter what ayah dressed me in, or how tidy I looked after my bath, within minutes I'd managed to get myself dirty again! This must have been very trying for her as most ayah's loved to show off their little 'charges' by dressing them up in their best clothes and bragging about how good, and how easy it was to look after their little 'missy baba's. Compared to some of the precious little golden-haired - they always look so clean don't they - children taken to the 'Railway Institute' to play I must have let her down badly, but thank goodness, she still loved me!

My sister and I shared a bedroom, which had a dressing room and toilet at one side; a door from the dressing room led into my parent's bedroom; my sister and I sharing the same facilities as my parents on this side of the bungalow. My two brothers had the same facilities on the other side of the bungalow, a door from their dressing room leading into the large lounge/dining room. Both toilets at either side of the bungalow had steps leading out onto the side of the building which gave the sweeper access to empty the toilet pans several times during the day; the 'night soil' people - who were of even lower rank than our sweeper - used to come in the dead of night to collect all the rubbish and excrement.

It was quite nice sharing a bedroom with my sister, but we girls could talk the hind leg off a donkey, once we got started. Which inevitably led to giggling? Although most nights we were too 'whacked out' to talk; going 'spark out' as soon as our heads touched the pillows… but sometimes… we'd talk for hours; softly at first, then going into fits of laughter over the slightest thing.

"Will you two girls stop talking and get to sleep!" the shouted warning from my mother in the next room, having the opposite effect, and made us even worse. We'd giggle hysterically, unable to stop ourselves, stuffing our hands into our mouths as we convulsed with absolute mirth. But the masculine tones from our father telling us to "be quiet or else…," had the desired effect! Covering our heads with the sheets we didn't dare disobey.

If you were to have asked me next day what on earth we were giggling about… do you know, I just couldn't have told you!

Growing up girls do an awful lot of giggling!

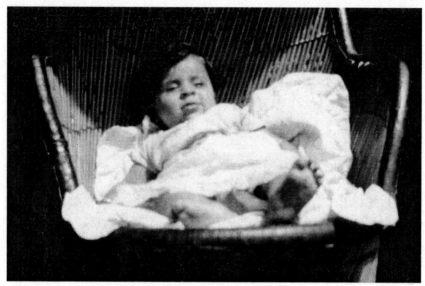

Me as a baby lying on a morah (cane chair).

Me in nun's costume.

Billy and I in front garden - in front of mum's sweet peas.

Billy and I in back garden - sitting on the hodhi (water container).

Bungalow we used to live in at Ajmer.

Father on his motorbike.

St Mary's Convent, Ajmer. Picture taken in 2000 - corridor now boarded up, with new pathway where garden used to be.

St Mary's Church, Ajmer. Picture taken in 2000 - with my sister Hazel standing nearby.

Gate House Lodge at Barnes High School. Deolali.

Founders Day and buildings at Barnes High School.

Open-air swimming pool at Barnes High School.

Edith Cavell House - picture taken in 1944.
I'm sitting second from the right of Sister Spencer.

P. & O. R.M.S. STRATHMORE, 23,500 TONS.

The ship that carried us to England in 1948.

CHAPTER FOURTEEN

Squirrels in the Jaffrey

The back veranda of our bungalow had a fitted 'Jaffrey,' a woven wooden screen, lined with a fine-meshed wire netting on the inside to keep birds, flies and insects out. There was a door set into it, which was kept closed at all times - mainly because of those pesky flies! It was a nice airy room, facing east; the rising sun flooding it first thing in the morning. It was here that we breakfasted, lounged about, did our homework, or just sat and chatted.

A couple of rows of shelves had been built high up on the inside of the Jaffrey screen, holding things we used every day. The lower ones held everyday items, the higher ones oddments, like confiscated marbles, catapults, letters and documents, and other bits and bobs, the clutter growing daily.

So one day mother decided to have a tidying-up session and found a squirrel had built its nest in one corner, on the highest shelf! She also saw a small hole in the corner of the Jaffrey where the squirrels had gnawed through. Thinking the nest empty - and that it had only just been built - she carefully removed a small part of the elaborate nest only to find there were tiny, squirming, pink-skinned baby squirrels nestling in the downy nest, the tiny sightless infants constantly climbing over one another; their shivering little bodies seeking warmth from one another. They looked so small and vulnerable, like miniature puppies with their bulging and as yet unopened eyes.

Quickly covering the hole she'd made, mother realised my father would give them short shrift. To him, squirrels were just so much vermin! He hated them with a vengeance, suspecting them of having stolen his precious bulbs from his garden; although he'd never actually caught them in the act, referring to them as 'tree rats', and a 'blooming nuisance'. He also said they nibbled everything they could get their teeth into; including electric cabling; having heard they had bitten through some electric cables in a house, which had caused a fire. So mum decided to keep the squirrels a secret from him, for now.

Of course, she let us kids into the secret - after all, she couldn't take a chance on one of us suddenly noticing we had squirrels, could she?

In time, the baby squirrels grew bigger, and became quite tame, allowing us to hand-feed them. The parents not so keen: snatching any food offered, then darting off to sit and eat it a safe distance away. Holding the tit-bit with both little paws as they nibbled away - button-bright eyes always alert - as they watched our every movement.

We even made clothes for the little babies - little jackets and pants - with holes cut out for their little bushy tails. They looked so cute!

How we giggled as they walked about like little miniature humans. Mother was so clever with a needle, she fashioned little 'cavaliers' hats, complete with small feathers, and when they sat upright - fully clothed - eating a nut from their little paws, we'd howl with laughter.

If only we'd taken pictures of them, but the camera was used very sparingly in those days.

Of course, father found out about them eventually, and he was as mad as a hatter, threatening to 'drown' the lot of them, but mother knew how to handle him, using all her wiles to appeal to his better nature; finally, making him promise not to board up their entrance hole.

"You can't do that Arthur," she pleaded. "Those poor little babies will perish without their parents."

A complete about-face in her attitude towards me when I was born with all that downy hair, eh?

So he agreed they could stay, but only on condition that after they'd flown the coop - or in their case the veranda - he would be allowed to reinforce the netting to keep the little 'varmints' away for good.

Squirrels 'ten points' - Dad 'nil' poi!

I think we all got a few nips on our fingers from the squirrels, mostly because we weren't expecting the little blighters to turn on their benefactors! And the babies continued to grow.

One evening, my father put his glass of whiskey down on the table nearby, and went off for a stroll around the garden. Returning, he saw one of the baby squirrels reaching over the edge of his glass, slowly sipping his best malt! Even he was amazed at the flagrant cheek of it all!

"Here Teresa," he called "Come and have a look at this." And by the time my mother arrived, the poor wee thing was teetering about all over the table-top. Bumping into things, and nearly falling off the side... but for her timely assistance.

The poor baby squirrel was drunk!

My father was scolded - it being 'entirely his fault' the poor little squirrel had drunk some liquor and might die.

"Oh how could you Arthur," she cried, thinking the poor thing would be dead by the morning.

"Me," he said looking surprised. "Don't be daft, as if I'd give the damn thing my best whisky."

Next morning, the baby squirrel looked no worse for its adventure - in fact it seemed perkier than ever. But dad kept his whiskey glass covered over for their entire stay after that!

Other babies were not so fortunate! I remember clearly the day a very poor 'untouchable' woman tried to drown her small child in our 'hodhi' (water container). This concrete container in our back garden held water for the plants. But as the pipes were buried very near the surface of the ground, the sun heated the water in them to nearly boiling point during the summer months. So the hodhi was filled and left overnight for the water to cool down before being used on the gardens. The water in the hodhi was always lovely and cold.

One afternoon mother was lying down on her bed - and I was supposed to have been doing the same too - because it was deemed much too hot to be outdoors. But I'd snuck out of the side door and was playing quite happily in the summer-house. Everywhere was quiet, the servants also having their midday siesta. In the heat of India's afternoon, even the animals conserved their energies, so there wasn't so much as a dog barking.

With the sun high in the cloudless sky, and the flies buzzing around the fallen sticky yellow fruit of the neem tree, I played quietly in the summer house - until I heard voices. Peeping out of my hiding place, I saw a young Indian woman who looked like an untouchable. (Hindu lowest caste) She was skinny, and very poorly dressed, with a small girl of about four or five by her side, and another very small infant in her arms.

I assumed she had come for a drink of water.

But as she proceeded to wash herself and the children, I thought it time to make myself scarce. Slipping indoors I bumped into my mother – who was up and about.

"What are you up to?" Mother questioned. "Er, er..," I stuttered, not really having an excuse for being out of my room. 'There's a woman outside by the hodhi!' I blurted out. And it worked! My mother's thoughts were diverted to something else, as she hurried out.

At first it looked as if the woman was washing her young child in the hodhi. But getting closer, my mother realised the women was not bathing her child! The older child was crying by now, and pulling at her mother's skirt, pleading with her mother not to harm the baby.

She was not washing the child; she was trying to drown it!

I think my mother realised straight away what was going on, and wrestled the small child - who was bleating, and gasping from her contact with the cold water - away from the Indian woman. The younger child was sobbing as she implored her mother to stop. "Nai, nai" (no, no) she screamed, and with all the noise and confusion, the other house servants were soon on the scene.

Mother was holding the poor wee mite upside down, trying to get the water out of its system. And as the child's mouth shuddered with the cold, it cried... sounding just like a little lamb bleating. The Indian woman had collapsed onto the ground, and the older child was huddled over her mother, crying and pleading with her.

The servants were able to make out what the poor wretched woman was saying, and translated for my mother.

It appeared the woman was a poor untouchable, whose husband had died a few weeks before. Being left with two small children, whom she was unable to feed, she had been begging around wherever she could. She was at her wits end as to how best to feed her children - her breasts had long since dried up, and the baby was starving - then she'd seen the hodhi full of water. Better the young child was dead than slowly starving to death she had thought, and after giving them both a drink, and drinking deeply herself... she'd decided to put the smallest child out of its misery, which was the point where my mother had entered the scene.

When the infant had recovered enough, my mother found clothes for both children, and heated up some cows milk for the baby; spoon-feeding the little mite herself. Then, after making sure they all had enough to eat, my mother asked our own sweepers wife - who was also an untouchable - to help find the poor woman and her children a roof over their heads.

Of course, money helped, and with repeated salaams as she bent to touch my mother's feet, the young mother wept as she took her leave, mother having told her to come back and report on their progress, from time to time.

A few months passed, and we had begun to think the poor woman had not been able to resist doing herself and her young children in so we were delighted to see the same young mother walking up the pathway from the back of our bungalow. This time, a huge smile lighting up her pretty face - which had filled out nicely with nourishment - and with the smallest infant walking too, they made a handsome threesome.

The children were clean and well-looked after, and looked extremely bonny, the younger one smiling, when my mother gently prodded its fat little tummy. And it was a different tale the mother had to offer this time.

A man had come looking for them after hearing about his brother's death. Deciding to marry his widow - who was quite a bonny girl - hence the smiles all round. We listened to the young woman's account of her changed circumstances and her giggling admission that this man was even better than his brother. Proudly patted her bulging tummy... to indicate she was once more with child.

How my mother laughed. It was the best news she had heard in a long time.

Sometimes we were given the odd treat too. Out of the blue father would announce "I think we'll have a picnic tomorrow!" It was invariably at evening dinner and after he'd had one or two 'aperitifs'. Of course we children went mad with delight, and the next morning we would scramble aboard a couple of tonga's and head off to the open countryside; my parents with the laden 'Tiffin box'(food container) in one tonga, and a couple of servants and us kids in the other. Being the two youngest, my brother Billy and I got to travel up front with the tonga wallah, (driver of horse-drawn carriage) which was great... until the horse passed wind. As it trotted along it used to lift its tail, and we would get the full force of its flatulence; and sometimes the blessed thing did its business as well so bits of 'that' went all over us too. I suppose that was the price we had to pay for wanting to sit 'up front'.

When we reached our destination the horses were taken out from between the shafts, hobbled, and let out to graze, their tails 'swishing' the flies off as they buried their muzzles into the juicy sweet grass which grew abundantly there.

Our picnics were often taken at a place called 'Happy Valley'. This was a natural valley; formed over thousands of years, long before the dam had been built. Then, monsoon rains had run down from the Aravali Hills to gouge the valley out of the land. The lovely mature trees, plants and grasses growing there making it the ideal picnic spot.

The dam was covered in writing from the many people who had visited in the past. Dates and signatures scratched into the surfaces testifying to the years it had stood there. Vast amounts of water, stored for agricultural purposes, now safely dammed to keep the rain water from flooding the small villages nearby.

We loved climbing up the groynes to add our names to the others already there. It's funny to think they are probably still there today!

It was a beautiful, green and lush valley. Some of the trees looked quite ancient; and spread their branches over a wide area, so there were lots of shady places to settle down under, and the horses chomped away at the grass, slowly getting further and further away; the drivers slept like babies as they knew they were being paid for doing just that.

We'd play games while our parents read, or chatted, joining us when they felt rested. Happy Valley was the ideal place to play hide and seek. There were so many nooks and crannies to hide away in. But of course, after going there so many times we knew most of the places off by heart.

But one day my parents stumped us.

We searched high and low, and couldn't find them! We kids were getting worried and ready to give in... and I'd begun to cry. But we decided to make one last-ditch effort; and found mum and dad hiding inside a deep well. They had climbed down some steps built around the inside of the well, and were sitting quietly chatting as they waited to be 'found'.

What if they had slipped?

Parents can be quite a handful at times!

After all that running about we were hungry, so we soon finished off the lovely curry puffs, sausage rolls, sandwiches, fruit and drinks etc. before running off to play again.

It had been rumoured that there was gold and precious stones to be found in Happy Valley; brought down by the rushing water long before the dam had been built; the water supposedly having loosened rocks from the very top of the hills, to wash debris and gems down into the valley, so we were forever hunting for the precious stones for ourselves; spending hours turning the rocks and stones over in the hope we'd find... something.

But apart from the odd spider, scorpion or centipede, we were not lucky. Although we did find some lovely bits of coloured glass - worn smooth with age - which I thought pretty enough to add to my collection of bits and pieces.

There were other picnics too. Sometimes whole families and friends all going together, which was great fun. All the women brought along something in the food line; vying with one another to produce the very best food - which they had made themselves or got their cooks to prepare; whole dekshies (saucepans) of curries, pillau rice, cold meats and other foods on offer, with proper tables and tablecloths brought along to hold the veritable banquet! Everyone sat down on dhurries (cotton rugs) to eat; except the 'older' ladies; their servants having brought everything but the kitchen sink! With folding tables and chairs for extra comfort.

Everyone dressed up in those days - even for picnics - the women in bright summery dresses and floppy wide-brimmed hats, while the men wore their 'whites' or casual wear and 'Panama' hats.

Games of ping-pong, badminton and croquet were taken along for the adults, while we children ran around playing 'tag' and other games - organised by some of the younger adults - like cricket and ghilly-dunda, an Indian game played with a stick and wooden bail. The bail was put on the ground - where a small area was cleared so one end of the bail was raised. Then, bringing the stick in your hand down with some force, you hit the bail... so it jumped into the air... then you swung the stick to hit it as far away as you could.

Then exhausted at the end of the day, we'd all climb back into the tonga's to head home.

Next day when some of the women got together, it was knives out for anyone who had overstepped the mark!

"Did you see Evelyn Hixon flirting outrageously with young Timothy O'Rourke?" Was met with horrified gasps as poor Evelyn - who had done nothing more than 'chat' - was dissected and criticised by those ladies who'd witnessed her harmless chattering with the Hon Tim O'Rourke on the previous day.

"Didn't think much of Mrs Everit's kidney curry." someone else would say bitchily, and off they'd go again... copious amounts of tea would be drunk as throats were talked 'dry' and delicate sandwiches and cakes demolished as the afternoon wore on.

At last the ladies having something more than just 'food' to get their teeth into.

Until the next picnic of course!

CHAPTER FIFTEEN

The Maidhan

The Carriage & Wagon Workshops sprawled for about two or three miles on the other side of the maidhan (field) and the high embankment on which trains from Delhi to Bombay ran. A large clump of trees growing where the restaurant-cum-café was situated.

Our bungalow was one of seven backing onto the maidhan; the bungalows having been built specifically for heads of departments and officials working for the Railways.

My father worked as head gate-keeper at the workshops at that time. Although I'm not sure if he was still attached to the Army, as he still wore his uniform? Khaki coloured shirt and trousers, complete with 'Sam Browne' belt and peaked cap; and carried a leather-bound cane. So I assumed he was still in the British Forces, but attached to the Railways too; receiving two military medals while in this employment.

His 'men' were also attired in uniforms. His 'Jemadhar' (Indian Officer) and second in command - a tall, powerfully built Pathan - wore a stiffly starched turban. He was always immaculately turned out; even his black curled moustache stiffened to attention!

From Monday to Friday, we were woken by the sound of the works whistle, shrilling loudly into the early morning, the first wake-up call for the hundreds of men working in the Carriage & Wagon Workshops in Ajmer. Many of the workers were unable to afford ordinary clocks let alone alarmed ones. The better-paid men arrived by cars or bicycles, while the rest had to make do with 'Shank's Pony'.

Apart from the six am early call, the whistle sounded again, at six-thirty with another short blast - a warning that time was running out - and the final start-to-work whistle went at exactly seven sharp. Any late stragglers being forced to make a mad dash before the big iron gates were closed with a bang; with my father's order of 'Bun-Currow' (close them) ringing out. Two men - on either side of the huge gates, then ran the gates on their runners shut, barring them firmly, fixing the doors with a long iron bar on the inside.

The resounding clash of metal, a veritable 'death-knell' for any man not quick enough to get in. Anyone who had been 'locked out', having to wait for the smaller gates – built into one side of the large gates – to be opened from the inside.

Late-comers were fined, with persistent offenders sometimes losing their jobs; unless they could come up with a pretty good explanation for their tardiness. Father, was no push-over either; he tolerated none of the feeble excuses from late-comers who were forced to wait with their explanations.

With hundreds of men working here, there was always someone left on the outside! These were then admitted – through the smaller door set into the large one – and processed. All the workers had numbered brass discs which were moved from the 'out' board to the 'in' board at the start of the day, the various departments within the vast workshops colour-coded. So it was the gate-keepers job to make sure the men were fairly dealt with. It was his job to note absenteeism, lateness, and illness, accepted only if authenticated by a 'chit,' or other official document from a doctor etc. Plus, the hundred and one things that needed to be recorded. The huge ledgers in his office recording everything that needed to be used by the staff to calculate wages, sick pay, compensation claims and any other disputes relating to the hours the men had worked.

So when the late-comers filed slowly in, their names and numbers were noted by one of fathers Chaprassi's. (Office servant/messenger) While my father; a tall commanding figure in his Khaki uniform; blue eyes seemingly to bore right through to the men's souls; would give each man just a few minutes to explain the reason for his lateness. Before issuing the man with a warning – verbal or written – or accepting the man really did have a good excuse.

Which were as rare as 'hen's teeth'!

Long-winded explanations meeting with 'juldi, juldi,' if he thought the man was wasting time; tired of the same old excuses being trotted out day after day. With no silly excuses tolerated.

Although one of the more unusual ones had stuck in his head, which he would often talk about - especially when in his 'cups'.

One particular day when faced by a wretched man of about fifty years of age - who looked like he'd been dragged through a hedge backwards - my father was surprised by the mans words.

"Arrey (oh) Sahib, you wouldn't believe me if I told you, the dejected man admitted.

Intrigued, my father urged the man, "Try me," speaking Hindi, as well as any Indian.

"Well Sahib, the man continued, watching the burra (big) sahib from under his lashes.

"Last night was the wedding of my cousin's cousin, and I celebrated too much."

The man's head was wagging about alarmingly by now.

"I drank too much 'shrraap' (grog), then bedded my wife."

"What was wrong with that," father questioned, fearing the man was coming up with yet another feeble excuse.

"Well," the man continued, beginning to look sheepish. "As I said, I was very, very drunk, and it was a very dark night... and... and instead of bedding my wife, I found myself in another's bed." The last words tumbled from the man's mouth in a single breath.

There's more to this story than meets the eye, father decided.

"But if you were so drunk, how come you knew you were in someone else's bed?" my father queried.

"Well sahib, it was when this big chap started hitting me." The culprit explained - his bloodshot eyes a testament to the alcohol-fuelled night before.

"I don't believe you," father interrupted.

"Hai sahib, I speak only the truth. But as I was saying, this man suddenly came upon us; it was the girl's husband." The man had started to sound more authentic, so my father let the man continue, rolling his hand in a circular movement, as if telling the man to get on with it.

The man hung his head as if in shame, looking truly repentant.

"Sahib, this other man...," the poor man seemed unable to proceed.

"Come on I haven't got all day."

"He... he... threatened to cut off my manhood Sahib", the man whimpered, starting to undo his dhoti.

"Stop, stop," father shouted, fearing the man was about to show him some evidence of mutilation.

"You're not telling me the chap actually...." Lost for words my father gestured towards the man's nether regions.

"Oh no Sahib, no Sahib I am still whole." the man said emphatically, smiling sadly through his tears.

"But it will be some time before I can sleep with my wife again." he admitted, the tears now running unchecked, down his face

"Because the fellow not only kicked me several times in a very tender place, but he also got some others to take me for miles into the jungle." Shuddering at the thought, the man continued... "Then they dumped me there...,"gesticulating with his hands, the man indicated his utter desolation at being dumped. "They left me there to be devoured by the wild animals. But by the grace of God, and by the heavenly spirits, I was able to walk all the way back without being eaten by the tigers."

The last few sentences had come tumbling out without the man taking a single breath in between. Falling to his knees, the man bent forward as if asking pardon!

"It was a very long walk back Sahib... and that is the reason for my lateness," the man concluded, as he gazed tearfully up at my father.

Trying to contain his mirth, my father ended the interview. He ordered the man to visit a local doctor in case of any complications and instructed the chaprassi to give the man a couple of days off work - without pay - knowing full well the man, who was already suffering from his folly, would suffer even more when his wife found out he had lost two days wages, and the reason behind it.

CHAPTER SIXTEEN

Afternoon Tea

By late afternoon the sun had travelled slowly over our bungalow to slip over towards the west, leaving the back veranda in shade. So it was here that my mother entertained her lady friends to afternoon tea.

Coming home from school, we would find three or four of her 'cronies' sipping tea from the best china and eating wafer-thin sandwiches and dainty cakes while they chatted about their husbands, other people, local events, the price of groceries and the servants.

Of course, we kids never got a sniff of any 'goodies', my mother and her friends having healthy appetites; especially one - a large and gregarious lady called Mrs Adams. Older than the other women, she was a biggish lady, with an even bigger appetite; who'd been widowed for many years; her husband having left her quite a tidy sum of money too. Perhaps it was because of her wealth, she felt she didn't have to conform to the norm, or the 'niceties' of the times. I prefer to think of her as an eccentric.

Things would be going along quite smoothly, everyone talking and laughing... Mrs Adams could certainly tell a tale or two, and then without any warning, she would lift one of her massive buttocks off her chair... let off an enormous fart... and carry on the conversation just as if nothing had happened!

The assembled women, much too polite to do anything, other than give one another surreptitious looks, or dab a dainty lace handkerchief to their noses, their only way of showing their disapproval, and let the incident slide. We kids - in the other room having our own tea - would be in fits of giggles, as we chomped happily on our jam sandwiches.

Mrs Adams was tolerated not because of her enormous wealth, but because of her big heart. 'Gertie' had married one - Tom Adams; quite a high-ranking soldier - when she was just a slip of a thing.

Rumour had it, that she'd been a real beauty then. Tom Adams had doted on his Gertie, and had loved the laughing, devil-may-care girl who had a heart of gold; staying happily married until his death, several years ago. False rumours also did the rounds then, many claiming that Gertie had hastened her husband's death with all the rich food she indulged him in. Anyone going to their house for dinner was blown away by course after course of the most fattening foods.

Tom had enjoyed his food too and had matched Gertie pound for pound in the heavy-weight stakes. Anyway... we all knew Gertie was absolutely devastated when Tom died - although not me personally, you understand, not having been born then - but anyway, leaving Gertie a very rich widow.

She'd been left with a very large house in India, several properties in England - left to Tom by his wealthy parents - some really lovely paintings and jewellery, and an income from which, the interest alone was enough to indulge her every whim.

Gertie Adams lived well, but was generous in helping others less fortunate than herself. Many a beggar had found himself quite a rich man when one of the servants of the burra memsahib, slipped him 'baksheesh' outside the gate - even after the servant in question had taken his cut out of it by palming a few notes out of it for himself first!

Of course, Gertie knew all about her own servants little fiddles, but she turned a blind eye, having been brought up practically a pauper herself. So she continued to help others less well-off, and was a jolly good laugh into the bargain, with her outright manner and great store of funny tales. Gertie had been a friend of my mothers for years, and it was to Gertie that my mum turned whenever she'd had a row with my father.

"Come in Teresa, come in," she'd cry, on seeing my mother and us kids standing on her doorstep yet again... usually late at night.

"Had a row with that big oaf of a husband again?" She'd say, enveloping my mother's slight frame in a bear hug. "Sami," she'd bellow, calling out for her faithful servant. "Bring chai, juldi, juldi."

As young children, we loved it when mum and dad had 'words'. Mum would flounce out of the house - taking us kids of course - and head for her friend Gertie Adams house, a short distance away.

"Serve the sod right, I've told you before to leave the bugger." Mrs Adams would bellow, as she ministered to my distraught mother.

"You're too good for that man, I keep telling you... Sami, where's that bloody tea?" She'd shout... all in the same breath.

Everything that Gertie Adams did was loud, and larger than life.

As always, poor old Sami would appear - his red turban slightly askew - bearing a tray with a big pot of tea, biscuits, samosas or any other delicacy he'd made earlier in the day; a big welcoming smile on his face, as if serving tea at this godforsaken hour was his greatest pleasure in life!

I swear the poor man didn't ever get undressed at night! Probably just took off his turban to lie down; in case of being summoned at whatever unearthly hour he was needed. Nothing seemed to faze the once batman, faithful servant, and friend of her late husband, Tom Adams.

After Tom's death, Sami had taken over the 'looking after' of his sahib's memsahib, seamlessly running the house and the rest of the servants with the help of his wife, Amilla. Even helping to choose the clothes Gertie Adams wore to some of the posher functions - having worked for many English people before, where he'd watched and learned carefully - Gertie herself never had had a 'good eye' for matching colours and fabrics. Left to her own devices, Gertie would have worn red, yellow, green and purple all together if she could get away with it.

Amilla, Sami's wife of many years, was a very dark-skinned Indian woman of about fifty years; and walked about as silently as a ghost. She would be summoned to make up beds for us all, while we kids tucked into our 'extra' supper; putting away some of the nicest sweet-meats of jellabies, gulab-jamons or other delicacies Gertie had had stored away for herself, until we were fit to burst.

With my mother's mind on 'other' matters, there was no one to worry about tooth decay or minor details then.

A veritable, children's paradise!

Amilla always wore white - on Gertie Adams orders - as did the rest of her servants.

As Gertie said, "That way I can see when they get their clothes dirty, no? Let them wear dark colours and you don't know where the hell they've been wiping their dirty fingers. Haven't you noticed my Sami always wears white?" Pausing to take breath, she continued,

"Also the khansama too, only in his case a cheap length of cloth, so he can make himself a dhoti, and they have to bloody well wash their hands."

It made perfectly good sense!

Sitting in Mrs Adams large sumptuous dining room; with its Victorian hangings and fancy falderals, was like a second home to us and staying up late was another great treat. We couldn't help hearing Gertie as she discussed the vices and virtues of 'that man', my father; giggling at the swear words we'd never hear at home! Well apart from the odd 'damn' from my father - followed by a stern rebuke from my mother; who never swore, or if she did, I never heard her!

"You really should leave the bugger," Gertie would insist regularly - 'bugger' being her favourite word - with 'bugger it' or 'what a bugger' used so many times, us kids began to think it part and parcel of the English vocabulary! So decadent and outrageous to hear swearing in those days! Bug-eyed and bug-eared we'd listen to the 'grown-up' talk, hoping this time, with our parents 'split-up', we would be spared school the next day!

Yes, to us children every 'cloud' definitely had its 'silver lining'.

Our own dining room area, with its pale green Indian carpet, crystal chandelier and dark polished furniture was a much more 'sober' room. It was reserved for us to have our evening meals, and for 'company'. The extra-long table extending so that you could sit a couple of dozen people comfortably round it. At Christmas time, the table really came into its own.

Our back veranda was the room we used the most. As children, we'd tumble out of bed, and after a quick wash, we'd congregate at one corner of the veranda, which faced east and the maidhan; with the sun just beginning to push fingers of golden light through the slats of the Jaffrey.

It was quite warm in the summer, but not as fierce as it could get later on in the day. In the cooler winter weather, we stayed in the dining room. It was here on the veranda we breakfasted and got ready for school at the 'hub' of all the daily events being discussed between our parents and the servants.

The servants came each morning to take their orders for the day; the khansama being given all the ingredients he'd specified for the meals he would be preparing for that day (with a trifle over for himself) or the mali would be given instructions as to what needed doing in the gardens.

One of my father's chaprassies always sat on the bottom step carefully polishing my father's leather boots, cane, and Sam Browne, until they shone brilliantly, waiting until we kids were ready to be escorted to school. The poor man then having to get back to the house and occupy himself until it was time for him to carry the heavy 'Tiffin-box' with our lunches to the school once more. Then, when we'd finished eating, he had to pack away the empties and carry the box all the way home once more. Even then, his job was still not done. For, just before four in the afternoon, he would be back at the school gates to escort us home again. He must have so looked forward to our summer time-tables, when we started school at the ungodly hour of seven-thirty in the mornings, and finished at midday, it being much to hot for lessons after that. Then, the poor chap only had to do the journey twice.

Before I'd started school I was privy to all the goings-on at home. Like the 'wallah's' who called around all day with their wares, and regular 'spring-cleaning,' of the house - which went on throughout the year.

What a tamasha (big show) that was!

My mother would have the servants drag practically every stick of furniture out of the bungalow, and pile it up in the back compound. Then the place was thoroughly cleaned, walls, floors and ceilings and the items outside were beaten by sticks and jarins (dusters) to make sure no living thing was lurking in between the cushions etc, before being re-placed neatly back into their former places. The only piece of furniture that could not be moved was the massive almirah from our parent's bedroom, which weighed a ton!

A waste of time I hear you say - not at all - for often there would be an insect lurking under a bit of furniture where spiders would weave their webs into the tightest corners under a chair.

Centipedes loved damp cool places, so even the chatties on the veranda were moved but not as often as the other stuff, besides, dad's favourite frog resided there. Dad had named him 'Tojo' after the Japanese Prime Minister at that time. Our own 'Tojo' the frog, would croak every so often when things quietened down and he

144

thought he was alone. I think dad had grown quite fond of that frog. At the end of the war, I remember dad saying it was time for Tojo to go too, but he stayed put under the cold water chatties, where he was safe from the snake that lived in one of our godowns. Every morning you could see the s-shaped tracks it had left behind as it had wriggled its way over towards the hodhi and back. More frogs lived around and under the hodhi, so I expect the snake came out to eat and drink at night. The servants, who lived in the other godowns didn't seem at all put out by the fact there was a reptile living in such close proximity to them.

The water chatties (earthenware pots) stood one atop the other in a metal frame, the porous pots keeping the water ice-cold, even on the hottest day. A large ladle would be hanging from one side, ready to dip into the pure sweet well-water which was topped up by the bhisti (water-carrier) every morning. The water came in goat-skin pouches, filled earlier that day from a deep well far out in the country; and transported by bullock-cart; the animal standing between the shafts of the cart on the road outside, chewing the cud, as it waited patiently for the bhisti to deliver water door to door at the houses.

The poor old bhisti, staggered under the weight of the filled pouch, as he padded bare-footed up the steps to where our water chatties stood.

He had a brown weather-beaten face, a small wiry body, thin arms and the bandiest legs I'd ever seen, probably from carrying all those heavy skins of water. But it was his feet that fascinated me the most. He had the most enormous big toes!

He always came bare-footed, and I used to watch the way he walked - well, more 'trotted', with the weight of the water-pouch - whenever he called, marvelling at the way his splayed toes seemed to actually grip the surface of the ground as he moved. Perhaps I should have gone into writing some sort of thesis into the 'cause and effect' on people and the jobs they did?

The bhisti always wore a clean white dhoti, with his upper body devoid of any covering, no matter what the weather. His ribs - sharply outlined against his chest - shone like brown, wet leather. Probably from the water splashing him as he half-walked half-ran with his pouch of water.

He wore a rather large red turban, very loosely wound around his head, which covered his ears. I often wondered if he could actually hear properly. The heavy water-pouch slung over one shoulder and across his back, made him list slightly sideways, but he always managed to negotiate the steps; deftly undoing the leather tie around the neck of the pouch with one hand, to empty the water into the chatties, making sure to press the sides of the goat-skin until the last drops were squeezed out.

He was a quiet, well-mannered chap, bowing low for his few pice, never uttering a single word; only inclining his head to one side – which could indicate yes or no.

At Christmas, when he received his 'baksheesh,' his head would go into overdrive, wobbling about alarmingly. His lined face lighting up with a big gummy grin. So we took it he was as pleased as Punch? I think it was the only time I ever saw him smile.

CHAPTER SEVENTEEN

The Wallahs

Living in India during the thirties the memsahib didn't have to go out to buy everyday goods, as practically everything was brought right to her door on a daily basis.

The bhisti (water carrier) brought fresh well-water daily, and the dhood wallah, (milk seller) fresh milk, cream, butter and yoghurt; all in time for breakfast. Later during the day a succession of 'wallahs' (person selling or giving service) shouted from the roads outside the angrezi (English) houses; with regular accepted sellers, coming round to the back of the house.

"Alloo (potatoes), adrak (ginger), lusoon (garlic), mutter-ka-fullee (peas)..." the marlin would intone, walking slowly up the road. Then, making her way to the back of our bungalow, she would heave the heavy wicker basket off her head, and with a sigh of relief, place it on the top step of the back veranda.

She had confided in my mother that she lived with her brother and his family, but had wanted to remain independent money-wise, so she had taken over a small-holding, where she grew her vegetables. The woman was about fifty years old, and as ugly as sin. Probably the reason why she'd never married, poor thing. And my father used to tease her unmercifully if ever he was at home when she called around selling her wares. She in turn would cover her face with the end of her sari - for modesty - and giggle.

"Mutter - ka - ullee kithna hai?" (How much are the peas?) Father would ask.

"Seer huzoor?" (One kilo sir?) She'd query.

"Hai, hai aik seer," (Yes, yes one kilo) .

And she'd give him a price, which always brought the same comments from him of... too much, too much, then, father would offer to sell her some of his own from the garden. Of course, she'd go into fits of giggles, and mother would chide father for teasing the poor woman. But as we always had such a glut of vegetables, which we were always giving away, father would invariably end up giving the marlin a few bringalls, (aubergines) or other vegetables so she

147

could sell them on for herself.

Another 'wallah', who came shouting his wares, was the man with the very large umbrella. We called him the 'chumma, chumma, guppa' man. He walked along with his umbrella calling out... "Aik-alumba - chumma - chumma - guppa," in a sing-song voice. We knew it meant something big and pulled, but didn't know what all the other words meant! Other than we had to have him make us one of the many things he could shape from the sticky taffy-type mixture he had nestling up over the spokes of the umbrella; the mixture sagging, as it slowly settled over the spokes at the top. He would get it down from time to time to give it a quick pull, twist and pull, before putting it back in its resting place. Then, whenever someone wanted to buy one of his 'works' he'd break off bits, stick them onto the stem of his umbrella, and fashion them into wonderful shapes, from a bicycle to a baby's pram, and anything in between! He would make whatever was requested; with just a deft twist of his wrists.

We thought it great fun and made a beeline for him whenever we heard him, learning his chant off by heart. What and where his fingers had been in contact with, never bothering us then! I mean, have you ever seen an Indian man blowing his nose? He places a finger each side of his nostrils, and blows; quickly wiping his fingers on his dhoti!

Even the flies that swarmed over the sweet toffee-like substance didn't bother us in the slightest.

Nevertheless, we kids were always clamouring for a few pice to buy something, although, there was an end to the amount of money we were allowed to have. Can you imagine how sick we would get if allowed all the dozens of things that were hawked around door to door?

The kulfi (ice-cream) wallah brought lovely pistachio ice-cream cones, which were cardamom scented, the small cones nestling inside a large chattie (earthenware pot) of broken ice; which kept them frozen. He carried the earthenware porous pot on his shoulder; transferring the heavy load from one to the other of his shoulders every time he stopped. It really must have been quite heavy.

The small cone-shaped ice-creams, being probably made in some unhygienic abode by his wife! But the old saying of 'what you can't see...,' applied as far as we kids were concerned.

Mother, of course, stopped us from buying from just anyone.

The biscuit 'wallah' was mothers favourite. He came on a bicycle, a small wooden box fixed onto the back of his seat; from which he'd produce the loveliest butter-biscuits, coconut ice, and tiny puff pastry triangles filled with a mixture of freshly grated coconut and sugar.

Biting into any of his products was sheer heaven!

He could converse in quite good English, although he was a man of few words. He had a wide range of regular clients, some of whom had recommended this particular man to us, and the fact that he always looked 'clean and tidy' probably had something to do with mother buying from him. He only ever came down our road once a week. Probably hawking his 'goodies' elsewhere, on the other days.

The durzi wallah came, sewing machine in hand, then squatting cross-legged in one corner of the veranda, he'd quietly get on with the sewing; mostly mending sheets and pillow-cases, or the sahib's shirts, the collars being 'turned' then, and the sheets sewn 'edges to middle.' Just before Christmas was his busiest time. He was much in demand to produce the bizarre costumes needed for the fancy dress balls, and other 'jollifications' that were held during the Christmas holidays.

The New Year's Eve Fancy Dress Ball was the highlight of the year!

The young children's event took place in the afternoon; with children being put into age groups. Then, the officials went around 'judging' everyone. There were always three winners from each group, so nearly everyone received a prize.

There was always much more fuss made over the grown-ups evening event; as most of them had gone to an awful lot of trouble with their costumes, I suppose. A whole load of 'historical' costumes were worn by the ladies of a certain age, with the men much more likely to plump for something funny. One particular wag made everyone laugh with his bizarre costumes - very well thought out - and thoroughly enjoyed by most... but one year some thought he'd gone a tad too far!

He came casually dressed - placard on his back - proclaiming 'Gone With The Wind' (the well-known film with Clarke Gable etc.). But, his version, had nothing to do with the block-buster film. For the man had a great big hole literally 'torn' out of the back of his trousers... leaving his 'cheeky chappies' in full view.

That really set the tongues wagging! Though most of the 'memsahibs' got more than their share of quick looks that night.

The first prize going not to him, but to a couple dressed as a Lord and Lady, complete with ermine robes and crowns.

The poor durzi had done a great job on their costumes, unless of course they really were a real Lord and his Lady? You never could tell 'who' you were rubbing shoulders with in India!

At the other end of the scale... there were the others. The poor 'untouchables,' according to the caste system among the Hindu's; these people were considered the lowest of the low, even from the time of their birth. Believing it was their karma and that by suffering in this life, they would be amply rewarded in the life to come.

Slightly higher up in the caste system, were the people calling door to door, buying anything from clothes to empty tins. Similar to our rag and bone men who called around with their horse and cart; only these people walked and carried a sack on their backs. Some of the things they bought were asked for specifically. Like empty Ponds cream jars, or empty tins of all kinds, Ponds cream, being a favourite of nearly every woman at that time. So as kids we would make sure mum used up her Ponds cream quickly, so we could trade the empty one in for a couple of pice, which went towards the latest film that week.

We were never allowed to buy any lollipops from the 'iced lolly' man. My parents saying the water used in his ice may be polluted. They were strict about what we could and could not have sometimes which probably saved us from having many 'gyppy' tummies.

This iced lolly man pushed a cart around with a few bottles of brightly-coloured cordials standing in a row and some big lumps of ice - covered over by a damp gunny sacking. Then, if anyone ordered a lolly, he would 'shave' bits of ice; using a tool not unlike an upside down wooden plane, the tiny bits of ice then being moulded in a long thin tin shaped cone around a stick. The ice was tamped down, and taken out in one piece from the mould, resulting in what looked like a clear ice lolly. Depending on the person's choice, the vendor would douse the ice with splashes of cordial, to produce an iced lolly of many colours.

We could however, buy some of the purple 'jarmouns' - a sour fruit that was shaken up with some salt, chilli powder, and lemon juice. The salt making the jarmouns taste sweeter.

There were variations on this snack, one of them being Kabuli channa. Large boiled chick peas; to which the 'wallah' added bits of cooked potato, and equal bits of pear, apple, and onion. All mixed with salt, chilli powder, and lemon juice. This was also shaken up, and put into paper cones for you to eat as you walked along. Lovely!

Because my father liked cooking, he often made a few things he 'missed' from home like potato crisps. He had a special gadget made in the workshops which enabled him to make the thinnest of chips - round even slices - that he fried to perfection.

We even had toffee-apples, although he nearly burnt down the make-shift hut he'd erected to keep the sun off him as he worked. The fire consuming the 'curtain' covering that was keeping the hot sun off his head!

Ice-cream was another great favourite of ours, and this was made by father in the shade of the neem tree.

The ice-cream maker was a wooden bucket contraption, with an inside container and handle. Ice chips and saltpetre were packed around the middle container that held the milk, cream etc, and we all had goes at 'turning' the handle that protruded from the side of the bucket. This spun the middle container round and round inside the ice until the ice-cream formed.

It seemed to take forever, but was well worth the wait! The first spoonful melting deliciously on our hot little tongues. The trouble was it was finished far too quickly; because if you didn't eat it quickly it soon melted!

Of course, in the winter when it was cooler, father made soup. Making an outside fire, he'd mount a stout dekshie (saucepan) of water on the top, then add every vegetable grown in his garden. Adding salt, pepper and other ingredients known only to him. A huge wooden spoon was used to stir the mixture, which was kept boiling for hours.

The resultant soup was enough to feed an army; the neighbours, friends and servants took big containers for themselves.

Stew, was another of father's favourites, but as the khansama could never quite get it to taste the way my father's mother Rose made it, he used to have a go making it himself. Used to cooking for hundreds of men, he always cooked up much more than our family could consume. Even the tastiest food can become a bit much day after day!

Mother had had to go into hospital to have a cataract removed from her eye, and while she was away father decided to look after his children. Luckily I was just an infant, and can remember little of the events. But my brother Billy was about four at the time.

The hospital visit went well until my mother questioned Billy about how he was getting on.

"Are you being a good boy for Mummy?" and "Are you being a good boy for Daddy?" bringing a quick nod of his head, but the question of...

"What did you have for lunch today?" brought a quiver to Billy's lips.

"Stew," answered the miserable little boy.

"And what did you have for breakfast?" Mother questioned the boy whose lower lip was quivering.

"Stew," he answered again, and unable to stand the torment of not having his mother home, finally reduced Billy to a howling mass... my father trying to do his best to get the crying child out of the ward of women all listening in.

"When are you coming home mum?" Billy shouted from the doorway...

"I'm sick of stew for breakfast, and dinner, and tea!"

Because he had made so much stew, father thought it wasteful not to use it up, and had been dishing it up to the children for a couple of days.

As I said - wasn't I glad I was too young to remember that episode!

CHAPTER EIGHTEEN

Lala Rams

When the noon whistle shrilled out it was a welcome signal under normal circumstances for the workers of the Carriage & Wagon Workshops to down tools, switch off engines, and take a well-earned break from the rigors of the shop floor. But sometimes, with the expected monsoons delayed, and with the temperatures soaring into the forties, conditions at work could be intolerable.

Stopping briefly to wash their hands and faces in the cold water from the many containers and red-painted buckets of water marked 'Fire' hanging ready for use in case of emergencies, the workers hurried outside, into the comparative cooler temperatures, each making for their favourite spot, preferably in the shade, where they could eat the food they'd brought from home, and rest for a while.

Some of the luckier ones who could afford to, ate at 'Lala Rams' - an enterprising Muslim's café-cum-restaurant - set up just across the road from the main gates of the workshops, in the shade of a clump of shade-giving neem trees. A prime spot Lala Ram had 'appropriated' some years ago, by promising the officials he would keep the prices of his food reasonably priced for the men working in the Carriage & Wagon Workshops in Ajmer.

The restaurant - specially built with sturdy metal scaffolding and topped by sheets of corrugated iron; which could really get hot during the summer months; was shaded from the sun by the dense foliage of trees. Here, Lala Ram and his team of helpers served up dozens of meals seven days a week; the main meal being served at noon. Work, on the huge amounts of food started well before dawn, to get the meal ready in time; with many more snacks being sold before and after the lunch break.

The place was kept buzzing from early morning till late in the evenings, with people working 'overtime' on special projects requesting hot 'chai' and breakfast snacks, which were served almost as soon as Lala Ram got the shutters off his restaurant in the darkness before dawn. The night shift workers ready for a cup of tea and a snack, before wending their way homewards.

Hundreds of 'cullards' (earthenware cups) used daily for the hot sweet chai loved by the Indians, were stored on the roof of the building. Like rows of rounded tiles, the earthenware cups sat row upon row lining the corrugated sheeted roof, fitting snugly one inside the other. So whenever a few more were required, one of the men released the small 'peg' that held them safely up on the roof, and slid a quantity of cups down, handling them with a much practised dexterity. The cups were only used once before being smashed; the pile of broken cullards growing daily; so not only did the men enjoy their 'cuppa'' but they were also able to get rid of their frustrations at the same time.

Orders for lunch had to be placed the day before, or at the latest, early in the morning. These taking precedence over casual customers who turned up at meal times expecting to be fed; although no one was ever turned down. Sometimes, the curry was thinned down to such a degree, the buyers grumbled, with Lala Ram turning a deaf ear to the complaints as he was never one to turn a rupee down, if he could help it!

A devout Muslim, Lala Ram was always fastidiously dressed, wearing the simple cotton garments favoured by many of his contemporaries. A long, loose white cotton kurta (shirt) with baggy white pantaloons, and strong leather chupplies (sandals) because he was constantly on his feet. A small white pill-box hat fixed firmly on the top of his head.

His hair was worn fairly short and his side-burns - which were grown and trimmed neatly - came down to meet the small beard on his chin. His slight squint was rather off-putting as people were never sure if he was really handicapped or just trying to look at two places at the same time, ensuring his employees were working! Very little got past the wily businessman, who expected his employees to work flat out while they were being paid. He also expected his men to be clean and neatly dressed - like himself - while working in his establishment, and had been known to send many a man packing if they turned up looking unwashed or grubby.

Business was brisk once the workmen rushed in after the lunchtime whistle sounded. With a limited time to eat, the men also wanted a little time to rest after their lunch. So the plates of curries, bargi's, dhalls and rice were placed before the hungry men almost before they'd seated themselves. The sounds of benches dragging against stone floors as the starving men quickly took their seats.

The long trestle tables and benches filling up rapidly as men from different backgrounds and religions mingled together; tucking into the excellent food being placed before them, those not yet eating added to the constant babble of voices over which Lala Rams could still be heard, chiding the already hard-pressed servers, constantly gesticulating and harassing as he rushed to and fro; holding up, rather than hurrying the men.

The poor waiters worked as fast as they could; being unable to move any faster if they tried.

But to Lala Ram, every man seated at his tables and being fed, meant even more rupees coming in! His agile brain working out almost exactly the profit to be made each day; having done a quick head-count in between serving and chivvying his helpers; the fragrant smell of curried mutton, aromatic spices, and pillau rice drifting through the hot air to mingle with the vegetable curries, hot dhalls and chapattis that were being whisked from kitchen to table.

Two of the waiters - practically running round the tables, each carrying a pitcher of cold water in either hand - filled and re-filled the thick, sturdy glasses sitting on the tables, which were being emptied almost as quickly by the thirsty men.

Watching the copious amounts of water being drunk, Lala Ram scratched his beard and wondered if he could think of some way of charging for it. After all, he reasoned... he still had to pay for ice with which to cool the water; and the wages of the men employed to serve it?

But as his wife had cannily pointed out... 'If the men filled themselves with water... would they not think it was the excellent food that had made them feel full?' So, much to his regret, he was forced to let them have the water free of charge. Better than a man leaving the table with an empty stomach.

With so many hungry men to feed, speed was of the essence. Besides, he wanted them to have enough time to visit his café next door too. Where a huge cauldron of boiling milk had been steaming for hours - a thick cream forming over its surface wrinkling the top as it cooled - ready for the hot 'chai' that would be drunk after their meal. There were piles of jellabies, luddoos, and gulab-jamuns and other sweet-meats placed temptingly by, just in case someone should still be hungry, with fresh samosas, sev and spicy nuts for those without a sweet tooth.

Lala Ram had built up a thriving business from just a small hut serving tea and snacks some years ago, because he knew hard working men had to eat if they wanted to carry on earning a crust, the tremendous array of foodstuffs never failing to win over new and old clients.

Even after a big meal, some men could not resist just one small sweetmeat to go with their cup of chai, (tea) which was served already 'cooled' for the men... by the process of pouring the hot liquid from one container into another - quickly and efficiently, sometimes an arms length away - as the tea went back and forth. A nice frothy top eventually obtained when it was finally poured into individual 'cullards'.

This scene was re-enacted each and every working day at the midday break, and it was Lala Rams proud boast that every man who'd paid would be fed with speed and efficiency in the hours break; or else he would be refunded his money in full. And Lala Ram, never one to part with money, made sure his helpers worked their socks off.

So far, no man had ever had to ask for his money back!

Nothing escaped Lala Rams beady eyes, and today, as the sweat rolled down his sideburns, he realised something was putting quite a few of the men off their usual hearty eating. Of course, it was the hot weather and the late monsoons, he concluded! Pray Allah the rains would come soon. Then, maybe he could double his money?

Luckily he'd made a deal with the local kulfi-wallah to supply him with large amounts of the cone-shaped desserts that lay nestling in their bed of broken ice; within a large earthenware container to keep them from melting. Scratching his beard once more he wondered if he should have ordered even more.

But what if the rains came? He might get stuck with them... Arrey... who'd be a businessman.

On the maidhan, (field) several groups of men who couldn't afford to eat at the restaurant had found whatever shade they could; squatting on the ground under the trees as they ate the food they'd brought from home. While away in the distance, the poor beggar women and children watched and waited, giving the men a little time to eat before they descended like flies to begin their daily task of begging.

Then, picking their way carefully between the small groups of men, they had to make sure their shadows did not fall upon the seated men. For these beggars were 'untouchables'; branded as being impure from the moment of birth, and the bottom of the Hindu caste system which prevailed in India at that time; even their shadows cast upon those of higher ranks being an insult. The scruffy unkempt beggar women - some holding small children on their hips - going from man to man as they begged for scraps which is what they got; the men tearing off just a small corner of a chapatti to throw into the corner of the dirty sari held out, or if they were lucky; even a whole chapatti. On very hot days the women benefited, the men unable to eat much... and for once the beggars and their families would eat well.

At one, the whistle would summon the workers back for the second half of their working day, leaving the maidhan empty once more. Except for a couple of mangy pie-dogs scavenging in the dirt; sniffing out the few crumbs that had fallen to the ground; even scraps of paper that had once held food licked clean then wolfed down by the starving dogs; whose ribs stuck out from their skinny bodies.

Up in the thermals, bald-headed vultures circled endlessly; their gimlet eyes searching the ground far below for traces of some small animal that may have perished in the killing heat. *Their* favourite eating places; the 'Towers of Silence' high on the hillsides - the charnel houses of the Parsees - where the dead were left to be picked clean by the birds of prey. The carrion-eaters, waited until the mourners had left, before swooping down with loud flapping of wings, to descend through the open-topped towers to where the body lay. Hopping sideways, the ugly red-faced bald-headed vultures would fight with one another for a place on the body; screeching and flapping their wings as they fed; their long necks covered in blood and gore as their sharp beaks tore great chunks out of their prey.

The food chain is endless!

The maidhan was used by us children in the cool of the evening; it being the ideal place to play. My brothers flew kites, while my sister and I drew out squares to play hop-scotch, and, if joined by other children, we'd switch to playing 'rounders' or sticks and stones.' For this game every player required a stick. The stick had to be 'resting' on a stone, as you moved towards the goal. One person - the catcher – watching for the chance to 'tap' you and shout 'out,' if he or she managed to catch you without your stick firmly on a stone. Daft game? You bet, but we did have fun!

Another stupid game was called 'statues'. One person would be chosen to stand with their backs to the rest of the players, some distance away, and count up to three. The players had to move towards this person swiftly; but stopping whenever they turned around after the count. Anyone seen moving was out, the aim being to reach the person as fast as you could while the count was on, then, standing perfectly still, like a 'statue' when the counter turned around.

Of course you were supposed to strike a pose... like a statue, the funnier the better, so it could get hilarious. But you were deemed to be 'out' even if you smiled.

One year father had some metal 'hoops' made for us all at the 'Workshops'. With little metal bits you held onto - one end 'twisted' to take the round metal hoop - allowing us to run along while pushing our hoops forward as we went. Gosh, we must have run for miles!

Many strange creatures lived in and around the maidhan. So we had to be extra careful if we moved a large stone or boulder, as we often found a small snake, centipede or scorpion hiding underneath. There were some big lizards too, these usually sat on the rocks and inflated their bodies if you approached; changing their colour from a drab grey to bright reds and greens as they tried to frighten off anything they saw as a threat. The funniest creatures being the little 'piggy-faced' spiders who built their lairs at the bottom of a steep-sided hole. These were just tiny little things about four or five millimetres long. The holes being only about three or four inches deep. The spiders kept the sand around the slopes smooth and slippery; constantly 'kicking' loose sand up with their hind legs. Then, as it waited - concealed below - some careless ant or insect would slip over the edge of the hole, and slide ever downwards. Quick as a flash, the spider would pop up to grab its prey, and drag it under the sand. If you blinked you missed the action!

Of course one of our favourite games was to 'pretend' to be an insect... we'd drop a tiny bit of stick or grass onto the slippery slope... watch it slide down, down... and the spider would pop up... only to find nothing there! I know it was cruel, but at the time we felt sorry for the poor insects that were being gobbled up by the spider with the face of a pig.

On one day every month the maidhan was transformed. It was the pay day for the workers at the Carriage & Wagon Workshops, and from early afternoon tradesmen gathered to set out their stalls. By about four - an hour before the whistle blew - the maidhan was packed with tradespeople, the locals also taking advantage of this monthly mela (fair).

There were dozens of sweet sellers, and vendors of everything from pots and pans to bolts of material. Clothing stall owners and fruit sellers all vying to be heard as soon as anyone started to walk around the stalls; the canny businessmen ready to lighten the workers of their hard-earned cash if they possibly could.

Until one day...!

The weather had been threatening for some time! The winds getting stronger with each passing hour. But with so much to lose the sellers decided to stick it out, and anyway, it had taken so long to lay out all their wares! Besides, they had taken hardly any money at all from the few locals who'd come earlier. It would soon be five and the men would come flocking to buy their goods, they hoped!

But suddenly from out of nowhere a whirlwind began its journey across the maidhan; gathering speed as it sucked up sand and debris from the ground, and then, much to everyone's surprise - and as the unfortunate vendors watched in disbelief - some of their goods were being scattered about by the winds... then snatched up and sucked up into the vortex; which was getting stronger by the second... whirling things high overhead. The roaring wind growing stronger and stronger as it travelled along the ground; carrying everything it had picked up in its path with ease, even bolts of material; which were unwinding as they were plucked from the ground... like so many giant coloured ribbons fluttering gaily as they soared hundreds of feet into the dust-laden air. Even men's turbans were being plucked from their heads – with people running hither and thither trying to grab back anything within reach; the vendors flinging themselves across their wares in an attempt to stop everything being blown away. Some people having to hang onto whatever they could to 'anchor' themselves from being taken up into the sky themselves.

Amidst the shouting and hollering, the stinging sand continued to blast like tiny bullets, forcing everyone to cower in fright, their hands over their faces as they bowed before the mighty wind.

Luckily, many of the vendors had run from the path of the whirlwind, and could only watch and weep as their livelihoods vanished in seconds. While some of the luckier ones - only metres away - had been spared.

And as we watched from the safety of our veranda, the whirlwind - shrieking like a banshee - fled like a thief into the distance; taking with it all it could carry!

CHAPTER NINETEEN

Barbie's & Base Behaviour

Barbequing food has been going on in India for hundreds of years. Long before the Australian 'barbie' and our own recent venture into 'cooking up' a few sausages and burgers on the garden barbeque at weekends.

Anything edible was cooked up on various contraptions - all doing the same as the garden 'barbie'. The market places being swamped with wallahs preparing various delicacies on small portable barbeques.

Leaving the Railway Institute after any function - no matter which road you exited for your journey home - you'd find vendors lining up along the roads in their dozens; selling freshly barbequed lamb, chicken and vegetable morsels to the late-night revellers.

Under street lamps, buzzing Tilley lamps, or just plain lanterns, the vendors managed to produce such things as succulent lamb kebabs, and other spicy delicacies, freshly cooked before your eyes.

Squatting behind a square charcoal brassiere - fanning the coal into a bright white-hot heat - on which long iron rods of ground meat sizzled, the vendors produced instant food to order. Carefully turning the rods until all sides of the meat was equally cooked - the smell of onions and spices making your mouth water, as you stood waiting for your snack - cooked just as you liked it. Then unwrapping a chapatti, from a pile warming nearby, he'd deftly transfer the meat into the centre of the bread; adding chopped onions, green chillies, lemon juice, whatever was your preference; before rolling it up ready for you to eat.

The tasty grilled meat - hot and spicy - eaten with much relish, as you waked slowly home with friends, everyone munching the snacks of their choice. Every vendor kept busy with queues of waiting people. There was always so much to choose from! Big round vats of smoking oil waited for the buggias; small round, nutty balls of ground chick-peas, onions, herbs and spices. The balls quickly dropped into the boiling oil where they sizzled away as they cooked. The golden brown nuggets, along with other variations were endless. Bringalls, potatoes, spinach and green chillies (for the brave) dipped into a spicy batter and fried. The cone-shaped paper container of piping-hot snacks, yours for just a few pice.

There were freshly made samosas, little three-cornered meat or vegetable filled pastries to crunch, and Indian sweet-meats, savoury peanuts, and gol-guppers. Small round balls of puffed-up pastry, crispy fried, which you dipped into a thin sweet and sour sauce, filling as much of the mixture into your pastry ball, before transporting it into your mouth. Lovely!

The smell of barbequing meat filled the air.

Some of our Church contributions found their way into the street vendors pockets too!

Every Sunday evening, the four of us children were sent off to Church for the 'Evensong' special for children. My mother tying the pink ribbons of my straw bonnet into a big neat bow under my chin, then she'd stand back to look at us and make sure we looked 'just right;' my older sister and I, nearly always in matching dresses; the boys in short trousers and shirts, highly polished shoes, and hair slicked back. Very twee! I quite liked my dress, but oh, how I hated that bonnet.

Mother would wave us off and we'd duly wave back... until we were out of sight... then off came that damn bonnet... which I would swing around by its ribbons. Then I would use it to carry things like stones, much to the disgust of my sister, until I was in the church grounds, or right by the church door, before reluctantly shoving the damn thing back on my head at the very last minute, because I had to.

The Church smelt of wax, damp, and decaying books. The air always felt quite cold inside, no matter how warm the day had been. But a feeling of calmness and holiness seemed to spread through you as soon as you walked through the massive wooden doors. From the very first step inside - I kind of tip-toed in - trying to think pure thoughts, but not always succeeding; as I imagined God - who saw everything anyway - would be even better equipped, on home ground!

The big sturdy wooden pews looked like rows of kneeling supplicants saying their prayers, the sunlight filtering through the windows hardly lit up the inside of the church.

Walking quietly up the aisle to take our places right at the front, we'd try and be quiet... but always ended up making noises with our shoes on the stone floor. All the while, the gentle organ music was ebbing and flowing through the vast space between floor and rafters - like some cloying perfume - wrapping you in its embrace.

Shadows seemed to lurk in and around the outer edges of the great room, where the light didn't quite reach. Only the religious figures in the stained-glass windows stood out, looking almost life-like as they gazed down from the long Gothic shaped recesses behind the altar; lit up from outside by the fading sunlight.

Taking our seats the dozen or so European children filling just two or three rows, we would sit quietly, waiting for the music to end, then watch as the figure of Reverend Marris glided silently into view, to stand in the chancel. And the very first time that happened, I nearly wet myself! Thinking God himself had appeared.

I thought Reverend Marris was at least one hundred years old - give or take a year here or there - because he looked so frail and wizened! He was always dressed in long white flowing robes, with a purple or red sash tied round his waist. The two long tasselled ends falling almost to his knees. His hair - very white - sat like a halo round his head, and his face was just a blur because of the bright images behind him. It made him look quite ethereal as he stood hands clasped together before him to address us.

"Good evening children." he'd say, inclining his head slightly in our direction. "Thank you all for coming to Church."

"Good evening Reverend Marris." we'd pipe up almost apologetically, taking the praise for being there although it was all due to pressure from our parents really. Feeling we were committing sacrilege by speaking in that hallowed place at all.

Then, as I gazed intently at him during the sermon, his body seemed to sway gently; his voice gentle and soothing, the words even and smooth... and as I tried to think piously, because that's what you did in Church, I'd sometimes surprise myself by thinking bad thoughts! But then I'd realise it was the devil trying to get through, so I'd squeeze my eyes tight shut, and pretend to be praying. Hoping he'd see I wasn't up for temptation, give up on me, and just buzz off.

But sometimes the devil did get the better of me, because I'd nod off... right in the middle of the service... only to be dug in the ribs by my older sister.

I'd hastily sit upright, giving her a dirty look, and try to concentrate once more. But you know what it's like once you try out the quick kip? Your eyes keep wanting to shut on their own accord! It wasn't easy.

The Reverends figure would begin to ebb and flow once again, his pale face becoming one with the figures in the stained-glass windows. He never seemed to know what to do with his hands! His long, thin white fingers were always playing about with the ends of his sash as he talked; letting the long tassels on the end run through his fingers - over and over again, although I don't think he even knew he was doing it. I suppose if I'd been more attentive to what he was saying - and not what he was doing - I would never have noticed anything but the lesson of the day.

When it was time for the collection 'bag' to be passed around, I always dropped my money - given by my mother - into it with a big show; making the money sound all 'clunky' as it hit the other coins already there; so the others could hear it dropping in. I particularly wanted my sister to hear me drop the collection money in, although I still managed to keep just a teeny bit back for myself.

OK, I knew it wasn't right, but there were better things to spend my money on than the starving poor. Besides at that time, I truly believed I was the starving poor!

We always sang at least two hymns, Reverend Marris accompanying us on the organ, and, as usual, my voice outdid everyone else's. So my sister would give me another, not-so-gentle, dig in the ribs again!

I mean... what is it with older sisters?

So I'd just mime the words silently, forming my mouth into the right shapes so that everyone thought I was singing anyway.

After the service, Reverend Marris shook everyone's hand, and thanked us for attending church again. I'd squirm a bit, knowing I'd still got some of his money burning a hole in my pocket. Especially when he told us we could each pick a posy of flowers from the church gardens, to take home to our mothers.

"But please children, try not to pull the roots up." He'd warn, which was quite a hard thing to do sometimes; as trying to break off a flower got pretty difficult, if you tugged a little too hard, the blessed roots came out too!

The gardens in the grounds of the church were looked after by malis and always looked immaculate, beds of brightly-coloured flowers begging to be taken. There were so many to choose from, that sometimes you didn't know where to start. But this was the part we'd all been waiting for, and we'd quickly gather our little bunches of flowers, wave goodbye to Reverend Marris, and head for home.

Well almost... there was just one more thing we had to do.

Leaving the church grounds by way of some side steps by a bridge, we only had to cross over the road and we were near the back gates of the Railway Institute. As sure as eggs are eggs, there would be a street vendor, with a large vat of boiling oil at the ready... selling those lovely buggias.

Soon, I was handing over my misappropriated money - I never could think of it as stolen - and tucking into those nice hot buggias as we walked home, feeling all holy.

"Where did you get the money from?" My sister would question suspiciously, and I'd look her right in the eye and say very sweetly... "found it in my pocket."

"But that was supposed to be for the collection." she'd say sternly, giving me a really dirty look.

"Must have missed it." I'd lie without any guilt whatsoever.

"Have a buggia Hazel." I'd offer, and of course she just couldn't refuse!

Sadly the holy feeling didn't last for very long, and soon I was up to more mischief!

I suppose like most children I couldn't resist being nosey!

My parent's bedroom had some lovely furniture in it, including the most beautiful almirah that had been made especially for my mother. It reached practically up to the ceiling; and it was here – high up on top, she chose to hide our Christmas presents every year. In fact anything of any importance was hidden up there, or locked away in a huge wooden chest in the 'store' room, safe from prying eyes.

Until I was old enough to start investigating!

It was a pretty dumb thing to do - but when you're all of six years old you aren't thinking of dying, are you?

Stacking one chair on top of another, I was soon high enough to poke my nose through the ornate carved gallery at the very top, my eyes searching for hidden 'goodies', like you do... and I spied something there. Under the accumulation of dust, spiders' webs, and dead flies littering the canopy; hidden in the very far corner - covered in dust because the almirah was too heavy to be shifted for spring-cleaning – was a rather tatty, dog-eared book! So blowing off the dust I slowly read the title. 'L-a-d-y C-h-a-t-t-e-r-l-e-y-s L-o-v-e-r.'

Hey, come on... I was only six, remember? I mean some kids today still can't spell when they are sixteen!

My disappointment was huge - but life's like that, isn't it? To me it was just another book. But when I was older and wiser, I realised just what a huge find it had been! It was THE book everyone had been talking about in the early thirties. It must have been read, re-read, loaned, borrowed, and swooned over, and talked about endlessly, until it had been read and abandoned by MY MOTHER! Who might have actually bought or borrowed the book and read the juicy x-rated novel! 'Attagirl!' - it was nice to know she'd lived - if you know what I mean?

Climbing down was not a good experience.

CHAPTER TWENTY

Monsoons & Lal-Boochies

For weeks the sun - an incandescent orange ball in the sky - had dominated the lives of everyone and everything as it moved across the cloudless skies daily, leaving only devastation in its wake.

A typical Indian summer!

Moisture from the land evaporated rapidly, to leave vast cracks in the ground, where once lakes stood. People sought shelter in shady places, even as the day started, unable to eat or sleep because of the intense heat.

Even pie dogs - ribs outlined against their skinny bodies and tongues lolling from the sides of open mouths - slunk into whatever shade there was; until the worst of the heat was past.

Overhead, eagles circled the thermals - their gimlet eyes on the earth far below - searched for some small bird or animal that had expired in the scorching temperatures, before descending from their lofty heights to pick the body clean.

Indians made 'Poogas' (offerings) daily, placing dishes of food and flowers before the altars of their gods, as they prayed for the monsoons to arrive, while some of the luckier Europeans, fled to the hill-stations and the cooler air of places like Simla, at the foot of the Himalayas.

But the less well-off had to put up with the atrocious conditions.

At night people sweated - tossing and turning about on their beds - unable to sleep in the sticky heat, those fortunate enough to have the luxury of ceiling fans, faired no better; as the blades clicked and whirred overhead, stirring warm air round and round the room.

So imagine the euphoria when the rain finally came!

Storm clouds would have threatened for days, with sheet and fork lightning criss-crossing the skies. The heat sticky, and so intense, that the slightest movement caused perspiration to drip from ones brow.

Then, just when you thought you couldn't take any more...the rain came; starting with a few drops of water... big blobs that came pattering down; as if to test the situation... these turning into larger drops – that came thumping down, like tiny bombs, to disappear immediately into the dry, powdery sand. The pace quickening as clouds released more and more rain; the drops of water falling faster and faster... to bounce off the ground with the impact!

As more rain-clouds filled the skies, the unrelenting glare of the sun was at last obscured, to give blessed relief for the first time in months. The rich, moist smell of damp earth filling the air, and lungs, with the sweetest smell imaginable! Everyone took big, deep, breaths, as if to savour and store that 'special' smell. So that on some later date, it could be taken out again and again to invoke memories of the first rains!

The land cooled rapidly, as more and more rain tumbled down from the skies.

Raindrops washed away the residue of sand from buildings, rocks and trees - whose leaves seemed to dance merrily in the monsoon rains - free once more from the suffocating desert sand.

We children couldn't wait... shouting with joy, and shedding our shoes, we ran - fully clothed - out onto the compound round our bungalow and into the welcome rain.

The cold spots of water took our breath away at first. But oh, how we danced. Loving every minute of this time, in complete abandonment, as arms outstretched, faces upturned and eyes closed, we opened our mouths wide; trying to catch some of the sweet rain-water in our mouths!

It was exhilarating stuff, a kind of temporary insanity!

My parents looked on - probably longing to do the same themselves, but as sahib and memsahib of the house, it wouldn't have been right and proper. So they smiled tolerantly, holding out a hand to 'catch' a few raindrops, but who knows... perhaps they did creep out under cover of darkness?

Even the insects wanted to join in the monsoon dance! Hundreds of little insects known as 'lal-boochies' (red insects) would appear as if by magic, like little red velvet cushions; of different sizes, on spindly legs, running here and there, with us in hot pursuit. If you stroked one very gently, you could feel the soft velvety smoothness of their backs, their bright red bodies resembling tiny strawberries. We thought they had fallen from the sky, along with the rain! I never did find out what they were, although it was suggested they might have been the source of cochineal – the scarlet used for colouring food?

'It's raining cats and dogs,' father would comment, and when I was a very young, I'd believe him... looking up eagerly; expecting to see small cats and dogs falling out of the sky, like the Lal-boochies.

The rain would fall harder and harder – in veritable 'sheets,' almost flattening you to the ground – and then we would be called in, tired but happy, ready to change out of our wet clothes. Then, drying our hair, we'd drink glasses of the loveliest homemade lemonade prepared by mum, as we looked out at the tumbling rain from the safety of the veranda.

The rain could continue for days sometimes. Then, we were forced to play indoor games like Draughts, Lotto, and Snakes and Ladders, and card games... and a game called 'Karam'.

This was played on a three foot square wooden board, with draught-like counters - which were dusted with talcum powder to make the round wooden pieces glide easily on the wooden surface. You were supposed to flick them with your thumb or finger, to hit other counters into the four pockets, at each corner. This we did with gusto - the counters flying over the built-up edges of the board as we got carried away; with arguments as to who had cheated - our voices drowned out with the sound of the rain drumming away outside.

The rain was a very welcome sight, especially for father.

At last, his precious vegetable garden was getting a good old soak! And mother fussed, worrying about the battering her flowers were taking, and making notes for the mali, or reading a book, glad that she could order the khansama to prepare something more substantial than the endless 'salads' we'd been having.

As dusk fell, with the rain showed no signs of abating, you could hear some lone Indian singing at the top of his voice away in the distance, his head covered in an old gunny-sacking bag, as he paddled happily home.

The next morning everything always appeared so much greener! And everyone seemed to be smiling.

The monsoons had come!

Father would have been up since dawn to listen to the news from 'home', the wireless crackling and spitting as he fiddled with the knobs. The blessed thing always seemed to need an awful lot of tuning.

The big neem trees at the side of the bungalow seemed to stretch up to the sky with renewed vigour; their branches and trunks now black with the rain water that had soaked into the porous bark; leaves bright green once more.

Even the birds - twittering high above in the uppermost branches - didn't seem to be quarrelling for once.

Servants scurried about, performing their daily duties cheerfully. Whereas before the rain, they'd dragged their feet lethargically, and who could blame them?

Father, having listened to all the latest news, ventured out to inspect the damage done to his plants in the vegetable garden - his pride and joy - at the back of the bungalow.

The vegetables were grown in oblong 'beds' measuring six feet by four feet with little brick-built pathways in between them; filled with every vegetable imaginable, father having planted the seeds and pricked out the tiny seedlings too, but mostly supervising the mali, who could be seen every morning from just after dawn - white turban bobbing up and down, loin-cloth tucked between his legs - as he weeded, hoed and watered the plump red tomatoes, purple bringalls, creamy-white cauliflowers, and dozens of other vegetables growing there.

Father of course took most of the credit!

Guavas, pomegranates and other fruiting trees bordered the outer edges of the back garden; screening the godowns, and servants quarters from the bungalow.

A pathway from the back compound went past the garden and hodhi, and then led onto the maidhan.

Father grew all the English vegetables, plus many of the exotic Indian varieties.

One year, his runner bean plants reminded us of the story, 'Jack and the Beanstalk.' They just grew and grew! Twining themselves around the stakes, and onwards... the clothes post... and along the clothes line too - some twenty or thirty yards long - producing enormous runner beans that hung down like so much washing, which made for easy picking.

Luckily, the dhobi (washer-man) took much of our dirty laundry away, leaving ayah just the hand-washing and as our clothes line was otherwise 'engaged,' she had to make do with other places to dry the clothes until the bean plants finished producing beans. It not being unusual to see small bushes festooned with bits of washing laid out to dry.

Strange things grew after the monsoon rains; like the pale yellow weed, long thin tendrils minus leaves which seemed to appear overnight. The weed grew rapidly over other grasses and plants in copious quantities - which we called 'Old Mans Hair'. It was smelly and earthy, and seemed very delicate; breaking easily, but didn't seem to be of any particular use. We had fun harvesting it though; seeing who could gather the most.

But that's kids for you!

CHAPTER TWENTY-ONE

Sweet Violets

My mother loved her flowers. They grew in great profusion in the front garden of our bungalow, largely due to my mother's diligence, and help of the mali of course. She refused any 'helpful' hints from my father, reminding him she never interfered with his vegetable garden. So he had to be content to let her do things her way.

More plants spilled over into tubs and pots that stood on the front veranda steps, the flowering shrubs and ferns being changed around as soon as they had finished flowering; or if they'd been damaged by the sun. Then they were placed in the 'summer house' to recuperate. So there was always something in bloom for much of the year.

To the side of the garden, the drive led up to the big iron gates, and the road beyond. We kids all enjoyed swinging from these gates – but only if father was out. The gates were deliberately set at an angle so they would swing open, the drive sloping gently down towards the bungalow.

The gates were a sort of 'demarcation' point, being a stopping place for the many hawkers who brought goods around the houses of the English community. The regulars, like the bhisti, (water carrier) doodh wallah, (milk man), dobhi (laundry man) and the other delivery people were allowed to walk around the bungalow to the back steps; where all transactions took place. Any unauthorised vendor stopping by the gates to 'call' out his wares noisily - but only between certain hours of the day - early afternoons were the time that most English people had a rest from the heat of the day. So around about four o'clock, the various vendors would be back, with their distinctive calls sung in lilting voices to entice the householders.

Just near the top by the gate, a small gully ran under the drive, which was not very deep; just shallow enough for a dog to have crawled under to have her pups. We only knew of their existence when we heard the little yelps coming from the puppies underground.

Of course, we used to wriggle our way through to see the

puppies when my parents weren't looking - which was terribly dangerous - especially if there had been a snake or two hiding in the cool dampness under there, too! Those puppies smelt lovely, all earthy and new-born, and the mother dog used to try and wag her tail - restricted by the tight space - as she too, welcomed us. We always took some little snack for her too.

But the tears came thick and fast when my father said he was going to 'drown' the poor little things. Unfortunately that's what people used to do at one time. As so many 'stray' dogs could not all be fed and looked after. But he relented, and said he would spare any that we'd managed to find suitable homes for, so we ran about - small puppies in hand - offering them to anyone who would take them. In the end we were left with just the runt of the litter which we persuaded dad to let us keep.

He was named 'Rover' of course, and he was the maddest dog you ever saw! None of his body parts grew in proportion to his appetite; he could clear his dish in seconds, then gaze up at you as if he'd never been fed. His paws were huge for his size, and his ears flopped over like a spaniels. He was a proper 'bitsa' dog... you know... bits of everything! But he had a heart as big as his big barrel of a chest. As he grew bigger, he'd be chained up in the shade of the neem tree - because he was always 'chasing off' somewhere. Even when the chains were changed for thicker and stronger ones - he still managed to break away and make a run for it, ending up miles away from home. Of course, he was always brought back, his collar having both his name and address on it, as required by the law at that time. Once, he ran amok in mother's front garden, chasing after butterflies. He made such a mess it was a wonder he was forgiven.

The flowers in the front garden were a riot of colour. The beds arranged formally, in circles, oblongs and diamond shapes. Sweet peas climbed dome-shaped frames made from bamboo canes. Beds of holly-hocks, sweet-scented stock, flocks, pinks and tiny white 'babies breath' flowers; all fighting to outdo one another, with bright yellow marigolds, brilliant red hibiscus and red cannas dominating by their exuberant colours and sassy presence. Big white lilies - the size of small plates - swayed elegantly; giving off the sweetest smell imaginable every evening, after the mali had watered them.

Then there were the large tubs of assorted palms; whose bark turned brown and stringy. The 'pretty as a picture' leaves - as big as umbrellas - with sharp needle-like points that could puncture your skin if you weren't careful. In fact, there were many thorny plants growing in India. Like the Indian plum tree. This had lovely fruits that were round, red and sweet when ripe, but getting to them was a real battle. Getting someone strong enough to shake the tree very hard would result in some of the ripe fruit falling, but there was always that 'big juicy one' that eluded you.

So near... and yet so far!

At the side of the house - under the partial shade of three neem trees - more fruit trees flourished in the hot climate; papayas, custard apple and mulberry, and a rather special bush that gave off a pungent 'curry' smell. This was a 'curry park' tree, the leaf used in curries and especially a lovely soup, called 'pepper-water soup'. It was tart and hot, and guaranteed to put an end to a cold; one of my mother's favourite soups.

But pride of place was given to the lovely violets, my mother's favourite flowers. They were grown in a raised bed, just nose-high to me when I was a small girl at the preparatory school. I could just about peer over the edge, and because of that, got a better look at the shy little flowers who liked to shelter underneath their heart-shaped glossy leaves. They were a beautiful shade of violet, and sometimes we spotted a little white one there too. The scent from them was divine. They seemed to thrive in the dappled shade of the neem trees, flourishing there for years.

Sometimes we were allowed to pick a small bunch to take to a teacher of our choice, but only if we were careful not to pull out the roots.

The pleasure I got was two-fold. Walking to school took about fifteen minutes, during which time I would bury my nose into the tight little bunch of violets I held, sniffing away to my hearts content! Then watch the look of utter pleasure my teacher got as she buried her nose into the sweet-smelling flowers too.

I never took flowers to the teachers at the convent, as they always seemed to have enough of their own. Besides, I didn't have a favourite teacher there.

Our bungalow was surrounded by a large compound, the dry, loose, sandy soil having to be swept twice daily by the sweeper - an 'untouchable'.

Every morning and early evening the sweeper removed any debris from the ground of the compound, using a long-handled broom; which left long arcing marks in the dry sand. Moving backwards as he worked, so as to leave none of his own footprints behind. Apart from making the place look neat and tidy, there was another reason for the 'twice daily' sweepings.

Footprints of birds animals and humans all left their distinctive marks - as did snakes, scorpions and centipedes; their markings different and easily detectable. Following the unmistakable markings generally led to the reptile or creepy-crawly and its hiding place - generally a stone or rock where they had hidden. So it was easy enough to dispose of anything considered dangerous, before they caused a nasty mishap.

There were all sorts of bugs to contend with, including caterpillars of all descriptions. A large green one with red spots all over its body would quickly walk over a branch, its body undulating like a little concertina. We were warned to keep away from the brown prickly looking ones. Sometimes, we found sticks all bound together and nestling inside the cocoon would be something waiting to be born.

Large lizards with big heads and colourful bodies would dash through the undergrowth and there were insects that gave off a very peculiar smell; similar to one of the Indian spices. Large black beetles lumbered slowly along, as if they hadn't a care in the world, and ants dashed about, carrying twice their weight, always rushing around madly. Beautiful butterflies flitted from flower to flower; the smallest bird ever joining them as it darted from flower to flower; its wings beating frantically as it hovered in front of the flowers; its beak buried deep inside as it gathered nectar.

They were humming birds, and really tiny! Sometimes you could see their nests - dozens of them hanging down from the branches of a tree. Elongated globes hanging down - like some exotic fruit - the small beautifully-made woven cocoons with just a small round entrance hole at one side , nearly always built over fast-flowing rivers and streams; or other inaccessible places, safe from any predators.

The golden orioles were shy birds, who loved coming out after a shower of rain; their brilliant yellow plumage a splash of colour against the green of the trees.   Bulbuls gave off throaty calls, and mynah birds imitated other birds and humans. While pigeons cooed, sparrows squabbled and parrots screeched.

We had hundreds of different species of birds in India, and many of them loved the fruit of our neem trees. The early mornings shrill with the cries of the squabbling birds; as they gorged on the ripe fruits; ending with huge amounts of the sticky fruit on the ground below! These big trees must have been a constant source of irritation for the sweeper, who had his job cut out trying to keep our compound clean; starting with the hundreds of the tiny white flowers that fell to the ground after they'd been pollinated; and then the sweet, sticky yellow fruit that dropped in their thousands as the birds feasted high up in the branches of the trees.

The back garden - my father's pride and joy - supplied us with nearly all the vegetables we needed. The fruit trees of guavas, pomegranate and plum bordering the vegetables in their long beds. The fruit trees were jealously guarded by my father; who had planted the guava trees himself; watching them grow big enough to fruit. But would never get to see the 'fruits' of his labour, unless he kept us little beggars out of his garden! Knowing we'd pick the green fruit and then discard it, when it wasn't to our taste.

So the garden was forbidden to us children, unless father was at home!

Everything grew beautifully in the sunny clime!   Juicy red tomatoes dragged the plants to their knees, and the cauliflowers had to have their leaves turned over to keep the white florets from yellowing and 'going over' in the bright sunshine. The peas in their pods tantalised us as they glistened in the light, and purple aubergines hung like fat little bats underneath the broad leaves of the plants.   Cabbages, as big as your head; kohlrabi and onions flourished, as did the big green capsicums; turning to orange and red as they ripened.   With the pretty white flowers of the potatoes promising a good crop later on. Small patches of lettuce, spring onions and radishes were planted at intervals throughout the summer, so we always had enough for our 'salads'.

The poor mali had to tend to both the front and back gardens, starting really early in the mornings; before the heat of the sun made it impossible to work. He wore a dhoti and small white turban while working, his body, arms and feet bare, and seemed to have a permanent stoop with all the bending he did. His dark brown body glistened with sweat as he kept going for hours without a break; stopping gratefully at ten o'clock for his tea break; supplied by our khansama. Then, clutching a hot tin of tea in both hands, he'd sit - his stooped back against the fence - as he dipped his slice of white bread into his tea, and 'gummed' it. He wasn't all that old, but had lost all his teeth, but it didn't stop him from enjoying his food.

Most outside work stopped at noon, with the sun riding high in the sky, it would be far too hot to be out, let alone work during the worst of the summer months. Except for the workmen of the railway 'Carriage & Wagon Workshops', who were forced to return to the confines of the over-heated workshops after their lunch break? After the one o'clock whistle silence would reign over the area for the next few hours.

For the lucky few it was siesta time, all except for a few pie dogs slinking over the hot sand of the maidhan as they searched for scraps, or some unfortunate Indian rushing across to the latrines - because he had to.

The servants rested or talked in low voices as they stayed in the shade of their godowns, and traffic halted in the worst of the summer heat, the tar on the roads melting in the fierce heat of the sun.

Poor Rover, who'd got into a fight after running off one day, was badly bitten everywhere. My mother did her best to fix him up, but flies had laid eggs in a wound right on top of his head. He was unable to get to it himself and by the time mother realised what had happened it was too late. She poured disinfectant into the wound hoping to kill the writhing creatures, but they'd disappear for a minute, then rise to the surface again, driving poor old Rover to distraction. He'd try and claw at his head, howling, and the sound went right through you.

So father decided it would be kinder to have him put out of his misery. Even now, I can still hear the sound of the shot that ended our poor dog's life. He was shot by father - with just one well-aimed shot - right under the neem tree, and the sound of it reverberated round and round the bungalow for what seemed like ages.

He was buried in the shade of the giant neem, so that he could be mourned by us as we laid flowers on his grave and 'talked' to him from time to time.

All the family missed poor Rover for ages afterwards, the house unusually quiet. And for weeks afterwards we half expected him to come gambolling over to greet us when we came home from school, forgetting that he was no more.

We did have many other pets though, my brother Billy kept pigeons in one of the store rooms. Some of them were lovely white fantailed ones, which could spread their rounded tails and danced for their partners, going 'gutter-goo, gutter-goo.' He used to open their cages in the morning and off they'd fly, circling the bungalow once or twice as if to fix their positions…then off they'd go - flying away with a 'buzzing' and 'shirring' of wings; returning back to their cleaned-out cages and fresh food and water. Talk about a 'pigeon's life!

We kept tame rabbits, and even had a tiny abandoned monkey once. Mother fed him with milk from a fountain pen filler when he was very tiny, but he grew no bigger than a little kitten. He had big inquisitive eyes, and sharp teeth; nipping anyone when he thought he could. We had tried to tame him, but weren't very successful, as he would sometimes go absolutely berserk! Clawing his way up the curtains and sitting in a spot far above our heads as he 'jabbered' away – baring his little teeth and screeching; so father was forced to give him away. I often wondered if he ended up as one of those poor little monkey's who used to wear a small round hat and beat a tambourine for one of the many 'dancing monkey' travellers in the market.

My sister Hazel, brother Billy and I were allowed to keep a small kitten each at one time, and gave each of them names. Hazel's kitten was called 'freaky' because she was a cat of many colours and had a twisted tail, and Billy named his 'tiger' because of its grey and white stripes. I'd named my little black and white kitten 'Guderber' because it was the nearest I could get to the Indian equivalent of galloper, or my interpretation of it!

Sometimes when we were at home and it got nearer the time for mother to feed them, we would up-end books between the door frames inside the bungalow and hold onto our little kittens - waiting for mother to start calling the kittens for their meal from the back veranda. She would scrape the plate with a spoon calling... "Come on kittens, time for your dinners." and the poor hungry kittens would pull away from our hands and gallop along... over all the barricades... the only way they could get to mother and their food... and we'd rush after them to see which of them had won! Me shouting, "Guderber, Guderber, Guderber, go, go, go!" for my kitten, with Hazel and Billy shouting for theirs too.

It wasn't cruel as the books were not very high, and the playful kittens got plenty of exercise which they needed; having spent nearly all day kipping!

CHAPTER TWENTY-TWO

Tomboy

Did I mention I was a bit of a Tomboy? Well, with a father who insisted on treating me like a boy, its no wonder I thought myself one. Even from a very young age, father had taught me to do 'boyish' things like, hunting, shooting, fishing, and boxing too.

Plus, I was pretty good at running, especially if I was trying to get away from trouble! And I could use a catapult - better than most boys.

I was pretty fearless for a girl... well... almost! I hated bats. They always flew so fast... dipping and swinging past you as they flashed silently past in the twilight. I'd put my hands over my ears, sure the bats were going to suddenly bite one of them... then literally... hang on. The ones I'd seen had little piggy faces, and scary teeth. I thought them repulsive! But their mothers probably thought them cute. Spiders, and other things despised by girls were OK by me. I could catch toads or frogs, handle worms, and tied string round the raised 'tail' of scorpions, to make them 'dance.' Out of sight of our parents, we put pins on the railway lines when we knew a train was coming. The small 'swords' they'd turned into when they'd been flattened, handy for miniature 'sword-fighting' games.

Heights didn't worry me unduly. I climbed the highest trees with my brother and his friends determined to be 'better' than them, so they'd allow me to play with them. My father had also taught me to use him as a climbing frame from quite an early age. Facing him, my hands held firmly by him, I'd place one foot on his right knee - which was bent slightly - and with father pulling me up, I'd quickly climb... up... another foot and toes on his wide leather belt…and then with a final step, and roll of the drums from dad - I'd stand on his shoulders, and turn round to face forward. Suddenly I was 'The King of the Castle'.

I was a fearless little beggar. But only because I knew he would never let any harm come to me!

All that stopped when I reached the ripe old age of ten. I rather think I was getting a trifle too big and heavy to be hoisted aloft then. Besides, I was quite a chunky thing by then! Mother thought it quite unladylike anyway! She also thought I should give up climbing trees and some of the more boisterous games I played with the boys, telling me it was about time I acted the sex I was.

In the cool of the evening, father would don a pair of khaki shorts, a cotton vest, sturdy sandals, and in the heat of India, go 'jogging'. He must have been the only white man to be seen doing that; my brother Billy and I sometimes accompanying him... although we much preferred the coming home bit. Mother would have tall glasses of lovely cool homemade lemonade, or 'mango fool' waiting for us to drink.

Dad taught me to box too, first 'shadow-boxing' then he would make my older brother - one arm tied behind his back so we were of equal strength - box each other. I, of course, had to prove myself, and would go tearing in... both fists flashing a right, left, right hook to my brother's midriff - which was about as high as I could reach - and him backing away from the little bundle of energy... me, calling out, 'it's unfair, it's unfair.' Of course it was, but not in the eyes of my father. All he wanted to do was toughen up my brother and make sure I learned how to defend myself. But to a fourteen year old boy with one hand tied behind his back, it must have seemed terribly unfair. I mean, he couldn't really hit his little sister could he? Having to put up with me jabbing away to his midriff - which was the only place I could reach. So when Ernest was sent to Mount Abu to join the 'Boys Brigade' he must have been more than relieved!

Then, with my eldest sister away at boarding school too, there was only my younger brother and myself at home. I loved nothing better than to be included in games with his friends. But sometimes he would tell me I couldn't join them, sneering 'we don't want any girls with us.' But a kind boy named Ian always came to my defence. 'Yes let her play with us.' he'd insist. 'She's not bad for a girl.' And once again I was 'in' with the boys. But it was becoming more and more difficult too, some of them giving me 'dares' to perform if I wanted to continue playing with them.

"Lets see you scrump some plums," someone suggested. I had to sneak through some thorny brambles, onto a farmer's field, to steal some of the sweet white crunchy plums growing there;

practically by the very door of the farmer's house. Squirming my way over the ground, the way father had taught me

I'd managed to wriggle quietly over the parts that were overgrown with grass and weeds, then, just when I was within striking distance of the tree, a dog started barking! Unluckily for me it was tied up to the very tree that held the plums, so I quickly backtracked before the farmer came to see why the dog was barking. The other boys having 'legged' it at the dog's first bark!

I even resorted to cheating, just so I would be allowed to play with the boys. There was always a 'dare' we had to do. We'd all got catapults. So the boys decided the first one to bring back a dead bird would be 'top dog'.

Of course, I had to show the boys I was better than them... and knew exactly where I'd find a bird. I'd seen it only days before, it was just a baby, and had probably fallen out of its nest. So I made my way there. I was so desperate to 'prove' myself, needing to be 'accepted' by the boys once and for all.

Silly me! I was the first back - with my dead bird - but the price I paid was very high indeed.

The boys laughed and laughed, they weren't fooled by my 'dead' bird. It probably had something to do with bird being stiff and starting to smell too. Oh, and the tiny ants emerging from its body can't have helped!

Father loved going out hunting or 'shikari' as it was called in India, my brother and I begged to be allowed to go along too. Occasionally, we were taken, much against my mother's wishes.

With my father and one of his men riding motor-bikes, and an excited child clinging tightly on behind each rider, we'd set off. The roar of the bikes and the fast approaching darkness was thrilling. We'd travel for mile after mile...past the lights of houses and watch them disappear from sight. To be replaced with dense jungle on either side of the road, until after what seemed like ages, the men would dismount from their bikes, and lift us off, before finding a suitable tree we could all climb.

We'd go as high as we dared, all the time it was getting darker and darker; the nights falling quite suddenly in India. Father would tie us securely to a branch of the tree - to make sure we didn't fall out - and then they would set the scene for whatever 'game' they had come for, which was mainly, deer. Although sometimes it must have been 'bigger' game as the men once put a live animal as 'bait' underneath the tree we were in, and then scrambled back up into the lower branches of 'our' tree, telling us to be absolutely quiet.

The waiting would begin.

Sounds of crickets chirping, and other night sounds were magnified in the pitch blackness, while away in the distance we'd hear some poor animal cry out; a high-pitched scream; suddenly terminated... by who knows what! It always seemed like hours and hours to us kids; as trying to peer out into the blackness of the night, and our eyes straining to see what was out there, finally gave way to sleep. The strong cords preventing us from dropping down to become prey ourselves! Later, when we woke, we'd find the men had climbed down from the tree, and we were alone in complete darkness. The only sounds to be heard were the snuffling noises under our tree!

Or at least that's what we thought!

Wide eyed and terrified I would hold my breath, and wish with all my heart my father would come back. Billy whispering "Did you hear that?" not making me a happy bunny at all!

Then in the distance, a tiny spot of light... that got bigger and bigger sent leaps of joy through me. I could see the two men returning by the light of the lantern they carried. Sheer, blessed relief. Sometimes, it would be in reverse. The two men would tell us to remain in our tree, as they climbed down, and we would see them disappear into the jungle, the light of the lantern getting smaller and smaller until at last it flickered and disappeared!

I don't really know which frightened me more?

But still we begged and pleaded to be allowed to go along on his next foray into the jungle.

One day father refused to take us, saying he was going after wild boar, and that it could turn 'nasty'. Although we didn't realise just how nasty.

Tracking wild boar was a dangerous pastime. So when my father and one of the other hunter's went out one night they knew they had to be very careful indeed. Following some of the pigs 'droppings' they walked slowly forward... when suddenly a wild boar shot out of the thicket of thorns and charged towards them;

taking both men by surprise. By pure chance they both veered away from the path of the charging beast; the other man making it to the safety of a nearby tree, which he climbed in record time. It was the biggest old boar my father had ever seen! But now it turned in its tracks sharply, it came charging back... straight for my father! He managed to raise his twelve bore gun and fire... and thought he'd hit his target... but the huge beast continued to come straight towards him.

He was a huge beast, his front teeth shining in the light of the torch attached to the gun. Father ran behind the nearest tree... with the boar right behind him.

"Climb the tree sahib, climb the tree!" the other man yelled, but father didn't get the chance, as the wild boar chased him round and round the tree. It had been hit, but continued to fight.

My father was unable to reload his gun as he dodged the furious animal, and was then forced to use the butt of his gun on the animal's hard skull. Battering the animal again and again, until his gun was smashed. Just when my father thought he never stood an earthly, the boar slowly teetered sideways, and dropped dead. My father's clothes were ripped to tatters from the thorny brambles, and with his face, arms and legs cut and bruised, he stood and panted as he looked down at the now twitching porker; half expecting it to get up and charge him again! Only when he was quite sure the beast was dead, would the other hunter climb down from his perch in the tree.

The two men managed to drag the heavy kill to where the motor bikes had been left and by the dawn light, they made their way home. My father looking like he'd been the victim!

A huge grin lit up his face as he proudly showed my mother the dead wild boar tied to the back of his bike. It had been so heavy that it shifted about - the men having to stop several times on the way back to re-tie it, before finally getting the behemoth home.

The next day, we and our neighbours all dined on fresh roast pork, the smell wafting through from the outside kitchen for ages, to tickle the palate. Then, with fresh vegetables and plenty of gravy, we tucked into the juicy meat. Crunching the crackling, and having second helpings of the lovely stuffing that only mum could prepare properly. Years afterwards, my father was reminded of that fearsome fight whenever he looked at the mangled remains of his gun which he was always going to have repaired.

Of course, we thought our father was the bravest man ever. But obviously, mother didn't share our feelings. She told him off soundly for taking 'silly' chances.

Father was always being called upon to settle disputes, intervene on someone's behalf, or shoot mad dogs. The latter often proving to be quite tricky! The poor rabid dog would snarl; its jaws covered in saliva as it bared its teeth. Charging anything as the madness slowly coursed through its poor emaciated body. In those days, the only kindness was put the poor creature out of its misery!

Armed with his gun, my father would make his way to where its last sighting had been, and try and get as close to the dog as he could.

Sometimes, the maddened animal would charge forward, snarling and ready to bite. So, with his gun already loaded, he had to make sure he got a good clean shot in first. If he'd been bitten, nothing could have saved him from contacting rabies, even the long course of injections afterwards, didn't always work!

I think all of us children had had to have tetanus injections in our stomachs as a result of being bitten by a dog. No chances could be taken that the animal who'd done the biting may or may not have been rabid! The injections were the most painful things too!

Living in India meant a visit to our local hospital at least once or twice a month. There were so many things that had to be treated. At certain times of the year tiny flies caused 'sore eyes'. A painful process where your eyes began to itch, burn, redden and get stuck down until you couldn't open them! We would be taken to the out-patients department, where they washed our eyes out with warm water, and had eye drops inserted on a daily basis, until it cleared up.

Then there were the unexplained bites that refused to heal, and sore throats. Once again we went to the hospital, where doctors 'swabbed,' our throats with a thick, obnoxious, sticky brown gunk. The taste was horrible, and as you gagged, the doctor swabbed all around inside your throat. Urghhh! Ears too, were given a good clear-out. I think they used a solution of peroxide, which fizzed in your ears something awful, and then you were sent home with cotton wool stuck in your ears.

I, of course, needed a whole hospital just to myself! Where my father had got into trouble as a young boy, there too was I...

following in his footsteps!

It started when I was about two years old. Mother noticed a nasty smell whenever she came near me, which got steadily worse; before the site was pin-pointed as my nose! I was taken to the hospital, and the doctors poked and prodded, but could not find what was causing it.

Until x-rays revealed I had a pea stuck up my nose!

Mother was horrified to think it had been well over a fortnight since we'd had peas for lunch. So I must have shoved this itty, bitty pea up my nose then. All the poking and prodding had simply sent the pea further and further away up my nostril.

The doc suggested my mother try the age-old recipe... a piece of bread and jam... and a liberal dusting of pepper! When we got home, that's what she did. I was given the peppery piece of bread, and grabbing it I sank my teeth firmly into that 'buttie' and sneezed and sneezed - until this stinky, rotten pea came flying out.

Everyone around me cheered, and I carried on eating my bread and jam, completely oblivious to the pepper, and the fact I was sneezing constantly, until someone took the peppered jam buttie off me, which made me scream of course. I'm told they replaced the peppery bread for the real thing, and I contentedly chomped away.

Another time, I was running about on the maidhan. It was still quite early, although the evenings close in rather suddenly in India, so the light wasn't particularly good at that time, so I ran right into one of the taut wires holding up a high pylon. Of course, it was my nose again! It was badly ripped and once again I was rushed off to hospital. Where they were getting to know me quite well. Anyway, my nose was stitched and I was sent home. But the wound just refused to heal. So back to the hospital I went again. This time, the doctor's decided to inject the nose with some antibiotics, me screaming blue murder as they inserted the needle; again and again; the liquid squirting out of the other side every time! No matter what angle they tried to inject, the liquid squirted right out again.

Of course I now know the nose is just a bit of gristle, so there probably wasn't anywhere for the dratted liquid to go! To this day, I still carry a tiny scar at the very tip of my nose.

Then, there was the time that I was bitten on my foot - again completely my own fault. I must have been about seven or eight years old at the time, and had danced on the stage as Carmen Miranda, you know... the South American singer/dancer who used to have hats of tropical fruit, and wear flamboyant clothes? Well I'd learnt how to imitate her, and had been persuaded to do her act on stage! Being ever the show-off, I gave it my all. Singing...'Mama Ye Carro, Mamma Ye Carro' and 'I, I, I, I, I, I Love You Very Much, I, I,I, I, I, I Think You're Grand...' Rolling my eyes and giving all the hand movements etc: I was a hit. I suppose all the applause I received on stage just went to my head, and I wanted more plaudits. But my poor family must have been fed up with my performances!

So serve me right when I decided to show off to them once more.

The trouble was we were sleeping 'al-fresco', that night - as we often did when the weather was uncomfortably hot. I'd hopped out of bed, and with just a dim light coming from the back veranda started giving the performance of a lifetime. I'd just hit a high note, when something bit me on my foot... and my voice changed tune... I screamed... a piercing wild cry that made everyone panic! Well if you'd heard me scream, I bet you would panic too!

I'd been bitten on the foot by something, but by what?

Identifying what the 'biter' was could be very helpful in getting the right treatment... so my father tried to find anything lurking on the ground around where I'd stood. While my mother put a wet cloth on the spot that was slowly swelling, and getting hotter by the minute. The pain was excruciating, so once again I was rushed off to hospital.

Without identification of what had caused the poisoning the staff at the hospital didn't quite know what to do. And my father was still searching.

It could have been a poisonous snake, scorpion, or centipede, or anything else for that matter. Anyway, by the time I was taken to hospital, my foot had swollen up and the red patch had spread all around the bite mark.

The poison was doing its work!

Luckily, the doctors were able to find an antidote, which eased the pain and the swelling.

And yes, I continued to go about barefoot whenever I could!

CHAPTER TWENTY-THREE

The Oompha Bands

On Christmas mornings in India we woke to the sounds of bands playing a medley of tunes, and our Christmas presents. Mine was nearly always a doll - and our stockings (one of dad's old socks) containing: an apple; an orange, a few prettily wrapped chocolates and a few nuts that would have slipped down into the toe, with a comic rolled up and sticking out of the top of the sock. We were over the moon, and quiet for about ten minutes or so examining the present we'd received before running into my parents room to show them what 'Santa' had brought us.

Billy my youngest brother always had an electrical toy; invariably a train, aeroplane or boat which I would covet! But which I never minded him having as he always allowed me to play with them anyway, as he was so good-natured. Mum having to save him from himself sometimes.

Getting dressed quickly we'd head for the front veranda to get a good look at the bands - small groups of Indian Bandsmen dressed up in matching uniforms - playing a variety of instruments as they stood on the side of the road, in front of the iron gates.

They played all the European military marches, until someone from the house went out to give them a little money. Almost before they'd gone on to the next house, another band would take its place. Throughout the morning more bands continued to call. The later ones playing for about fifteen minutes before walking dejectedly away because there was no more money to be had. My parents having a limited supply of goodwill, and money!

The house would have been bustling with activity for weeks before the actual day. In fact, the preparations would start well before October; with homemade mincemeat made for mince pies, and various pickles being put up. The Christmas pudding was also made well in advance of Christmas. Everyone in the family taking turns to have a go at 'mixing' the ingredients in a big china bowl. Then we'd watch as mum dropped in a handful of tiny silver coins. The puddings were then steamed, and hung up until needed for

Christmas Day. This was one thing the khansama wasn't going to ruin! In fact, mother always seemed to sack the cook just before Christmas. I think she quite enjoyed taking over the cooking for Christmas anyway, and she was helped by my father who had been an army cook for many years.

One cook was dismissed for removing a mark off a plate – by wetting the end of the jarin (tea-cloth) and rubbing off the offending spot – witnessed by my mother. She was absolutely livid! Another, was skimming a bit too much off the top of the daily shopping money, and yet another didn't look clean; no matter how many new clothes were bought for him; my parents coming to the conclusion that he just used the clothes for everything - even to sleep in.

The servants were each given three sets of clothes every Christmas, as part of their 'Christmas' presents; one to wash, one to wear, and one as a stand-by, along with a months extra wages.

Anyway, I think mother much preferred doing her own cooking; she was an extremely good cook too. With so many tomatoes growing in the back garden, she was a real dab hand at making tomato sauce; which she bottled - giving quite a lot away. Her Christmas dinners were enjoyed by all our visitors too, as we always seemed to end up with unexpected guests.

There were other 'goodies' prepared a few days before Christmas, like the big succulent hams that were glazed and dotted with cloves, and a sweet called 'cull-culls'. Small balls of pastry rolled along the prongs of a fork, and deep fried. Then, when they cooled, they were dipped in a coating of wet sugar, and left to harden; when cool, they were crunchy and sweet.

We had all the usual trimmings like crackers and a proper iced cake; which we were allowed to decorate. The little silver balls dotted around it making it look really festive! There were the other things mother had grown up with in her Portuguese home too, wonderful light crispy 'waffles' with a dusting of icing sugar. Lovely 'puttoo' rice cakes with freshly grated coconut and sugar, also, 'hoppers', a beautiful white pancake made with rice flour, coconut milk and eaten with either a savoury or a sweet filling, and lovely roasted spicy nuts.

Mother bought all her dried fruit and nuts from the N.A.A.F.I stores, and the market, locking them away in the big wire-panelled box in the storeroom. Sometimes she would let us have a small handful each as we sat around the fire in the evening, the small pine nuts taking ever so long to shell. They were so tiny too, but lovely and sweet once you'd managed to get the shell off. They were just too small to use nut-crackers on.

It used to get quite cold in the evenings sometimes, and the time spent around the fire making our Christmas decorations was a magical time.

My parents would supply us each with a small dish of flour and water, and bundles of ready-cut bits of coloured tissue paper. It was a race to see who could produce the longest bits of chain. We children sat on the hearth-rug in front of the fire, moving away if the flames got too hot, and soon there wasn't a sound except for the rustling of paper. These were joined together and were used to decorate the house for Christmas; and because we'd all helped to make the chains, it was even more thrilling to see them finally go up.

The tree was decorated about a week before Christmas Day.

Sometimes, on those nights around the fire, we would beg mother to tell us ghost stories. No one could tell stories like her. One of us would rush to put out the lights, then, with just the glow from the flickering fire, she would begin. As the story progressed we'd creep ever nearer to my mother's chair, until we were practically clinging to her skirt.

"That's enough for tonight," she'd say later, and then we'd look at each other, too scared to move. Washing ourselves very quickly, we'd get undressed and into our 'jammies' in no time at all; jumping into bed to cover our heads with the sheets, terrified, in case one of the evil spirits came to get us. But next day all would be forgotten as we begged mother to tell us some more of the ghostly stories.

There would be a regular procession of callers on Christmas morning, several of father's men coming to pay their respects to the sahib and his family on their 'special' day. They always came with trays of lovely dried fruit, nuts, and lumps of sugar candy, and garlands of marigolds which they put around our necks; always starting with my father - as head of the house. Then, in turn garlanding my mother, and so on, until I came up in the rear; being the youngest, the garlands getting smaller and smaller as they got towards me. Of course, father always gave them money in exchange, which again was the done thing.

Friends and neighbours called around too. Everyone excited about Christmas. The drinks would flow, and everyone got merrier and merrier, everyone slightly inebriated by lunch time, when there would be upwards of a dozen family and guests sitting down to Christmas dinner! It was the only day we had our 'dinner' at 'lunch' time. Everyone would wear paper hats, pull crackers, and laugh a lot. Finally, when people left, they would shake hands all round, wishing each other 'The Compliments of the Season', and press a little money into the hands of the children present. A quaint custom, but nearly always done when visiting one another for special occasions.

When we children were given money by some of our guests, we thought we were in seventh heaven! Running off to our rooms we'd count out how much we'd received, and depending on how drunk the guest had become, the amount of the 'gift' varied. Once, I received a bundle of rupees, there must have been well over twenty rupees there. My eyes popped out of my head. I could buy a whole sweet shop! But my joy was short-lived. My parents thought the man in question had made a mistake, and I was made to return the money. I was so disappointed.

There was always so much happening over the Christmas period with events for the children at the Railway Institute starting a good week before Christmas. On Christmas Eve a children's party was held in the grounds. With Father Christmas coming on either a camel or an elephant, with sacks full of toys. Large trestle tables groaned under the weight of plates of cakes, sandwiches, trifles and other foods. Another table held all the presents.

But first we had sports. With races, high-jumping, and long-jumping for all age groups. The sack race and three-legged race getting everyone tangled up as the competitors fell about. The first three winners over the finishing line would have their names taken for the prize-giving later on.

Then, it was time for the lovely party food. One by one, our names would be called out, and we'd go up to receive our prizes and a present from Father Christmas.

We only found out many years later that these presents were paid for by our parents. Organised by the Railways, the events were also helped out with donations from the families, money being taken from my father's wages each month. But in those days we never really appreciated just how lucky we were in having all the lovely parties and the facilities of the 'Railway Institute'.

On New Year's Eve, the fancy dress parties were held there for both the children and the adults; the childrens' being held in the afternoon. All the children paraded in their costumes around the lush green lawns, to the applause of our parents and friends before being put into age groups, for the 'judging'. The people doing the judging would then whittle the entrants down to just three in each of the age groups, before pinning the appropriate numbers onto the winners.

Somehow, our family always managed to bag a few prizes, thanks to my mother's inventive brain. She came up with really great ideas, and with the help of the durzi, our costumes got us noticed. One year, I was dressed as a little old lady; complete with glasses perched on the end of my nose, lace mittens, a long skirt, mop cap and shawl, and carrying a tiny teapot. I was the lady on the tin of 'Mazawattee Tea'. My sister was dressed as an Indian lady, and my younger brother was dressed as a pair of scissors. I even went dressed as a nun once!

Of course, when we did win mother was delighted. But not as delighted as we were! Clutching our 'extra' prizes, we were on top of the world!

My sister was very athletic, and regularly won all the races in her age group. One year, she won the prize for the long-jump, high-jump, and the one hundred yards dash, with the hop-skip-and jump making it four out of five events. She kept going up to receive her presents, one after the other, with us cheering and clapping like mad! Some of her prizes were duplicated - the people buying the presents not knowing the same child would win nearly all the prizes - she had two jewellery boxes, so she gave one of them to me.

Everyone came back down to earth after the festivities, and we were always careful to take all decorations down on the twelfth night! We wouldn't have wanted any bad luck, would we? Going back to school was dismal after all the jollifications, and it always took a couple of weeks to settle back down to study.

Christmases always seemed to take so long to come around then!

CHAPTER TWENTY- FOUR

Odious Creatures

I suppose we got used to the endless varieties of birds, animals and insects living in India, although some of them kind of 'freaked' you out! Stroking strange dogs was never something one did out there, in case it had been in contact with some other rabid animal. Sometimes, even playing with family pets could prove hazardous!

All of us had been bitten when we were children; sometimes just for stroking a dog that we'd known for ages, the weather making the beast act out of character. Then we had to be taken to hospital for treatment which entailed being injected in the stomach for a set number of days; and a watch being kept on the dog in case it became rabid!

We were still living in Ajmer, and our favourite place to play was on the maidhan; a large open field at the back of our bungalow. All sorts of insects, lizards, scorpions etc: inhabiting it. And many more visited it after dark, and in the early evenings.

We would be playing on the maidhan outside our bungalow, and suddenly...bats would come zinging by. Flashing right past you, so you could feel the air move! We believed the bats were after our ears so we'd cover them over with our hands, and run indoors. I think they were the only things I was really afraid of!

As soon as twilight descended, large groups of flying foxes took to the skies, flying off to where the fruit was ripening in orchards and fields. Some of the poor farmers having to keep all-night vigils as they walked about their fruit groves hammering metal covers, or anything else that produced enough noise to frighten away the destructive birds.

Then after dark, we could hear the jackals wee-a-waaing as they left their day-time hide-outs to come looking for food, followed by the raucous 'laughter' of the hyenas. These were creatures similar to the dogs, but had thicker and longer necks. They were ugly creatures too, with their spotted, mottled lop-sided bodies. The noise they made was almost a laugh, followed by a rasping cough, and you didn't want to be out there with them. Luckily, they hated us humans nearly as much, and only ventured out long after we'd had all settled down for the night.

Laying in bed you could hear the jackals calling out to one another in the distance, their calls getting closer and closer. Then, outside in the darkness you would hear the noise of a dustbin lid crashing to the ground as the beasts rummaged for scraps.

My eldest sister was really terrified of getting out of bed after dark, and used to make me accompany her to the toilet! Sometimes she would whisper, "Rose, get me a glass of water." and I'd refuse.

"Get it yourself!"

So she would resort to bribing me - which of course was what I was waiting for!

"Please Rosie, I'm so thirsty. I'll give you anything if you'll get me a drink!"

"Like what?"

"Oh, anything you like, just get me a drink of water, will you?"

"Can I wear your new blouse?"

Now the blouse in question didn't even fit me, but I was determined to get something, if I was to traipse all the way through the house to fetch my sister a drink of water. After holding out for about another five minutes, she'd finally give in.

"Oh, okay, you can borrow my blouse, but if you get it dirty, or tear it…!"

I'd then slip out of bed and fetch her water. Although I never knew why she was so afraid of the dark!

Even the servants thought I could see in the dark... because of the colour of my eyes which were green. Saying "The little missy baba has got the eyes of the tiger!" But of course that wasn't true. I was as blind as a bat after dark just the same as everyone else!

The funny thing is... that even after being bitten on the foot by something - we never did find out what it was - I still walked around bare-footed at times. Of course I was made to wear sandals or shoes outside, but I much preferred nothing on my feet, and still do!

I hated those solar topees (sun hats) we were made to wear during the summer months. They might well stop us from getting sunstroke, but they were cumbersome things, being made of compressed cork and covered in a white twill, or khaki material; with a sort of webbing on the inside that kept your head from touching the top and sides; with a brim to protect your eyes, and another that covered the back of your neck. There were also little air-holes along the side to stop your head from perspiring too much.

Mother used to wear hers with a veil around her face when she ventured into her garden to cut flowers for the table, and a thin pair of gloves, because there were always mosquitoes lying in wait in the darkest spots in the garden. These mosquitoes were malaria giving bugs, so mosquitoes nets were fitted to our beds when the monsoons seasons gave them a chance to breed in their thousands. The little beggars used to get in too no matter how careful we were to tuck the netting into the side of the bed.

Then there were the locusts!

After being in recession for years... they suddenly swarmed... leaving their breeding grounds in the desert, to take to the skies; flying for miles until they dropped out of the sky - to strip fields within minutes.

One very warm day, a swarm of locusts was sighted and the word spread like wild-fire. Well almost as quickly as the locusts themselves! The telegraph wires buzzing along the line as they informed everyone of the coming destructive force.

Which is all my father needed!

Quickly and with military precision he organised everyone to do their bit to stop the advancing enemy - all of us delegated our separate tasks - then with the help of the servants father had small fires laid in and around the vegetable beds; ready to light at the first sight of the flying insects, his theory being the fires and smoke would prevent them from landing anywhere near his precious garden!

On seeing the flames and smoke, the insects would give his patch a miss, and go elsewhere.

But no one had told that to the locusts!

All us kids along with the servants were pressed into service and given tins to beat. Father had found a couple of those wooden things you swung around in your hand - which some people use at football matches - they made a rasping, grinding noise, that could frighten anything away.

"Make as much noise as you can," father instructed, and for once we were more than happy to oblige!

"Get your hair covered," mother was told, and she quickly

fetched hats out for all of us.

We didn't have long to wait!

Soon we could see the swarm, high up in the sky. The sky was black with them, and you could hear the whirring of their wings. Like a big gathering cloud they blotted out everything... there must have been millions of them!

"Light the fires." father ordered, and soon fires were blazing up and down the length and breadth of the pathways between the vegetables. Smoke billowing up from dozens of different places, making our eyes water and our noses run!

"Everyone get ready, here they come." And, even before he'd finished speaking, we saw hundreds of the creatures dropping out of the sky. The noise they made was eerie! Their yellowy, green bodies with great big bulging eyes and long legs made them look evil!

Beating our tins and the noisy rattlers like crazy - our watery eyes seeing twice as many of the creatures - we all ran up and down the garden paths, treading on the insects that were already crawling along, father - in his army ten boots stamping on them like some demented thing. The poor mali in his bare feet trying to do his best, by picking them up and placing them in a bucket of some mixture my father had concocted... suddenly they were in our faces and hair, clinging to our clothes, and swarming over the lovely luscious vegetation that had been grown so lovingly by my father and the mali... the whole place was absolutely crawling with them.

They must have had a special call to let the others know too, as more and more seem to arrive as if one of them had sent word on ahead.

"Come on down! There's a lovely bit of grub down here. Just follow your noses."

Every bit of greenery was covered in those bug-eyed monsters, chomping away.

We must have gone mad for about half an hour or more - who was counting? But we were fighting a losing battle! The ground was covered by the crawling, hopping bugs; all making for the nearest bit of greenery.

"Everyone indoors," father finally shouted, knowing when he'd been beaten, so we beat the things off each other and retreated inside to watch from the safety of our bungalow. Watching helplessly as the locusts consumed every stick of vegetation they could get their teeth into. We were all tired and weary from our marathon fight against the advancing enemy. The servants probably thought the pagli sahib was doing the 'King Canute' thing, or the Indian equivalent!

Within a few hours the garden looked like it had never been there! Plants had been stripped clean of leaves, and as the fires died down, you could hear popping noises as some of the locusts wandered into the embers. It was amazing that these little creatures had been able to eat so much in such a very short time.

Father had to keep a stiff upper lip that day, and I saw our mother gently take him by the hand as she consoled him, the loss of his beautiful garden, and all his vegetables, being hard to take. Mothers front garden had fared no better, the locusts had done a good job there, too.

Funnily enough, I cannot remember another swarm of locusts while we lived there.

My biggest pet hate of course, was lice! No matter how clean my hair was, I would somehow manage to attract those pesky things!

I was at the local day-school at the time, before my stint at boarding school and although all the parents were quite fastidious with their children, there was always one child that brought the 'things' along! Being kids, we'd go into a huddle - our hair touching - and hey presto, before you knew it you were scratching your head furiously. So mother used to get the nit-comb out as soon as we came home from school.

I had to kneel down - my head on a large square of white cloth - covering my mother's knees, as she combed through my hair. I was always squirming about, in tears, as that comb pulled every hair of my head, scratching my scalp raw. If mother found anything at all, it was 'the only option'. My hair was doused in kerosene, a stinking, vile concoction that was intended for starting fires!

My poor scalp would burn where the comb had scratched, and my eyes would water continuously. But regardless of discomfort, I was made to wait the required time for the horrible stuff before it was washed off. Then several washes later - hopefully with the lice long dead - my hair still smelt terrible. It seemed like ages until I lost the smell of the kerosene from my nostrils.

Happy were the days the nit-comb failed to turn up nary a one of those little 'burrowers'. But why it was always me that got the dratted things I'll never know! My brothers or sister always seemed to be completely free of the odious creatures.

CHAPTER TWENTY-FIVE

Zut! And the results!

Father did like a wee dram, or three, of an evening, so you won't be surprised to read about some of the antics he got up to when he'd imbibed the odd 'one over the top'.

The 'local' brew he liked and drank from choice, was made in one of the breweries way out in the countryside of Ajmer; probably, because if it had been any nearer, the fumes emanating from there would have got the whole town drunk!

Father got his 'brew', which we referred to as 'Zut', in a couple of large glass bottles; it had the strength of more than 150% proof! The mixture was lethal! It could have been used for aviation fuel! So it was a good thing plastic hadn't been invented in those days. I'm sure it would have melted the bottles!

I'm not sure how he actually obtained this alcoholic drink, I only know that regular as clockwork and after sundown, he would sit - a smile of utter contentment on his face - as he sipped the colourless liquid. Getting more and more genial as the evening progressed!

And thus he'd sit, until dinner was served.

No one went near him for the first half an hour at least. We all knew the drill by now! And mostly good things came about after dinner. Like the aforesaid picnics etc. So, if any of us had been stupid enough to have done something wrong, we gave him a wide berth until around evening dinner! Especially if he'd come home to find something had been broken or even worse... one of us kids had been into his precious garden to steal the unripe fruit off his trees!

I swear he counted those guavas or pomegranates! But more likely, it was the 'evidence' of the bitten-into and discarded fruit. We hadn't the sense to hide the fruit we'd tried; and finding it not to our taste - probably because it was still quite green and sour - we'd just throw it away, and try another... and so on!

As an adult now, I fully understand his getting mad at us, I mean, what a dreadful waste! But then children do not have the logic of adults! And when all the fruit ripened on all the trees - as they did - there was so much we just 'gave' most of it away. That was after my mother had turned the guavas into 'guava jelly' and 'guava jam'.

Just thinking of that lovely sweetly scented fruit, with its white or pink insides full of seeds, makes me realise just how lucky we were to have whole trees of the stuff virtually 'to hand.' They are so expensive to buy nowadays!

Anyway - back to the drink. As I said, father did love his wee dram in the evenings. It was even taken whenever we went anywhere, Mother carrying it in a small bag. Father having gotten into the habit of having his usual dram or two after sun-down. So, wherever we went, the 'zut' came too! Especially if travelling away from home by train; just in case it couldn't be purchased anywhere else.

There was a ban on drinking in certain states, whisky and other alcoholic drinks being much more expensive if they were imported from England.

When we travelled anywhere by train, father was entitled to free first class travel.

"We'll have two tongas to take us to the Mail Train in the morning," father would order one of his chaprassies. In those days my father only owned a motorbike, so it was 'tonga style' transport for nearly everywhere we went, unless someone gave us a lift in one of the 'official' cars.

The tongas would be at our bungalow in plenty of time to allow us to drive leisurely to the railway station.

Once there it sounded as if all hell had broken loose!

Hundreds of people mingled outside and inside the railway station, with increasing numbers coming and going.

Shouts of "Carry your bags sahib?" from the red-turbaned certified baggage handlers - wearing brass numbers as proof of identity - would precede an onslaught from them as they converged on the occupants of the tongas. Offering to carry the sleeping bags and other travel bags we had brought along; dozens of arms reaching out to grab a piece of luggage.

"Stop!" Father would command and the tone of his voice brooked no 'junter-munter' (nonsense). He'd choose one man with a small cart, and supervise the loading, leaving my mother and us to follow behind. Then he'd stride off to the Station Masters office, returning with no less than the important man himself.

The Station Master would then escort us to the reserved railway carriage, personally placing the small slip of paper which said 'RESERVED' in large letters inside the slot by the door. Of course by this time the engine driver and the guards would all be hovering nearby, making sure their 'boss' could see they were all doing their jobs.

"See that this coach is kept under surveillance," the Station Master would order one of the guards; who would throw a smart salute to both the Station Master and my father, as our luggage was put aboard. The rolled-up bedding in their canvas outer casings lifted up onto the overhead luggage racks. The Station Master would then salute my father saying..." Please let me know if there is anything I may do for you sir." And father would return the salute – thank the man for all his help, and shake hands; making sure he had a piece of rolled-up paper money ready to palm into the man's hand.

Well if you want first class service, you have to pay for it don't you think?

Anyway in those days it was 'expected'. It was all back-handers!

We were always allocated a whole compartment to ourselves! This had ample seating for four or more, with two overhead bunks that could be pulled down when required. There was also a tiny toilet, cum wash room in an adjoining compartment too. When you looked down into the toilet, you could actually see the ground flying past underneath! Everything you did, like urinating or the other, fell straight onto the chuckies between the railway lines.

Of course, you weren't supposed to use the toilet when the train was at a station, no matter how much you wanted to, even though some of the stops were half an hour or more!

When mother felt like a cup of tea, the engine driver of our train always provided plenty of boiling water from his engine; his assistant trailing along the carriages with a jug of steaming hot water.

With train journeys in India taking days to complete, one of these 'larger' coaches was essential for comfort, but when my eldest brother and sister were away at boarding school the one train compartment was more than adequate for four people; my brother Billy and I quickly 'bagging' the top bunks.

We always took our own bed linen, pillows and blankets, which were placed inside long canvas bags - already made up - so we only had to undo the leather straps holding the rolled-up bedding together and spread it out on the bunks. It was great fun... at least for us kids anyway.

My brother and I would be up at the windows, watching the melee going on outside on the platform. It looked as if the whole country was ready to travel with us that day. It was always the same each time we went by train! Every day there seemed to be people travelling about.

There was always much shouting and gesticulation from the people at any of the stations we went to, and those we passed on our way through, every passenger seemingly had some difficulty in trying to board the trains. The people already occupying the coaches, tried to stop any more people from entering their space claiming the compartment was already full to capacity, the voices of angry passengers trying to gain access to carriages, and the shouts of vendors, selling their wares reaching a crescendo, as they shouted to be heard.

"Chai, chai!" the vendors shouted, as they hawked tea and other morsels to the captive passengers aboard the trains; pushing small trolleys of steaming tea canisters and mounds of cups and saucers, which would be hurriedly collected even as the train pulled out of the station, little brown arms reached through the open windows and doors of the compartments as they urged the clients to finish their tea and return the crockery.

Sometimes, when the tea boy hadn't timed his descent from the train as it thundered out of the station, he would be forced to stay on until the next stop... and catch the returning train, with the treasured cups.

Luckily, most Indians were obliging enough to finish their tea in plenty of time; although many of them took their tea in some of the small cullards, which could be disposed of through an open window.

There was always a great deal of spitting and 'hawking', of another kind, too, even with huge notices up everywhere written both in Hindi, Urdu and English. Promising the culprits hefty fines if they did not conform to the rules! Spitting was an Indian past-time. What with the chewing of paan and beetle nut! Great splashes of red stained the roads and pathways where the red liquid had been 'squirted' out from between teeth.

Probably why the stations all had notices up saying 'NO SPITTING ALLOWED'.

With trains arriving and departing from other platforms, there were always people running about in a panic... having gotten onto the wrong platform, mad dashes over the edges of the platforms and over the lines - fraught with danger - as they desperately took short-cuts to their respective trains. The guards shouting at them as they ran, literally into the path of the huge locomotives which luckily for them was slowing down as it came into the station.

One day, a particularly frail old lady's son was having some difficulty in getting his mother into the adjoining carriage, and mother could not bear the agony any longer!

"Do you think we should offer that old lady a place in our carriage?" mother said, "It does seem as if the train is over-full today?"

"Are you mad?" father replied, "Let one in, and you might as well leave the carriage yourself! We'd soon be overrun!" Mother knew when she was beaten. "Besides, I've already booked this coach for us as there are only four bunks here, where do you suggest we get another bunk from?" And father would pull down the blinds, and leave the guard outside to deal with the matter.

Soon, the train whistle sounded... loud and clear... nothing was allowed to delay the Mail Train. Peeping out, there was no sign of the frail old lady, so we assumed she had managed to get on somewhere in the end!

"See I told you the matter could be resolved," father said, but you could tell he was secretly pleased. He wasn't really as mean as he pretended to be. The guard would wave his flag, and the engine driver would give a long loud blast of the whistle, to let everyone know the train was departing. With a sudden jerk and judder, our train would begin its journey. The engine huffing and puffing as the steam came rushing out under the engine wheels, the massive engine doing its best to get the wheels turning; then with a grinding and squealing as the huge locomotive took up the weight of several carriages and hundreds of passengers plus the 'mail', the wheels turned and the train slowly pulled out of the station, the vendors still shouting their wares to the departing occupants on board.

Sneaking looks out of the side of the blinds, we could still see people huffing and puffing as they tried to board the moving train; there would be no 'clingers-on' allowed on the outside of this train. This was the 'The Mail Train'. A very 'fast beast' indeed; travelling at over one hundred miles an hour at its optimum speed. So it would have been utter madness for anyone foolish enough to try and 'catch' a ride on the outside of this fast train.

Watching from the windows, my brother and I would be transfixed by the familiar scenery we passed, sometimes singing songs - at the top of our voices - as we let off our own steam; the train went right past our own bungalow sometimes. Children from rural country villages ran to wave to the trains passing - the children never having ridden on one of the trains themselves. Then, as the familiar gave way to the countryside and beyond, we listened to the sound of the wheels going 'clickety-clack, clickety-clack' over the railway lines, slowly lulled to sleep after our early start and the exhaustion of the day.

If we'd stayed at the open windows long enough, our faces and hands would get covered in black dust from the soot and debris emitted by the engine. But we loved those old steam trains, and our long journeys into yet another adventure!

Every station we stopped at, no matter what time of the day or night, even in the very heart of the country, heralded the arrival of young Indian boys and girls with small baskets of fresh produce, homemade sweet-meats, fruit and sticks of cut sugar-cane and the usual 'Chai-wallahs'. Even though some of the smaller stops only warranted a very short stop of fifteen minutes. With just this train going through, the poor urchins had to do some fast and furious selling. And as the night wore on and the passengers slept, the vendors at stations where we stopped tried to keep their voices at a lower level to let people rest. Sometimes when I woke in the night it was because the train had stopped at yet another station. I would be able to hear the sounds of vendors calling out their wares in softer tones, with the muted conversation of passengers buying or just stretching their legs outside on the platform. Of course I had to look out to see what was going on, but I'd soon nod off again once the train started to move.

Father liked to stretch his legs sometimes too; going for a brisk walk along the length of the platforms. Then, when the trains whistle sounded, and he was nowhere to be seen on the platform, we would be really worried in case he had been left behind, although he nearly always made it back in time.

Except for one time when he'd left it a bit too late and the train pulled out of the station, and he still hadn't shown up. Billy and I craned our necks out of the windows looking for him as the train slowly pulled out of the station, but there was no sign of father anywhere! We all thought he'd been left behind, so it was a great relief when he came back to our compartment at the following stop, an hour or so's journey away. Mother was furious, and told him off in no uncertain terms for worrying us all.

With our train journeys sometimes literally taking days, we ate in some of the station restaurants; father asking the station master to wire on ahead to the next biggest station to order a meal; which would be ready and waiting when we arrived there.

With the stops being anything from fifteen to thirty minutes, we had ample time to eat, and return replenished to our own compartment, before the whistle to 'board' blew. And as we knew the train driver was also taking a well-earned break, we knew the train wasn't going anywhere!

Once, coming home, our train reservations had got mixed up, and mother had to travel in a 'woman only' compartment. My brother and I were allowed to stay with her, my brother being quite young then. My father stayed in another compartment further down the train. But whenever the train stopped, father would stride over to our compartment to see how we were, and all the Indian women would pull the end of their saris over their faces; which was the custom for them.

He also came to get his wee dram... mother pouring a small measure of his zut out, which he would drink swiftly, before returning to his own compartment. The two of them having decided it was better for my mother to keep the small bottle of 'zut' in her possession; probably because she didn't trust him not to finish it all off in one go!

After a couple of stops, with father duly getting a nip each time, one of the Indian women became curious.

"What is it the sahib is drinking?" she asked.

Never sure which of the women in the compartment was against alcohol, mother quickly said... "Oh, he comes to take his medicine."

"Truly, the sahib is such a good man to take his medicine without any fuss, memsahib. My own husband makes such faces and refuses whenever I want to give him a dose of castor oil."

"Will you please stop looking so pleased with yourself when you come for a drink Arthur," mother admonished father on his next visit. "I've just told them you are coming to take your medicine." So my father was obliged to pull faces, and look as if the 'medicine' he was taking was now beginning to get to him.

Of course, my parents had a good old laugh about it later on.

One of the other times my father had had 'one over the eight' was when a neighbour had called in one evening.

Mr Peacock lived just down the road from us, and also worked at the Carriage & Wagon Workshops. We kids were great friends of his children, and often played at each others houses. They were a large 'fun' family, with swings, acrobatic rings, parallel bars and slides taking up their compound; Mr Peacock not as keen on gardening as my father.

The two men had a convivial evening together on the back veranda in the cool of the evening, until my mother; fed up with listening to yet more boring talk of 'work' decided she would call it a day.

Bidding the men good night, she left them to finish their conversation and drinks. After all, Mr Peacock didn't have far to go.

She later recounted that she must have dropped off as she listened to the hum of their voices outside on the veranda. When she awoke a couple of hours later, she realised my father had still not come to bed. Hearing murmured voices on the other side of the house this time; she looked out of the window, and in the light of a very bright moon, perceived the two men at our front gate.

She couldn't hear what was being said, but assumed they were bidding each other good night, so went back to bed and fell asleep. Waking much later to find my father had still not come to bed! Slipping on her dressing gown, she walked through to the front veranda, and saw the two men walking back along the road - their voices carrying as they strolled along from the direction of Mr Peacock's house! She was baffled, and decided to wait until the men eventually reached our front gate.

She watched them shake hands and thought - oh good! It wouldn't be long before my father came in!

But listening closely she was able to hear...

"That was decent of you to see me home Robert," my father said to his friend.

"Not at all dear chap, happy to do it," replied Mr Peacock.

Thank goodness for that, thought mother, and was just about to go back to bed, when she heard... "Are you okay to go back home?" Father's very slurred accent came to my mother, who by now was thoroughly confused.

"Certainly old chap" coming from a very drunk Mr Peacock.

"Well, I'll just make certain and walk you back," father gallantly offered. Soon, the two men were stumbling back along the road towards Peacock's house.

Glancing at the clock, mother saw it was now nearly two in the morning! So she put on a pair of shoes and slipped on some clothes. After all, a lady couldn't be seen in her night attire! She then waited for her husband to return.

Sure enough, after about fifteen minutes the two men arrived back at our gates.

They had been walking each other home for the best part of the night!

She hauled my father indoors, and told a thoroughly confused Mr Peacock sweetly that she was sure he could find his own way home.

Regaling her friends for years afterwards with the story of the two men seeing each other home until the wee small hours!

At one time, there had been quite a lot of pilfering going on from the Carriage & Wagon Workshops. Neither the police, nor the internal affairs people were any the wiser as to how the goods were being taken, but father was determined to put a stop to it once and for all. Deciding he'd try to catch the crooks red-handed. With the help of my mother, he dressed up as an Indian beggar; in ragged clothing and a big turban round his head; blackened his face with boot-polish, then took himself off to the side of the Carriage & Wagon Workshops where he found a suitable place to sit and watch. Beggars were plentiful and there were so many of them about, that no one would take any notice of one more!

Father was certain this was where the stolen goods were being taken from, or thrown over the high wall by 'insiders'. The position he'd chosen gave him a good view of everything at the side of the workshops, so he sat down against some logs to wait.

His Jemadhar (Indian Officer) and second in command, was hiding nearby; just in case the sahib got himself into any trouble and required help.

It was a busy road, and even at this late hour there were many people passing. To keep occupied and to keep out the cold, father took a swift nip from the small bottle of grog he'd taken along, and was beginning to feel quite merry as the time passed.

A few people walked past on their way home, calling out "Goodnight Fisher sahib" but nothing untoward happened, and by three in the morning father was snoring his head off!

The Jemadhar decided it was time to take the sahib back home. Waking father, the Jemadhar said he'd take the second watch, persuading my father to go home. The man having to help with getting father back home as he was all over the place!

"Thank you Jemadhar for bringing the sahib home, he didn't catch anyone then," mother said with a chuckle, seeing the state father was in.

"No memsahib. I think the game was surely up right from the start - even before the sahib drank his sharrup" (grog). The man hesitated, not wanting to give his sahib away, but knowing the memsahib was no fool either.

"The disguise was excellent, but not good enough for all those budmashes, (baddies) for everyone that went past the sahib was saying... "Good night Fisher sahib."

"But how could they have known it was him, his disguise was good," mother queried?

"As I said memsahib, the sahib's disguise was very good," the Jemadhar said with a smile. "But have you yourself ever seen an Indian with such blue eyes?"

CHAPTER TWENTY-SIX

The Sacred Groves

The people of India have always believed trees to be the abode of gods and ancestral spirits, so there must have been hundreds of trees full of spirits in the sacred groves all over India.

The 'looking after' of the Sacred Groves nature conservation at its very best; something that has been practised in India since the beginning of time; ecology a very important part of the ancient Hindu culture. Although 'Sacred Groves' are to be found all over the world as well.

We're talking ecology on a grand scale!

Generation after generation of villagers and tribes-people have looked after these 'tracts' of land, passing down their religious beliefs about the land they will continue to protect for hundreds of years to come.

These tracts are a form of 'Ethno' forestry, but without writing a complete thesis on the subject - which I would be unable to do anyway - I can only speak of the ones near where we used to live in Rajasthan.

To simplify the subject we need to think of the sacred groves like botanical gardens where all kinds of wonderful trees are grown and looked after with great care and attention. But unlike botanical gardens, these forests and tracts of land have not had the trees 'planted' there for a purpose. These trees and plants and the diverse wildlife they sustain have been growing in the 'sacred groves' for hundreds of years. Ancient trees growing in their natural habitat for decades; the protected species of plants, trees, and the animals they sustain, along with other life-forms; all living in and among the fertile land to a ripe old age - unless they venture out from their wonderful ecological abode.

No pesticides are ever allowed to be used here!

Because these forests are 'sacred' the people living in and around them treat the forest and its inhabitants with great respect. None of the animals are ever harmed, and the trees and plants are left to flourish without harm or hindrance. The villagers are not allowed to tear down branches or chop wood from these forests, only kindling that has fallen to the ground can be gathered. Ripe fruits can be eaten too, and wood for temples or other religious buildings can be used sparingly.

There are many benefits to be had from living near these 'sacred groves'. Plants in the groves are said to increase the quality of oxygen in the village atmosphere; so the humidity and the cool atmosphere can be enjoyed by the people living there. The plants absorb dust, so the grove acts as the lungs of the village too.

Other advantages can be found, like the ancient remedies derived from trees and plants grown in these forests, used for aeons in the making of ayurvedic medicines; with new and exciting medicinal cures still being found today in some of the protected species of trees and plants.

Some of the plants and animals thought to be extinct have been found in these 'protected' areas, with butterflies, insects and other creatures being added to the growing list of 'things' discovered recently. Who knows... we might yet find that 'elixir of life' that has eluded us from time immemorial! Or at least find the cure for the common cold?

There are literally thousands of 'forest dwellers' and 'keepers of the forest' all over the world who for centuries have lived in and taken care of these natural forests. Knowing that if something is 'taken' from the forest, and not replaced, the forest will cease to exist in time. The trees not only giving shade, but oxygen to the world on a grand scale.

So the destruction of trees in the 'clearings' and 'burnings' that are now taking place along the Amazon and elsewhere in the world does much damage to the ecosystems that benefit mankind everywhere.

Not much is known about the people of the Bhill tribe who live in and around the foothills of the Aravalli Hills. These 'forest dwellers,' are said to be descendants of the Rajputs. Legend has it, that one of the Rajput Kings formed an alliance with a beautiful woman of the Bhill tribe. The subsequent marriage and offspring began yet another offshoot of the Bhill tribe, so for generation after generation the Rajputs would only allow people of the Bhill tribe to be treated on a par with their rulers, a Bhill tribesman allowed to be the right-hand men to the ruling classes.

Although the pure Bhill is today much of what he has always been; a savage forest dweller. They are a stunted race, but well-built, active and strong and quite black in colour! They generally have high cheek-bones, wide nostrils, broad noses and coarse features. But they also have a fine sense of humour!

The women had many more tattoos done on their bodies and faces than the men... perhaps because they can stand the pain better?

All over India the Sacred Groves are looked after by different tribes, all diligently minding the land in their areas; generally some forested land in and around the hills. The tracts in Rajasthan called 'Orans' which have remained undefiled for hundreds of years. A special 'Kesar Chirkav' blessing; where saffron water is sprinkled over the forest, is religiously made, the tradition finding its origin from the Temple of 'Kesari yaji', a place of worship for the Bhill tribal community in the Udairpur District of Rajasthan.

The Bhill people who live on the foothills of the Aravalli Range are a proud and independent race. Many of them survived by making the small clay figures beloved by all Indians; for when their 'festivals' are celebrated. Brightly-painted figures of Gods and Goddesses, elephant headed figures, and dozens of others finding their way into the houses and shanties all over India.

The poorer Bhills live in make-shift dwellings that are washed away regularly by the monsoon floods every year. But still they return to live in the same place year after year - all intent on keeping the sacred forests or 'groves' safe for future generations.

Women of the Bhill tribe used to come down to Ajmer once a year to collect coal-dust from the homes of the Europeans. Probably to mix with other things and use as fuel for cooking, this of course could have been the forerunner to the famous 'Bronski-Bullets' we were all introduced to in the fifties and sixties?

Many of the householders were only too pleased to have their coal-houses cleaned out. Ours being a sixteen foot square building, where the women would squat inside - noses, mouths and hair covered - as they sieved through the contents of our coal-house. They only took the dust, leaving the coal neatly piled to one side. The coal dust must have been suffocating in that confined space, because when they finally emerged from the godown, they would be covered in layers of coal-dust; their clothes, hair and faces now blackened by dust. But they remained ever jovial, even after their arduous task. The whites of their eyes and their teeth showing as they laughed and joked amongst themselves.

Sometimes, the women would splash a little water over their faces; taken from the hodhi to clean some of the grime off their faces; wiping the water off with the end of their sari's; which were coated in coal dust, so it made them look even worse! They'd all fall about laughing, knowing they all looked equally dirty, their laughing eyes and teeth flashing as they salaamed their thanks.

I often wondered if they jumped into some stream or river to wash off the excess coal dust off themselves and their clothes.

Talk about happiness in the face of adversity!

Some of the plants and trees in India considered sacred are the Tulsi, the sacred basil, revered for its medicinal and spiritual value. The leaves are a remedy for coughs, and if eaten after meals can assist digestion. Put into cooked food or water it can prevent spoiling. The Tulsi plant is believed to be an antidote to snake venom; and when burnt repels insects. It is also said to be so pure, that the slightest pollution can kill it.

The Bel tree - also known as 'bilva' or 'wood apple' is a medium sized deciduous tree. It has thorny branches and trifoliate leaves, and its fruit are large and round with a greenish-grey woody shell. The Bel also has medicinal properties. A poultice can be made for the eyes, and are good for diabetes, and can reduce fever. The wood of the Bel tree is never used as ordinary firewood for cooking purposes, and only allowed for sacrificial fires.

The Peepul is another sacred tree. It grows quite tall, and its heart-shaped leaves have long tapering tips which shiver and rustle in the slightest wind. The Peepul is used extensively in Ayurveda.

Ayurveda or health and healing, the word 'ayus' meaning 'long life,' and 'veda' meaning 'knowledge', so the science of Long Life. Ayurveda deals with the measures of healthy living, along with therapeutic measures that relate to physical, mental, social and spiritual harmony. Ayurvedic medicines are widely used today for all sorts of ailments.

The bark of the Peepul tree yields tannin which is used in

treating leather, while its leaves, when heated with ghee, are applied to cure wounds. Vishnu is believed to have been born under the Peepul tree, and the gods are said to hold their councils under this tree, so it is associated with spiritual understanding. It is said that Krishna (Supreme Person and highest God) died underneath a Peepul tree. The cutting down of this tree would be a sin equivalent to killing a Brahmin, one of the five deadly sins of Panchapataka.

The goddess Lakshmi - known also as the goddess of wealth, light, wisdom and fortune, as well as luck, beauty and fertility - is believed to inhabit the Peepul tree on a Saturday. So it is considered safe to touch the tree then. Women ask the tree to bless them with a son by tying a red thread or red cloth round its trunk or on its branches.

Another practice to repel bad luck is the marrying of the Peepul and Neem trees, the fruit of the Neem representing the Shivalinga (male) with the leaf of the Yoni, the power of the female. After the ceremony, the villagers circle the trees to rid themselves of their sins, and any bad luck that may be hanging around their village.

The Peepul tree is also sacred to the Buddhists, because the Buddha is believed to have attained enlightenment under it; and hence it is known as the 'Bodhi' tree or tree of enlightenment.

Palms of all kinds are sacred; some of them living more than a 100 years. Dating back to the age of the reptiles, there are more than 2,800 kinds of palms, which vary in size, leaves, flowers and fruit. Palms provide ornamentation, shade, and building materials, fibres for making ropes and brooms and for making watertight ships made from palm. Strips of leaves are woven into mats, hats and baskets. The oil palm provides oil for food and lighting. The 'Palmyra' palms sugary sap is used in foods, drinks and intoxicating beverages, while the seeds are used for buttons and carving. The coconut palm gives rich fruit which is used for many purposes like cakes, soap, salad oils etc. Other palms are the date palm, and the cabbage palm.

Palm trees have been sacred since the Christians of Jerusalem spread the palm branches before Jesus during the last days of the Crucifixion.

The Neem is one of three most sacred trees in India. It is used against a multitude of diseases, and has a variety of uses. Accordingly, it is called 'Arishta' in Sanskrit, meaning 'Healer of

Diseases,' and 'Mwarubaini' in Swahili, meaning 'Healer of Forty Sicknesses'. It is a tall, evergreen tree, with small bright green leaves which have a bitter taste if chewed. Pretty, small, white flowers turn into fruit and go from green to a bright ripe yellow; the sweet sticky pods attracting birds in their hundreds.

Being evergreen, the tree gives welcome shelter from the hot sun, and it is said that the Neem tree once sheltered 'Surya' the Sun God from demons, according to Brahma. It is also said to be sacred, because six goddesses live in it. The presence of these goddesses makes the Neem a test of truth, for if any should utter falsehoods beneath the Neem tree, they will fall violently ill.

Ah-ha, so that's where I went wrong? Think about all that time I spent playing underneath our Neem trees! And all the lies I told! Goodness I'm glad to still be alive!

The Neem tree is cherished as much for its shade, as its medicinal properties. The leaves have insecticidal and antiseptic properties. A Neem twig makes a very effective toothbrush, as its fibres clean, and its juice works as both mouth freshener and a germ-killing dentifrice. Drinking water infused with Neem leaves is said to purify the blood and heal the skin afflicted with measles and chicken-pox sores. Even now, the Neem is at the centre of a global controversy regarding ownership over its use. There is talk of 'biopiracy' and well there might be, as the Neem is well known for its medicinal properties; and the ailments it is effective against are: constipation, diarrhoea, indigestion, nausea, malaria, fever, haemorrhoids, headaches, ear, eye, and respiratory disorders in children, rheumatism, chronic syphilitic sores, ringworm, scabies, and epitasis. It is used to relieve boils, suppress bile and eliminate intestinal worms and phlegm, diabetes, and in blood purification... phew!

But even more, the Neem is known for its biopesticidal properties. Just one of the active ingredients in this species is highly effective against 200 species of insects; including mites, nematodes, fungi, bacteria and viruses. Every day, new remedies are being found using different properties of the Neem Tree. There is big money to be made from medicines and other pharmaceuticals. With Biotechnology the stream of technology that bases billions of pounds of profit from products derived from plants and trees, the fight goes on.

But let's close on a sweeter note, and talk about the Sandalwood tree, or 'Chandan' in Hindi; this evokes a world of ancient mystery, sanctity and devotion. It is most definitely a sacred tree!

Sandalwood is a fragrant wood and comes from evergreen trees which attain a height of forty to fifty feet, and a girth of three to eight feet. Sandalwood oil is most commonly used for incense, aromatherapy and perfume and is also used for fine woodworking, the perfumed wood holding its fragrance for centuries. It is considered an alternative medicine to bring one closer with the divine being, used primarily for Ayurvedic purposes and in treating anxiety. In Buddhism, sandalwood is said to transform one's desires and maintain a person's alertness while meditating.

To produce valuable Sandalwood commercially, with high levels of fragrance, the trees must be at least 40 years of age, but 80 years or above is preferred. The very whiff of Sandalwood is enough to conjure up pictures of harems and perfumed nights and the wood holds its divine fragrance forever.

All Sandalwood trees in India are government owned and their harvest is strictly controlled. Sandal essential oils prices have risen alarmingly in the last few years, with the Sandalwood from Mysore in India being generally considered to be of the highest quality available.

My mother used to have a small rosewood box lined with sandalwood for some of her precious jewels. It had the most wonderful carvings of roses and leaves over the top and sides. Over the years of handling the outside wood turned quite black in colour, but the smell when the box was opened was quite magical. It was the one thing we could never have to play with, and after her death the box just seemed to vanish! We know mother would never have parted with her precious little box, and although her jewellery came to light soon after, the box was never seen again!

CHAPTER TWENTY-SEVEN

Red Sails in the Sunset

I don't think my eldest brother Ernest never forgave our father for making him go into a military style boarding school - a sort of Boy Soldiers Academy; where the teachers gave the young men a sort of 'grounding' for life in the forces proper. The people running the establishment were nearly all ex-servicemen, so the regime was quite a tough one.

And Ernest just hated every minute of it!

'Mount Abu' - the place he was stationed at - was a beautiful Hill Station, situated at the highest point in the Aravalli Hills, and built on a plateau 1722 metres above sea level. It had everything... from rivers, lakes, waterfalls and evergreen forests, to an ideal climate. But the fact it was in one of the most beautiful spots in India didn't cut any ice with Ernest. He always complained, but only to my mother; and never when father was around.

He was a strong, handsome boy of fifteen or sixteen then, a lock of his dark hair always falling over one eye; giving him a rakish look. He was strong and broad-shouldered like his father, and the girls loved him! Although, at that time, he was far more interested in his food and whatever sports he could play.

With such a disparity in our ages, I never did find out much about his likes and dislikes, other than the times he was at home. Even then, he wasn't the easiest person to get along with.

The school at Mount Abu was quite a strict one, proficient in the teachings of all aspects of war, along with ordinary schooling too, which did not leave much time for enjoying other more frivolous, pastimes.

My eldest sister went to the sister school of St Mary's in Mount Abu.

When they came home for the holidays, Ernest would keep mother entranced with all he'd been up to. She in turn, delighted to have him back, would hang on to his every word, making sure he got all the foods he liked best.

"Fancy that," she was heard to say - several times, as he regaled her with tales of what had taken place at his 'camp.' The many tales of 'derring-do' exaggerated to the ninth degree, I've no doubt. But that was Ernest! Every time mother was about to leave the room, he would insist she remain to hear yet one more of his 'tales'. So she was forever being called back with "Mum, you've got to hear this," as he kept her enthralled with the entire goings on at Mt. Abu School. No one else was allowed any of the 'limelight' when Ernest was about. And he was indeed, very funny at times!

He had been allowed to bring his trumpet home, and would stand on the maidhan - the sound being much too loud anywhere near the bungalow - where he would give us his rendition of 'Reveille', and 'Lights Out'. The trumpet calls bringing others running out to see what all the 'tamasha' was about.

Ernest also had a habit of sleep-walking, especially if he'd been over-excited during the course of the day. Then sometimes - always after midnight it seemed - would get out of his bed... walk slowly towards my parents bedroom... and positioning himself by the foot of their bed, gave his rendition of a song called 'Red Sails In The Sunset' at the top of his voice.

After the first few times this happened, my father got quite annoyed at being woken out of his sleep; mother would silently slip out of bed and gently guide Ernest back to his own bed.

"This is getting quite ridiculous," said father, "Just tell him to go back to bed."

"He's sleep-walking Arthur," she'd say quietly. "You mustn't disturb him while he's still asleep." Apparently, being a trained nanny, she knew all about sleep-walkers and how best to deal with them. She would quietly lead Ernest back to his own bed, time and time again.

Of course, Ernest was known to repeat his operatic aria - several times during the same night - my father getting more and more irritated as the night wore on; mother just got up and led Ernest back to his bed once more.

It was always the same song too.

On waking next morning, Ernest said he couldn't remember anything, although I'm not at all sure about that. Feeling there was more to it than met the eye, with a sneaking feeling that his late-night carousing was in fact deliberate and more to do with getting back at his father for sending him away to that Boys Military School. The singing itself being nothing whatsoever to do with sleep-walking.

Funnily enough, these episodes only seemed to come on when it was getting to the end of his holiday, and before it was time to return to the hated school.

The whole family all dined together then, sitting round the big table for our evening meals. I was just five years old then, inquisitive eyes peering out from under a short fringe, as I sat at the table - cushion underneath me for added height - my legs swinging away as I could never sit entirely still.

It was always a formal meal, with my father at the head of the table and my mother sitting at the opposite end. I sat nearest my mother - so she could keep an eye on my 'eating' habits - with my sister on the other side next to me and our brothers sitting opposite us.

The protocol and serving of meals in our house, was always the same; the bearer offering the dish first to my mother, and then to my father. Then after they'd helped themselves, my sister was served; before my mother served me, and lastly my two brothers. The dishes - covered with lids - were then left in the middle of the table, should anyone require second helpings.

Now, I was either a very slow eater, or played about with my food, because before I would be about halfway through my meal, when my mother would be heard asking... "Would you like some more meat, Ernest?" Or it might be potatoes or vegetables, or whatever we were eating, my eldest brother having finished his plateful of food already.

Of course, he could not be seen to be actually asking for more! It was done much more subtly than that. As I got older, I realised there was a whole new language that was being used at our dining table. Without speaking at all, Ernest or my brother Billy could convey to my mother exactly what it was they wanted! Making sure my father was busy with his own meal, before catching mother's eye. Then, they would look from her to the dish sitting in the centre of the table, and back to his empty plate. Mother would then say, "Would you like some more meat?" curry, or whatever it was we were eating that night; without my father twigging what was going on. Born during the Victorian period and very strictly brought up, he didn't believe that children should speak unless spoken to, and certainly not at the table. Not even to ask for second helpings!

Of course, when I tried to send signals across the table I chose to try my father; after giving him the eyes this, and eyes that, he asked exasperatedly "Have you got something in your eye?" Swinging my legs ever faster I said... "No, but I'd like some more pudding please - couldn't you tell?"

Father was also able to put us kids completely off our meals sometimes, especially if it was a lovely fresh prawn curry. When the steaming dish was brought in, he'd say quite innocently... "Have I ever told you what the prawns feed on?" Of course, one of us invariably said, "what?" Forgetting about the many times we'd been duped. Then off he'd go, describing in great detail that prawns loved nothing better than eating 'dead men' that had drowned in the sea, with my mother trying to get him to shut up with one of her glares! Or sometimes just the word 'Arthur' with that special intonation in her voice that meant she was not pleased by what he was about to say.

We'd heard it many times before - with my father saying 'sorry', but when he'd had a glass or two, he seemed much more inclined to ignore it - it was like a game they played! You know... one taking the high ground!

We kids of course just pushed our plates away... saying... "We don't want any prawn curry," much to mum's annoyance. And father would pull the dish towards him saying, "Good, all the more for me then!"

Of course, being the youngest, I could do no wrong in my father's eyes according to my siblings, so whenever they wanted something... it had to be me who did the asking. Not that I was always successful.

But there was the one time when he would have given me anything at all. I must have been about six or seven at that time and was very ill indeed.

The doctors said it was diphtheria and as my temperature was very high and I was gasping for breath... they didn't hold out much hope for my recovery.

Anyway, the kind doctors shook their heads, and said... "Give her anything she wants, it's just a matter of time," looking sadly, at my poor parents. They in turn, wanting to make the last days of my

219

life as happy as possible, asked me what I'd like most of all. Lying there in bed, all sweaty and hot, I'm sure I must have been delirious because all I could think of having was a pair of red sandals! I mean... unable to walk at that stage... and my first thoughts were - red sandals? So, with one of my parents hovering by my bedside, the other was dispatched to purchase the sandals; which were eventually obtained, but only after scouring every shoe shop in town.

They say I clutched at the red shoes to my bosom, smiled, and fell asleep.

My siblings were not impressed at my choice, and thought there were more important things I might have requested, deciding I was the answer to all their prayers!

"Ask for an aeroplane," whispered my younger brother next day.

"Say you want some tinned fruit," my sister cajoled.

Which I eventually managed to persuade my parents was what I wanted.

"She's asking for tinned fruit," beamed my father. "She must be feeling better."

"What sort of tinned fruit would you like?" mother asked.

"Peaches," I whispered back - already primed by my sister - and within the hour a tin of peaches had miraculously appeared.

Now this was no easy feat I'll have you know. Tinned fruit in those dim and dusty days were not so readily available then! So my tin was scrounged off someone who'd been saving it for that 'special occasion'.

My mother did her best to get a few of the moist bits past my dry, chapped lips, but I was too ill to appreciate all the effort that had gone into obtaining it at the time. The tins of IXL fruit from Australia were all huge ones at that time too, but my siblings had no trouble polishing off the remainder; my parents not really having much of an appetite at that time!

"Thanks for the peaches," Hazel said, and Billy whispered later. "Ask for ice-cream tomorrow."

Oh, they sure made the most of my illness, I can tell you! And even though the doctors hadn't counted on my determination to stay around to wear my red sandals, I eventually did.

Then there were the times father had to go to 'camp' as he called it. We knew it was something to do with army training and involved 'bivouacking' somewhere with a load of other army men for a few weeks or so. But more importantly, when he returned home he'd bring his chocolate rations home for us. With whoops of joy we would rummage through his bags until we found the lovely bars of chocolate. We would be given a whole bar each! Such extravagance! I mean, mother always 'rationed' our intake of sweets, so we only ever got two bits of chocolate at a time. Even at Christmas!

Not having seen each other for three or four weeks, the grown-ups had much to talk about, and we would be left to savour our bars of chocolate, the first few bits gobbled down as-quick-as-a-flash. Then, we'd try and make the rest last for as long as we could, by just leaving it to melt on our tongues, or nibbling away, taking miniscule bites all around the edges, watching the rest of the bar getting smaller and smaller. The smell would waft slowly up our nostrils, and the taste was sheer heaven!

No chocolate since then has ever tasted so good!

We loved playing marbles when we were children, as I loved the beautiful colours. We'd scoop out a small hole in the shade of the neem tree, and play 'marbles' for hours. Or at least until I'd won a whole pocketful from my brother Billy! And they weren't all obtained fairly either! My brother being so trusting! I'd wait until he'd gone inside to spend a penny, and 'appropriate' a couple of marbles he'd left behind.

Well, he could hardly go off to spend a penny with his trouser pockets bulging with marbles, could he?

One day, my sister informed us that she knew where she could find buried treasure! My younger brother and I were so excited. "Show us, please show us!" we begged her, so she would oblige, digging up a few coins from the loose soil under the neem tree.

"That's brilliant!" we enthused, thinking we'd all soon be as rich as Croesus!

Hazel proudly took us from one site to another; slowly unearthing small amounts of money, and our excitement grew and grew. We were so sure she'd hit on the formula for getting rich quick!

"You clever thing!" we exclaimed for the umpteenth time, after more money was turned up. "Show us how you do it?'

Then mother called us in for lunch.

"Come in and get your hands washed," mother called, "lunch is ready."

"Oh blast and bugger!" I exclaimed, much to Billy's disgust, who never swore. And Hazel walloped me once more on my leg. Something I was becoming used to!

"I'll tell mum you were swearing," she threatened, but when she saw my lower lip start to quiver, she'd relent, "...and don't say anything about finding the money," Hazel warned us, and we silently trooped in to wash our hands ready for lunch.

Gobbling our lunch that day with added speed, brought a reproach from mother about 'not making little piggies of ourselves,' so we tried to do our best to eat a little more slowly, every mouthful feeling like a shovel-full. But eventually we were done, returning to the 'dig' as soon as possible. But something had gone drastically wrong! Hazel had lost her ability to 'find' any more money! She ran from one side of the compound to the other getting more and more frantic each time she dug the soil away to find... nothing! She finally burst into tears.

"Don't worry," we assured her, "we don't really want to be very rich," which only made her cry even more. It was some time later that she finally came clean; she had 'buried' the small coins herself, marking out the spots with a few drops of water so she could identify the actual site later on, but hadn't bargained on the sun drying up the water!

While we'd been indoors having lunch, the sun had sucked up any moisture there was, leaving no trace of the tell-tale spots of water under which the money lay, so Hazel lost the best part of the pocket money that she'd saved up.

I've often wondered if some other child playing there in later years found the buried treasure, and if anyone discovered the big hole that my father had dug under the neem tree at the side of our bungalow?

It was during the Second World War; which seemed to be getting nearer to us in India; and father thought it would be just a matter of time before it reached our shores in Ajmer. "It's definitely getting nearer," he insisted, as he listened to the news on his wireless. The news from 'home' was a must each and every day; after much twiddling the knobs on the set... until he'd got rid of the hissing and screeching noises he'd manage to get 'tuned' in. Then, ear glued to the wireless, he'd relay the latest news about the war.

"They've bombed London again," he'd tell mother, his voice full of gloom. "Won't be long before they start flying those blinking planes over here." Not knowing I'd overheard every word. Mother hadn't wanted us kids worried about the war, but personally I couldn't wait for the war to come! After all the 'happenings' in England, at last we too were going to be involved!

We'd heard about the fall of Singapore, and the fighting in Burma, so had expected to see a bit of activity in India. Now the building of a bunker was all the proof we needed.

Father wandered around the garden looking for just the right place to site the 'bunker' and he was soon pulling a piece of string from his pocket.

"This will be the ideal spot," he declared. Then with the aid of wooden pegs, he marked out the area to be dug, which was at the side of the bungalow underneath a neem tree; giving final instructions to the mali.

It took several days, with the poor man carrying basketfuls of soil to deposit around the garden, the hole getting deeper and deeper as father changed the depth when he thought it insufficient. I thought we'd probably come out at the other side of the world if the mali continued going!

Then at last, it was ready.

The hole had steps leading down to the main body - a long ten foot deep, by about three feet wide trench, which was narrower towards the steps. There were square holes cut into the sides for storage purposes, and even a small round hole - for toilet purposes - but only if we were forced to stay in hiding for several days.

All that was left to be done was the roof; for this father had ordered some corrugated iron sheeting lengths, and these were covered with sand-bags. It all looked quite 'pukka'.

"I do hope we never have to spend too long down there," mother remarked as she gazed down into the now dark bowels of the earth, but father was unable to persuade her to 'try it out for size'.

"If you think I'm going to go down into that thing, you've got another think coming," she declared, as she headed back to the house.

We kids of course couldn't wait to try it out.

Of course the bunker had to have fresh water and enough rations for us to live on, if we were to be confined there for days on end. So father arranged for special water and food containers. I think he quite liked the idea of being 'included' in the war too. He was leaving nothing to chance! The only thing that really worried him was the thought of his grog factory getting a direct hit. Well I did hear my mother say that to a very close friend of hers!

But it was not to be!

In time the novelty of having his very own bunker - with the war no nearer - made father less interested in it, and I had a new little 'home' of my own to play in; the fact that it was deep down in the earth, and a trap for every creepy crawly, like snakes or other biting bugs, didn't worry me in the least.

Luckily, we never needed the bunker for ourselves, and after the war, my father decided to return the compound to its original state.

I was away at boarding school at the time, and cried my eyes out when I came home for the holidays to find the hole had been filled in. Partly because I was sure I'd left some of my most precious possessions down there in the 'storage' holes, but I'd also lost my favourite hidey-hole. I mean, it was the last place my mother would come into, so a very good place to hide away in when I'd 'blotted' my copy-book. Which I was always doing!

Any future excavations done there will no doubt thoroughly confuse the diggers when they find my possessions deep in the earth. They will probably think they've struck buried treasure!

CHAPTER TWENTY-EIGHT

Boarding school!

After preparatory school, I was sent to the St. Mary's Convent school in Ajmer, to be taught by the nuns.

I was now a skinny little runt, but wiry enough to enjoy the games we played at P.E., chucking the 'bean bags' through our legs to the last girl in the line etc: I was good at most sports, but real crap when it came to ordinary lessons!

I got more raps on my knuckles, especially over needlework, than I care to remember, most of the nuns being quite strict. In fact, one or two of them were quite vicious! Even after my 'punishment' I'd end up standing outside the Reverend Mothers Office most days; which was at the end of a very long corridor.

Open arches to one side of the corridor led out onto tranquil gardens - which were beautifully kept - and were looked after by two nuns, whose sole job was to look after all the outside grounds surrounding the convent buildings, in between prayers of course! This included a large vegetable garden too; where they produced enough vegetables for themselves and about ten other nuns who lived in the convent buildings.

Of course, the gardens were out of bounds to the pupils. Can you imagine what would have happened if we'd been let into the garden with all those lovely red tomatoes, carrots and other delicious things? We hungry girls would have cleared everything much faster than any locusts, I can tell you.

I liked these two nuns, they always seemed quite happy - compared to some of the others - and could be seen on most days, digging, hoeing and doing all the heavy work between them; going into peals of laughter every so often, seemingly, unafraid of Reverend Mother. Both were German, and spoke to one another in their own language, but in broken English to the pupils.

They always seemed to be working in the gardens outside the dreaded office whenever I was going for punishment too, and would see me walk hesitantly towards the Mother Superiors door.

"Ach, wot haff you dun now?" the shorter of the two asked once.

"Made a mess of my sewing," I'd answered.

She said something in German to the taller nun, and they'd both tittered quietly.

"You are not li-kink the sow-ink?" She said, and I shook my head sadly.

"Ah so." she said kindly, giving me a little smile as if she understood.

I think somehow she, like me, wasn't all that keen on sewing, and knew the nun who took us for sewing was a bit of a tartar! Anyway, I could tell she felt sorry for me.

Knocking timidly on the Reverend Mothers door, I'd wait apprehensively, until I heard the Reverend Mother call "Enter."

She was a short, squat little figure wearing an immaculate habit of pale grey. Her little round face was pushed out from the tight snow-white wimple framing her face, her naturally pink cheeks glowing with health. Her black head cover always fell in equal lengths on either side of her face; covering her shoulders. She wore a big rosary on a long black cord around her waist; which hung down to about knee-length; and another one round her neck. She was obviously very devout, although I once caught a glimpse of her doing a little dance! There she was, pirouetting away in her room, as she hummed a tune! Having forgotten I was still waiting to see her. Of course, when she saw me with my mouth open, she pretended she had slipped accidentally? But I know what I saw! I think as a young girl she'd maybe wanted to be a dancer - and because she hadn't been good enough, had become a nun instead!

When she walked - she took quick little steps, her black well-polished shoes the smallest I'd ever seen on an adult! She must have worn a size two shoe?

I would open the door tentatively, and step into her neat little office. She was nearly always seated behind her desk - which was set at an angle facing the door in one corner - and would look up over the top of her little round wire-framed glasses, pressing her neck in a downward motion so as to be able to see over them.

"Aaah, Rosemary it's you again," she would sigh wearily, taking off her glasses to get a real good look at me. Or maybe because then, she wouldn't have to look at me? "What have you done this time?"

"Please Reverend Mother I was told to report to you because Sister Amy said I was talking in class." We always had to get the whole bit out to let her know what class you'd been in, and every misdemeanour had its own punishment. Even if you'd been caught uttering just one word! She never asked for our version of course, always believing the teachers version. Sometimes we were unfairly blamed!

My red knuckles - on both hands, which I was holding behind my back - were still smarting from the knocks Sister Amy had administered from the ruler she always carried; because I had not made my stitches smaller; and I didn't want the Reverend Mother to know I had already been punished for something else! My needlework could also get terribly dirty no matter how many times I washed my hands. So I'd get a rap on the knuckles for that too. I really think Sister Amy got a kick from battering us poor girls!

"H'mm, well wait outside until I can think of a suitable punishment," the Reverend Mother would say, eyeing me as if I were some sort of alien creature. So, closing the door quietly - I'd already made the mistake of shutting it noisily once before, and got three extra strokes of the cane - I'd go to stand in the corridor, not in the least surprised at having to wait outside her office, having waited there before. I think the waiting was all part and parcel of the punishment. Giving me that much longer to worry about what the punishment I would eventually get. The general punishment being three, four or five strokes of the cane on the palm of your hand. Although sometimes I'd wait perhaps fifteen minutes - hoping the Reverend Mother had forgotten all about me, and she would still give me the cane.

I think in my case she was running out of options!

As I said, some of the nuns were really sweet, but some were right Tartars!

There were a few teachers who weren't nuns, coming in daily to teach at the all-girls school; all of them kept on their toes by the Mother Superior, who was known to prowl the corridors of the school at times, listening out for troublesome pupils.

The door of the classroom would suddenly open, to reveal her standing there if the noise levels in the classroom were just that bit too high.

Immediately, there would be a scraping of chairs, as everyone - including the teacher - rose as one. No one ever sat back down unless they were told to do so. Sometimes, the Reverend Mother just wanted a quiet word with the teacher, but if the noise levels had been broken, she would face the class and just 'look' at us. She'd stand there, hands clasped together in front of her until every cough, splutter, giggle or word died on our lips. Then, she would say, 'Sooo... you can be quiet when you want to be then?' Her voice deadly calm - I'd never ever heard her voice raised - she'd then turn to the teacher and say very quietly... "If you have any further disturbance in your classroom, please send the miscreant to me." Then giving a slight nod of her head towards the teacher, and with a flurry of skirts, she was gone.

When I was younger, I often wondered what miscreant actually meant. In later life I discovered it can mean quite a number of things, so I suppose she covered the whole gamut by using the word 'miscreant'.

Some of the classrooms nowadays could do with a Mother Superior to control some of the more unruly kids and noisy behaviour that goes completely unchecked.

Before she went to boarding school, my sister was in one of the higher classes, and mixed with pupils of her own age, so I only got to see her at lunch time. Our school lunch was brought to us from home by one of our servants, carried in the 'Tiffin box' complete with tablecloth, napkins, plates, knives, forks, spoons, and drinking water; the food being kept hot in small round metal containers, which would be beautifully arranged on the table when we came out from our classes at lunch-time. Our servant waiting on us then sitting nearby until we'd finished eating. Then, he would put everything back into the 'Tiffin box' to take back home.

We always had a nice selection of food brought to school, but someone else's lunches always looked much more exciting! So we would do 'swopsies' much to the displeasure of our servant, who thought he would be blamed if we ended up with 'gyppy tummies'. Mostly we had to act with great decorum... as we never knew if we were being watched by the nuns.

When I was eleven, I was dispatched to boarding school. Complete with two sets of everything; and my name sewn into my clothes for added precaution. But found I had to wear the school issue uniform, and great big baggy navy knickers!

My school was a place called 'Barnes High School', in a place called Deolali (now called Devlali). This entailed a long overnight train journey from Ajmer to Bombay, then another shorter train journey from Bombay - or 'Mumbai' as it's now called - to Deolali station.

Yes, I know... everyone associates the name as synonymous with 'doolally', which is often used to describe madness. But Deloali really was the name of the 'PLACE'. And I still have one of my old exercise books with the name emblazoned across the front cover to prove it!

Deolali was not far from the port of Bombay, just a short train ride away. So it was used as a sort of 'holding bay' for troops who were sent there before continuing on to their real destinations; or kept there before being shipped home to Blighty.

It was a small one-horse town, the size of a matchbox. There wasn't very much they could do at these camps or accommodation, other than a small cinema and a few shops, the usual troop's canteen, and the heat. Hence the poor wretches were bored out of their tiny minds, and were said to go 'doolally,' while waiting to be dispatched wherever it was they were meant to be.

You see, there usually is a simple explanation for everything!

I was eleven years old, and very nervous as you'd expect, trying to look calm, when my heart was really in my boots at starting at this big school. It seemed so far from home now! Plus, one never knows what to expect at a new place either.

Would there be bullies there? Father had told me to remember my boxing if there were! "Hold your own," had been his advice. "Never let them know how frightened you are on the inside; always look as if you are in control." Such good advice when I'd been at home in my normal surroundings.

Now I was scared out of my wits! But a very sweet girl called Thelma came up to me and introduced herself. Then later on, she introduced me to the rest of the dormitory, everyone giving me a smile, and a hello. It was the start of a new term, so there were other new girls too, which made me feel a whole lot better.

'Barnes High School' sits atop a hill, and the Founders Day was in 1926. It used to be a co-educational school, and still is I think. A big 'Gate House Lodge' sat at the entrance to the school, and there was a long drive which led past the School Hospital building and sick bay on the right. The girls' dormitories faced that of the boys, but were separated by some quarter of a mile. Towards the right hand side - coming from the gate house - there were the classrooms, dining halls, and the younger children's dormitories.

All the children were allocated a 'house' and I was in Edith Cavell House; so we all wore red sashes for easier identification. The other 'houses' were also called after heroines, so there was 'Florence Nightingale' house, and a 'Joan of Arc' house, although, for the life of me, I cannot remember the name of the fourth house.

We were allocated dormitories according to our ages, with a couple of prefects in charge, who slept up on a platform at the end of the dormitory. A Mrs Wooley, our housemistress, was in charge of our building, so it was her job to oversee all the girls in her section. She had a book in which she kept everything written down, from our bowel movements to our periods. If you went for more than a couple of days without a bowel movement, you got a dose of castor-oil! Horrible, nasty stuff it was too; all thick and gloopy and colourless, served up in a thick glass. Mrs Woolley would tell us to hold our noses against the smell - which was revolting - and swallow quickly. Easier said than done!

Everyone tried to cheat by claiming they'd had bowel movements, but Mrs Woolley was no fool; she gave us regular doses of caster-oil anyway!

Then, there were the inevitable nit-hunting days too. Everything that could possibly happen was covered! Our school uniforms, the clothes for washing, and personal hygiene checked too. Nothing was left to chance!

We all slept in single beds on either side along the dormitory, with our heads to the wall, all our possessions in a small tin locker by the side of us. Having to look after our 'spaces' and keep our beds looking tidy, as nothing was ever allowed to make the dormitory look untidy. Something like the army!

The adjoining toilets, showers and sluices were great places to do your revision or 'mug up' before exams. Anyone doing exams next day would be 'cramming' away till after midnight; or earlier if some 'stinky' person had had to use the loo! There were a row of shower cubicles down one side, and five or six wash basins along the wall. With just four toilet cubicles along the other side, for about twenty of us girls; which were never enough, especially in the mornings; when many of us were left standing cross-legged in a queue as we waited impatiently! The dire threats we issued, if one of the girls was taking too long, was not at all ladylike! All the walls were tiled, and it was here that we used to place our washed handkerchiefs to dry. When you peeled them off the wall the following morning, they would look as if they'd been ironed.

A large jug of milk was brought to our dormitory every morning, with a hard biscuit each, which had to last us over the next hours 'study' period downstairs before we went in to breakfast. Then, Mrs Woolley came along with her little black book and the inevitable caster-oil.

Our 'study' classrooms were on the ground floor, under our dormitories. Here we studied from seven in the morning until eight, before marching off in our 'houses' to breakfast, with a further hours 'study' period after supper in the evening, before we retired to our dormitories for the night; that was at either end of a long days classroom work!

We breakfasted in the big dining hall between eight and eight-thirty in the morning. The boys at one end of the hall, the girls opposite. The teachers always sat up on the 'stage' for their meals. So they could keep an eye on the 'goings on' down below.

As you'd expect, it was very noisy in the dining hall. With hundreds of pupils tucking hungrily into breakfast, so with the din of knives forks and spoons being frantically applied, the steady hum of conversation, plus the scraping chairs etc., it was more like bedlam, but we were allowed to speak in there; albeit quietly!

Breakfast consisted of some bread and butter, marmalade if you were lucky, and tea. If your parents could afford 'extras' you could have scrambled eggs. I did not have this privilege, but I did get scrambled eggs only because the girl sitting beside me - whose parents were paying for this extra - couldn't stand the scrambled eggs they served, so she would quietly pass her plate on to me. The eggs weren't particularly good. Having bits of onion, tomato, and even potatoes mixed in to bulk it up, but I didn't mind. I was a young growing girl!

The lunches and dinners were no better... everything was bulked out with lentils, with all the food looking and tasting like stew! I'd swap my bit of bread with someone for a crust, and scooping out the inside, I'd fill the crust with a mashed-up concoction of potato, lentil and gravy; secreting this inside my blouse so I could have a snack during our evening study period.

And I wasn't the only one!

Throughout the study lessons, the lids of desks would go up – so the teacher in charge couldn't see us - as we chomped our way through our 'butties' which were now quite warm from their hiding places! I was a 'gutsy' little beggar! It's a wonder we didn't get food poisoning!

Mr and Mrs Bailey were the headmaster and headmistress at that time, and they were both extremely strict - especially Mrs Bailey, who could wither you with a glance! Luckily, I never, ever got her in any of my classes, as she taught the older children. But she was always there on a Saturday, sitting up on her balcony as she called out our names for 'pocket money'.

We were made to line up in our 'houses' and had to go up the steps smartly to get our few 'annas' each week - the amount of money being what our parents had agreed on. Mine was about four annas, which was roughly about 30p at that time, which I blew in the tuck shop within five minutes of receiving it.

Luckily I had brought sufficient toiletries with me to last the 'term', so my money could be spent on the lovely stick-jaw toffee made especially by the lady who ran the tuck shop. There were other things there I would have loved to have bought, but the stick-jaw toffee lasted a lot longer than anything else!

We had to line up in our 'houses' every morning, after breakfast; ready for 'sick parade'. Anyone feeling unwell would be marched over to the sick bay to see Sister Spencer who was in charge of the hospital. She was a fat, jolly person, who tended to the usual cuts and bruises, mumps and measles; and the real and imagined pains of growing teenagers; which she did rather well! I remember having mumps while at school, and having to stay in the school hospital for over three weeks, being kept busy by Sister Spencer with some sewing. Which I was now quite good at; thanks to all the rapped knuckles I got at the convent! I embroidered a complete set of table mats - with cut-out chrysanthemums - for a twelve-place table setting over the period I was incarcerated in the hospital, which was a good way of getting out of studying!

I loved our cookery teacher Mrs Fernandez. I think she was a Goan lady and she had lovely disposition and a passion for teaching us to cook. And jolly good she was too! I still have one of my exercise books from her class, showing the dishes we had to prepare, and some of the exams we were given. The afternoons passed quickly in her classes, and I was taught by her to cook and understand the ingredients I was using. Thereafter, whenever I was home on the holidays, I would be in the kitchen 'cooking' up some delicacy like banana fritters doused in sugar, or some other equally calorie-loaded tea-time treats!

The 'servants' children were the only other ones who were ready to try my concoctions!

The swimming pool at Barnes High School was right in the middle of a river. Somehow, they had managed to concrete the bottom and sides, so the water was being replaced all the time! 'How cool was that!' I loved swimming classes and sports too.

We were all very competitive at that time, none of this: 'children should not be made to feel inferior by competing' business.

Children thrive on competition!

We loved the competition, with the different 'houses' fiercely competing against one another, as the rest of the school children shouted encouragement for their 'houses'. And although I was just a 'titch', I could run with the best. But I could still never beat a girl called Catherine Palmer Wilson. She was a big girl, who came from South Africa, and no matter how hard I tried - I had to take two steps to every one of hers - I could never beat her! Luckily, she was in our 'house,' so we didn't lose any points.

Being good at sports meant Catherine and myself were the first two picked if ever there were 'sides' being made up, which was quite gratifying.

The only time I was left out was when we played hockey! I think I was just a tad too aggressive with my hockey stick, although I received quite a lot of knocks on my shins too! It was a great game to play if you had a grudge against someone. I remember when several girls 'ganged up' on one of the 'unpopular' girls; who exited the field in tears. She certainly managed to keep a civil tongue in her head after that!

I often wonder how it would be to have a 'woman only army' fighting wars! With their ability to think 'laterally' and fight really dirty, the enemy wouldn't stand a chance!

At school I was just one of many, until my big brother was transferred to Deolali. He was in the Army, and had been put in charge of supplies, finding time to come to the school occasionally to see me. Although as I said previously - there wasn't that much to do in Deolali!

I'll never forget the first time he came!

I was summoned to see Mrs Bailey, our headmistress, and went along with some trepidation, only to find my big brother - in his army uniform - taking tea with her and her husband on the balcony of their suite of rooms! He was always a handsome chap, and the old tartar was completely bowled over by his charm!

Ernest gave me a big wink as I was asked to join the tea party, and seemed at ease with our starchy 'head'. So there was I, sitting up there enjoying tea from a dainty china cup - much to the envy of my friends and the rest of the school - as the 'hoi polloi' looked on.

My brother came to visit often, always bringing the head mistress and staff 'things'. Like heaps of tinned goodies and anything he thought they might like. Plus food items for me too.

Our 'midnight feasts' in the dormitory after that were amazing! Eating toothpaste off the ends of our toothbrushes was a thing of the past! Now we could indulge in the best of everything! Using our fingers, we'd scoop out cold baked beans - followed by fistfuls of delicious jam - this too, straight from the big three or four pound tins. Then licking our fingers and hands clean, we'd retire to bed satiated and happy.

My brother was also allowed to take me out occasionally on a Saturday, when I got to tuck into egg and chips, or other restaurant meals. Sometimes, we went to the cinema and afterwards, I'd get to look around the vast store rooms that Ernest was in charge of, picking whatever took my fancy! Coming back to school loaded down with everything hungry girls wanted when they were far from home. Sitting down at night I'd regale the other girls with what I'd done during the day, and hand out sweets and chocolates to my best friends.

I was always popular then of course!

But by then, I was an 'old' girl. All of thirteen years!

I'd accumulated a few nick-names by then too, like fish face, fish-eyes, and bug-eye - all because of my surname Fisher, and my very large eyes! But hey, they didn't worry me in the least! As they say 'sticks and stones may break my bones, but words can never harm me!' Looking at a picture taken of me at that time I don't know why I wasn't as big as a barrel? Eating was my hobby!

I thought I'd be in big trouble when Ernest started dating one of my teachers; which I thought was a big mistake; but that too, turned out fine for me. The teacher in question signalling me out and asking me if I'd like to finish her 'supper' of lamb chops or one of the other delicious meals. The teachers were allowed to have their meals on a tray in their quarters. I think it was about this time that I decided I was going to become a teacher! Well, if I could order my own food!

I'm sure she deliberately ordered more than she could ever eat herself, just so as she could treat me, and I could see she fancied my brother by all the questions she fired at me! Did he have other girls, etc: Of course, I knew exactly what to say, my brother was a great coach!

But despite all this, I still got home-sick, crying into my pillow along with most of the other girls in the dead of night. Perhaps that's why the prefects sometimes sang to us. There was a girl called Peggy, who had a lovely voice, and sometimes if she wasn't too tired she'd sing us all to sleep. The songs were all invariably something to do with love. The prefects being older and always talking about boys; so I suppose their songs were sung as they thought of their sweet-hearts.

One of our prefects was a rather well endowed girl called Patsy. I really envied her 'sticky-out' boobs! Mine of course were like pancakes! Patsy was a large gregarious red-head who wore her hair in two pig-tails, and if there had been a 'burping' contest Patsy would have won it hands down! She'd start burping from the time she entered the dormitory - and continue until she reached her bed at the top of the room - some fifty yards away; throwing herself down on her bed with another almighty burp! But we all loved Patsy, she was really funny, and you could hear her coming - long before she put in an appearance.

I remember Barnes High School on the hill in Deolali with great affection. Our school motto used to be 'Onwards and upwards.' We couldn't wait for the end-of-term dance and party - which was held in Evans Hall - before going off home for the Christmas holidays. Everyone was so excited, and my packing took all of five minutes.

What had happened while we were away? Would our friends back at home still be there? Would our parents see any changes in us? The train taking us from Deolali to Bombay was filled with over-excited children who would be met by parents or travelling companions there, then scattered to every corner of India, from whence they'd come.

But we were always very glad to be making the journey back again to all our friends at school, when the holidays were over. The meeting point at Bombay station filled once more with chattering kids waiting to get back to Barnes High School, and the start of a new term.

CHAPTER TWENTY-NINE

Jitterbugging & Chewing Gum

Coming home from boarding school for the holidays was always magic! I'd run about excitedly, looking at all the things I'd missed while I'd been away. Renewing friendships, and trying to look 'cool', now that I was almost 'grown up'.

I was the only child at home sometimes, my other siblings now living away from home. My eldest brother Ernest was now in the regular army. Hazel my older sister having joined the W.A.A.F.I was stationed in New Delhi, and Billy was doing an apprenticeship at one of the larger electrical colleges attached to the railways.

During one school term my father was transferred to a small place called Dohad - not far from Bombay - on a temporary basis. The bungalow there was quite small, but as I was the last one living at home then it was more than big enough for the three of us. The train journey from school didn't take so long now, and as I threw myself into my mothers arms for a big hug - dad who'd come to fetch me home - beamed.

They'd had my bedroom, dressing room and toilet decorated in my favourite colours, and my window looked out onto an orchard of guava trees, great big, well-established ones. Everywhere you looked in the house was a big bowl of guavas. The whole place smelt of guavas!

I bet my father didn't waste his time trying to count them!

When my younger brother came home on his holidays, we used to frequent the 'Railway Institute' in Dohad. Yes even a small place like Dohad had its own Railway Institute! This lovely little Institute could be accessed from our back garden! A short hop, skip and jump... and we were there! And although a smaller version than the one in Ajmer, we liked it. With a bunch of other kids we used to roller-skate round the tennis courts. Just going round and round getting faster and faster. Then, tired but happy, we'd go inside the Institute for a glass of orange juice; the bartender having had a 'chitty' from father to say we could 'run' a tab.

Of course, we were very generous, treating some of our friends too well, until dad got the bar bill! All hell broke loose when he discovered the amount we'd allowed the 'tab' to go up to! Even though we tried to bluster our way out of it, by blaming it on the bartender, our privilege at the Institute was withdrawn, and we were 'barred' from going there.

I got my own back on father by climbing up one of the guava trees, and singing 'South of Pango Pango...,' and a song called 'Amapola, You Pretty Little Poppy...,' over and over again. Songs he hated... until he relented, and said we could go to the Institute, but there was to be no more 'tick' for us. Everything we had must be paid for out of our own money. In those days, pocket money was not really a done thing, and the only money we could hope for was birthdays and Christmases. So we resorted to cadging off our mates!

I remember my eldest sister coming to visit when she was on leave. She looked 'Ab-Fab' in the latest clothes. Her fingernails painted and smelling of perfume! But the best part was she could 'jitterbug' like a professional. Stationed in Delhi, where everything was 'happening', must have been really something! We were so proud when she came to the Railway Institute, all dressed up to the nines, with all the boys from five to fifty-five ogling her as she sashayed in.

Once I had to run all the way home to get her a pair of flat shoes, because she'd worn high heels that evening; coming back out of breath. But boy... was it worth it! She'd managed to get a good dancer to partner her, and when the band started up, those long legs of hers started bopping. Everyone's eyes popped, and left the dance floor to watch. A circle forming round the dancing pair! It was like something out of 'Grease'. They'd never seen the likes of all those steps! Fast, furious and fantastic! She was a hit! It was sad when she finally had to rejoin her 'buddies'.

Yes, the American influence was slowly taking over in India. We had many American forces stationed all over India, and they were even more generous than our own boys when it came to giving away things. I remember once, an American Troop train stopped right opposite our house – on the other side of the maidhan in Ajmer - and our servants went running to see the 'big loud men' who were leaning out of the windows wolf-whistling at anything that moved.

Eventually, the train moved off - but not before our servants had received bars of chocolate, tins of condensed milk, and what were called 'K' packs; a little box that contained rations for an American serviceman for a day. This would consist of all sorts of things, as there were several of these 'K' packs, one being for breakfast, and anther for dinner or lunch etc: Basically they contained the food required for one soldier; sometimes, a small tin of spam, tinned cheese, biscuits, and even chocolate - accompanied by toilet paper and the inevitable chewing gum. Our servants traded in some of the tins for money; the food not really being to their taste.

We loved the chewing gum, and even tried out the American slang words - until my father ordered us to stop.

Once, going back to boarding school, the train we were on was packed with American soldiers - all going to the depot at Deolali too - so we got acquainted. They turned out to be really nice boys, and father quite liked the way they called him 'Sir' all the time. I, of course, got all sorts of things to take to school, including silk stockings, Hershey chocolate bars, lipstick and several American comic books - really sought after by everyone at school, and at home.

Back in Ajmer, after our brief time in Dohad, we had a different bungalow, not too far away from where we used to live. I was still a bit of a tom-boy, but was beginning to dress more like a girl. I think I can pin-point the day I realised that I really was a girl.

I was at home on holiday from school and one evening tried out some nail polish, painting my fingernails bright scarlet. Waking up next morning the first thing I noticed were my bright red nails against the white of the sheets on my bed. And as I turned my hands this way and that way, the better to view them, I felt quite feminine!

The durzi was summoned to sew some dresses I'd designed. With one particular blue one with a sort of 'trellis-work' over the shoulders, very modern! I used to wear my hair longer then, the 'odious creatures' having finally given up on me. Wearing my pale blue dress and some subtle touches of make-up - so my parents wouldn't notice - I began to feel different, giving the performance of a lifetime as I sauntered into the Railway Institute one evening. Normally I'd dance around with the other girls, but this time, my dance card was soon full! Talk about swank! Knowing I was now being seen in quite a different light was G.R.E.A.T. As I was taken onto the dance floor, to be whirled around and around, I felt quite giddy!

And a boy actually asked if he could see me home!

But I had to refuse - my brother Billy having chaperoned me out that evening, and would of course, be taking me home again - because he'd been given strict instructions. What a bore? Still, I had had a great night, and there was much, much more to come.

I couldn't wait to get back to school, to tell all my friends there about my wonderful holiday. Waiting at the level-crossing gates was the boy I was really stuck on. I'd told him the time my train would be leaving, and there he was to wave me off. How magical was that! Father of course turned a blind eye and pretended not to notice me waving back. I think he realised his little girl was growing up!

From then on, I had 'crushes' on school teachers, boys at school, and even the odd girl. But being a girl was proving to be just as much fun as being allowed to play with boys. I couldn't believe it when the boy I was with treated me like an adult, and listened to my every word, as if I was suddenly some sort of genius?

Getting home, I'd look closely in the mirror... expecting to see some beauty looking back! But it was just me; great big green eyes staring back, scar on the tip of my nose, a sort of lop-sided look to my mouth, and nothing very special, just me.

Little monkey!

CHAPTER THIRTY

Burning Ghats & Evil Spirits

We children spent a fair amount of time in the cool of the evening playing on the maidhan. The big area with its huge boulders, nooks and crannies and nullahs being a great place for hide and seek and other games.

When the wind was right, there was kite-flying. We made our own kites sometimes too, with tissue paper and bits of stick - tied with bits of string. Any small 'tears' glued together with some sap from a cactus plant growing nearby. If you broke a small leaf off the plant a white sap oozed out. This was quite sticky, and used to set quickly, so was ideal for sticking paper together. Another source of glue was the gum from one of our neem trees; the amber liquid forming globules whenever the bark was damaged. Or we could revert to the old favourite; flour and water!

"Hold my kite and let it go when I tell you to," my brother Billy would order, because I was the youngest, and off I'd go... walking ever so carefully backwards as I held the delicate kite between my hands in case it tore.

"Stop," my brother would shout when the string had played out enough. I would then have to hold the kite high above my head, waiting for his next command. "O.K." he'd shout, and I'd release the kite, which should have climbed high into the sky - the wind taking the flimsy contraption easily - as my brother tugged away at the string. Sometimes the kite did sail up, up and away, but disasters often occurred... and I was always blamed!

"Stupid, that's not the way to do it," or "You let it go too soon dunderhead!" being just some of the unfair comments I had to put up with when it was really his fault.

Being a girl had its advantages though; my fingers were much more pliable than Billy's when it came to kite mending, compared to his clumsy efforts. Growing up I found I was a natural with this kite-flying lark.

We used to grind glass to mix with a paste, before coating the string for about fourteen or fifteen yards underneath the kite. This was used in a game called 'kutta' literally 'cutting' the string of another's kite. This game was played by old and young alike in India. There could be hundreds of kites of all shapes and sizes in the sky flying at any time, then suddenly people 'engaged' their kites in a fight.

Many of the kite-flyers stood on the tops of flat-topped roofs so they had the added advantage of a stiff breeze; playing out their long strings as the kites were taken higher and higher into the sky. You had to strain your eyes to keep track of the miniscule dots the kites became in the distance.

The game of 'kutta' would commence when two kites got entangled. Each kite flyer trying to do his best to literally 'saw' off the opponents' kite - their strings having been coated in glass - to send it fluttering down to the ground. Where it would land; to be caught by some urchin, or got entangled in the branches of some tree; trees everywhere in India sporting bits of colourful shredded paper, the torn and battered kites that once proudly rode the thermals, but were now firmly stuck fast in their branches.

There were plenty of accidents too, with kite flyers getting so carried away they sometimes forgot they were standing on their rooftops! The shallow parapets no barrier once someone had strayed too close to the edge!

Growing up in India in the early thirties meant making do, with whatever you had, whenever possible. It wasn't the throw-away society of today. Even though the Europeans living in India seemed to be well-off, compared to some Indians, they still had to make the most of what they had. Things from catalogues sent out from England taking months to arrive. Even after an item was of no further use to us, our servants would continue 'making' something of it.

Empty tins - mostly baked beans or fruit - were scrubbed out; the jagged edges left by tin-openers banged down and made smooth, were used as drinking vessels or storage. European clothing was given a make-over, and discarded furniture took on a whole new life after it had been re-painted and covered with Indian designs. An ugly old chest covered in brilliantly-painted flowers looking like some of the furniture you see today that sells for hundreds of pounds! Even our bland left-over food was spiced up by the methar's wife who added chillies and spices to make it more palatable for them.

They seemed to like our puddings though, rice pudding being a favourite of their son Nuthoo. He was about four or five years old and always licked his plate clean as a whistle afterwards. Rotating the plate as his busy little tongue flicked in and out at speed. I suppose it saved on washing up too! Of course when I attempted to do the same I was soundly told off for my trouble.

It was the custom for the employers to supply a hot cup of tea to all the working servants every day, so the khansama would brew up the biggest pot of tea at around ten o'clock every morning. It was made really strong too, with milk and sugar added and a slice of 'white' angrezi bread being handed out to each servant with it. Nearly all the servants would bring their own containers - generally rescued from the garbage - mostly an old baked-bean tin. Although some tried to buck the system by producing a large 'fruit-salad' tin which would have depleted the whole pot in one go! So it was stipulated that only one size of tin would be allowed. Not a bad size when you consider how much a baked bean tin can hold!

Our fresh bread came all the way from a bakery in Naisairbad, as did the newspapers, and my mothers weekly 'Times of India,' and our comics. We received the Beano, Dandy, Dennis the Menace and others. Knowing exactly what day and time they arrived; and would be up at the crack of dawn to make a mad dash for them when we heard the noisy old motorbike the delivery man rode. A fight between Billy and myself nearly always ensuing as to which got first pick!

"I'll stop all comics if this goes on," mother would threaten, but she never did; being too immersed in her own weighty paper. The comics kept us enthralled for most of the day. American comics much in demand too, so we would try and swop our 'latest' batch for a few of them. With all the derring-do going on in the comics it's no wonder we tried out our own dares?

"I dare you..." got us into some really tight places! One evening my ten year old brother Billy got onto the back of a pony that had not been 'broken in' properly. A car back-firing spooked the poor animal into bolting... with my brother clinging firmly on for dear life. Down an unmade road the beast bolted, kicking up its hind legs... my brother slipped from the saddle... his foot caught firmly in one stirrup. Billy was dragged along the rough road for yards on his back, before his foot finally came out of the stirrup; by which time his back was raw and bleeding.

My eldest brother and sister were horrified... and terrified of what our parents would do, because they hadn't prevented Billy's accident. Luckily one of the neighbours came running on hearing his screams, and lifted him indoors; applying iodine to his back; so you can imagine his renewed screams! Iodine being that terrible medication that hurt even more than any cuts or bruises! As Billy was a 'delicate' child my mother swooned when she saw the extent of his injuries. My brother and sister were both punished.

But it hadn't deterred us from any future escapades.

Hindu funeral processions often passed on the road that ran past our bungalow, on their way to the burning ghats. The family of the deceased walking behind the figure - bound in white and lying atop of a wooden stretcher. The head of the family would throw handfuls of coins and sweets out to encourage even more Indian people to join in the procession. Everyone chanting 'Ram, Ram Sutta hai', as they walked slowly along.

"Wonder what they do to the bodies?" Billy whispered one day.

"They burn them," I answered; a little miss know-all.

"Yes but how?"

"I don't know I only heard mum saying one day that burning the bodies was the best thing for everyone in India."

"But why? Anyway I don't want to be burned."

"Not us silly, English people get buried in cemeteries."

"So why don't they bury Indians in cemeteries too?"

"The same reason they aren't allowed in the Railway Institute I suppose."

"Wonder what they look like when they get burned," Billy said looking at me with that look, and you could practically see the thoughts spinning around in his head!

"We'll never know will we? I can't imagine we'd be allowed to go there."

"But we could sneak over there...?" Billy said looking all mysterious.

Every time we heard the familiar chant of 'Ram, Ram, Sutta Hai,' we would look at one another as if to say... 'Shall we?'

Curiosity had got the better of us, until one day everything slotted in nicely. We saw another procession and decided it was now or never!

The burning ghat was situated quite a distance away, but we had our bikes. It was a summer holiday so there was no school; and our parents were both away for the day! We wouldn't get a better chance! So getting our bikes we followed the funeral procession.

It was a warm day and as we didn't want to overtake the procession itself, we stopped several times in the shade of some trees until we were not too far away from the actual place. Everyone at the funeral seemed intent on watching the proceedings and took no notice of two small children hiding some distance away.

After what seemed like ages with the sun burning through our flimsy clothes we saw the flame being applied to the pyre. Clouds of smoke eventually turned into leaping flames that surrounded the body, as the flames shifted and danced.

But nothing happened!

We'd spent all afternoon waiting for just a pile of wood to burn!

"I'm going home," I said sulkily, turning away; and heard my brother's loud intake of breath! Turning back I followed his wide-eyed gaze... back towards the leaping flames; the body on the pyre was moving... a white figure amid the red flames was slowly sitting upright! Reluctantly removing our gaze from the rising body we looked at one another and the very look on each others faces was enough to make us jump up in fright, and make a mad dash to where our bikes lay. Terrified of that rising figure and thinking we'd be punished for witnessing some sacred ceremony, just by being there! What if the dead person was coming to get revenge?

Without a word we jumped onto our bikes and peddled frantically - looking over our shoulders from time to time - as we high-tailed it back to the safety of our home. We couldn't tell our parents as we were even more terrified about what they'd do to us; so had to live in fear for days thinking something terrible was going to happen to us.

There are so many myths and legends circulating in India about evil spirits after all.

With goddesses like kali - the black-faced evil one; then there are the Djinns (mischievous spirits) and others too. Djinns take great delight and pleasure in punishing humans for any harm that had been done to them in the past. So they could shift-shape. You could never be quite sure what shape they might take, when they came to you seeking revenge. So Indians believe if you tried to live a good wholesome life perhaps, just maybe... the Djinns would leave you alone. But of course it is better to stay on the safe side as well. Belief has it that spirits do not like loud noises... so any Indian going home alone after dark always sang at the top of his voice to keep those dratted spirits away!

Iron is said to be one of the repellents to keep evil away from a house, so a small piece of iron or a knife buried under the step leading to the door is considered beneficial. No self-respecting evil spirit would risk going over that threshold!

'Saithan' (the devil) is said to be another shape-shifter, with so many people ready to take advantage of the innocent; he could be any one of the strangers you meet? It is believed that wearing the colour saffron could give you some protection. And children - who are thought to be the most vulnerable - are protected from the 'evil eye' by the use of heavy black kohl markings around their eyes. This was said to repel the stare of any evil spirit looking to harm the child.

There are some very crafty spirits too, especially the 'Churails'. These generally take the shape of a woman so they could wear the fully-gathered skirts to hide their feet; which pointed in the opposite direction to those of normal people. If someone thought they were being followed, and glanced around to see who was following, but saw the person's feet pointing in the opposite direction he automatically thought that person was walking away! Big mistake! That was what the Churail wanted you to think. The crafty Churail was in fact creeping up on you. But by the time you realised your mistake, it was too late anyway.

'Gayal' another spirit came to haunt anyone who had 'messed up' with the proper burial rites of someone who had died. Returning to wreak his revenge upon the sons and others that had let him down! The threat of Gayal usually ensures that the proper funeral rites are performed.

'Pacu Pati' is a powerful vampire, deemed to be the lord of all beings of mischief. It is said to appear at night in cemeteries and places of execution.

Then there is 'Rakahasa' who is yet another vampire and whose name translates as 'The Injurer'. This spirit assumes the form of a beautiful woman, luring men to their death. She is said to live in certain trees and can induce vomiting and indigestion in people who stray into its territory.

There are many, many more, but I wouldn't want you to have nightmares!

Anyway if you have lived a blameless life you've nothing to fear. And you too could always make some sort of peace offering, couldn't you?

'Poogas' are offerings made to the gods and other deities. These are made daily by Indian people all the time. Sometimes for a woman to be blessed with child - preferably a son - or that the crops could grow abundantly and especially for the monsoons to arrive after a very hot dry summer. Some Indians will not do anything without first consulting a sooth-sayer or fortune teller to find out which month, day or time is the most propitious for a marriage, birth, celebration or other events taking place.

CHAPTER THIRTY-ONE

Murder most foul

The worship of the Goddess Kali - depicted with a terrible expression on her face, with her black tongue sticking out of her mouth, and a necklace of snakes and human sculls around her neck - was associated with the Thugee movement in India during the twelfth century.

Followers of this cult robbed and murdered travellers as sacrifices to Kali and in her name many other atrocious acts were committed; all carried out by using rigidly prescribed forms and ancient religious rites on their victims, before and after the killings. This was said to have been revealed to them by a complicated set of omens left by the goddess herself, with even a portion of the 'spoils' they took from the poor travellers being allocated to Kali herself.

According to the 'Guinness Book of Records' the Thugee (robbers and assassins) cult was responsible for approximately 2,000,000 deaths. Although it is believed they existed a hundred and fifty years earlier than it was first thought, with the British suppressing their activities in the 1830s. But it was not uncommon to hear about these activities - on a far lesser scale of course - still being perpetrated in India during the thirties.

Nowadays, Kali is revered as a benevolent mother-goddess. The name Kali or Kala being the name for the colour black. Some say that she is the 'Ultimate Reality' and Source of Being.

Then there were the 'goondas' or hooligans and the dacoits or armed robbers which was once quite a profession at one time, refined in India by a chap named Phoolan Devi. The title for the most legendary dacoit of all was held by Daku Nirbhay Gujjar. Between 1939 and 1955 he had notched up 1,112 dacoities, 185 murders, countless ransom kidnappings, and was involved in ninety police encounters; even killing thirty-two policeman.

The most frightening of the robberies were carried out by Thugees who came by night, taking advantage of the hot weather and open windows. Being dark-skinned they would shed all their clothes, then cover themselves with oil before slipping quietly into the house with the intention of robbery. They often held a knife between their teeth... just in case! They moved quietly - camouflaged by the night and their dark skin - so were able to slip away - aided by their oil-slicked bodies if anyone dared to apprehend them. Often using the knife they carried.

It was no wonder most Indians avoided the darkness, and would be safely tucked up in bed if they had no good reason to be out after dark. If by chance they were forced to be out and about they always tried to stay in groups - talking loudly. If alone they sang loudly; believing this would keep any evil spirits or dacoits at bay.

Most dark nights you would hear some poor lone soul singing badly as he tried valiantly to stop his teeth chattering through sheer terror of being set upon by 'something' or 'someone'.

The Indian 'bud-mashes' (bad men) were not alone in the robbery with violence stakes then... there were others doing the same thing all over the world.

In England during the seventeenth and eighteenth centuries the word 'Highwayman' was used to describe criminals who robbed travellers along the public highways, also called bandits and footpads in London. The more famous of the English ones were Macheath, also known as 'Mack the Knife'. Then there were Dick Turpin and Robin Hood; while Jack the Ripper did his foul deeds in and around the dark streets and alleyways of London.

In Australia the 'Bushrangers' were outlaws who used the Australian 'bush' as a refuge to hide from the authorities, between committing their robberies; also targeting small-town banks or coach services. Many robbers were escaped convicts fleeing from the early Australian penal colonies. These men unable to support themselves in the harsh wilderness turned to stealing supplies from remote settlements and travellers. Then with the gold rush of the 1850s and 1860s, they were able to cash in on the poor hard-working pan-handlers; stealing their hard-earned gold dust. Famous names included John Gilbert and Ben Hall who were shot; while Ned Kelly was hanged in 1880.

Meanwhile back in Ajmer, there were also robberies, killings and murders committed; but not that many against the Europeans who were more than well protected; hence the chowkidars who patrolled through the night as they kept watch. Although many of these 'happenings' were not known to us at that time, only one was committed anywhere near where we lived; although the odd incident was heard about from time to time.

Our small purpose-built Post Office was situated about four or five hundred yards away from where we lived, and had just the one room; some twelve foot square, with a small windowless toilet attached. There was just enough room for one person inside this small enclosure, and the Postal worker used to sit behind the grilled window as he dispensed the stamps or postal orders etc from behind the grille; the shelves all within easy reaching distance. The telegraph machine always sat beside him on his desk/ counter top - ready to relay messages at all times. The small gap under the window only big enough to allow letters or parcels of a certain size; the window could be opened wider to allow larger parcels; but was rarely used; the larger parcels nearly always taken to the big Post Office nearer town.

When our servant returned one afternoon to report the Post Office was closed, my mother was curious. She knew the opening hours of the Post Office by heart, but decided the postal worker had probably had an extended lunch break, so decided to wait till later.

One of fathers men was requested to do the errand a while later. The Chaprassi (office servant) in his smart khaki uniform and stiff moustache, bristling with officialdom didn't take long to reach the small office, where he proceeded to rattle the window to summon the Post Office worker within; peering in through the dirt-encrusted window when no one appeared.

It was a cloudy day with the sun hiding behind some clouds making it difficult to see into the small unlit room.

By this time several Indians - also wanting to do business - had gathered outside the building; some coming just to see what all the 'tamasha' was about.

"What's up brother," called one chap.

"Well, the Post Office should be open by now and no one is answering?" The Chaprassi replied.

"Hai, normally we see the man when he comes for his lunch," called another onlooker.

"Maybe he's asleep," offered a third.

"What with all the banging I'm doing," scoffed the Chaprassi as he bent forward to look through the double thickness of the dirt-grimed glass window and iron grille, into the office once more.

"Hai, I can just about see the lazy chap. He's sitting there with his blanket over his head having a great nap." He laughed at the gathering crowd who all laughed with him. But further banging still did not bring any response from the sleeping man.

"Perhaps something has happened to him," called a man in the crowd.

"Well yes I can see that," replied the Chaprassi, "he could have had a heart attack or something."

"Have you tried the door?" Someone asked.

"Yes, but it seems to be bolted from the inside."

"Here let me have a look," another chap said, pushing his way through the big crowd now there. And wiping more dirt away he peered through into the room; placing both his hands on either side of his face the better to see inside.

"Yes, I see his red blanket..." he began, and then let out an almighty cry as he staggered back away from the window in terror.

"What, what is it," asked the Chaprassi. But the man was shivering in fright and could hardly speak.

"It's not... it's not... it's not a blan...ket..." he stammered... "Its blood...blood, its blood I tell you," his voice dropped to a whisper. Staggering back from the window - his face looking shocked - he looked around at the other shocked faces and suddenly got his voice back.

"He's covered in blood, it's not a blanket, I tell you it's blood, and it's everywhere," he shouted to the crowd.

As everyone clamoured to see for themselves, the sun came out of hiding and lit up the room for all to see and soon everything became clear. It *was* blood, and it seemed to be covering everything in the room.

Taking charge the Chaprassi told some men to stay at the crime scene; although elephants couldn't have dragged anyone away that day; while he went to get help. Then he legged it to the nearest place he knew - my fathers office at the Workshops, where he blurted out his story.

My father summoned the local police via the telegraph service, and sent the Chaprassi back to wait until the police arrived.

When the two policemen arrived, they strolled over to the building and began questioning everyone who had been present earlier, before making an attempt to gain entry into the obviously locked and bolted door. Deciding it would be impossible to break it down they decided the window might be a better option, but it took them several attempts with a crow-bar to force an entrance; one of the policeman having to go in the broken window to open the door from the inside.

The man had been warned to be careful not to disturb anything as he slipped in... then slipped about in the sticky mess of blood that covered everything. Trying to avert his eyes from the gruesome sight of the headless body still sitting in the chair - his head cleanly sliced off at the base of his neck. The head had rolled onto the floor where it stared up with unseeing eyes; and what was first seen as a red blanket covering his shoulders, was indeed blood. Bright, red blood that had spurted from the severed arteries to cover the body in the chair, the ceiling walls and everything in the room; before seeping slowly to the floor where it lay congealing. The only footprints evident were those of the policeman who had entered via the broken window; his were the only footprints crossing the threshold - made as he exited the murder scene.

It did not seem possible that so much blood could have come from one person! The head had been so cleanly sliced off and so quickly that the poor mans heart must have continued pumping blood to make it spray everywhere! As the door was still bolted from the inside - until it was opened by the policeman - who on earth could have killed the man? Even the sharpest sword would have had to be swung in an arc to decapitate someone's head from their body?

The opening in the metal grille of the window was not nearly wide enough to allow someone to wield a sword or sharp knife through? It would have had to be the tiniest person who was able to squeeze through the gap through which transactions took place, it being barely twenty inches in length, and about five inches deep.

Had this been the work of Thugees? If so, how had they managed to kill in broad daylight? Decapitate a man locked up safely in a well-protected building? Without anyone having seen them come or go? Outside was a busy thoroughfare used by many people who passed the Post Office as they went to and from about their business?

This case remained unsolved as far as I know for many years. Although many explanations were bandied about over the years, as to why and how this murder took place at all.

Maybe there was something about the myths and legends in a country as complex and complicated as India?

CHAPTER THIRTY-TWO

1948 Leaving India

Many Indians believe the world is created and destroyed every few million years. According to some religious Hindus and some Hindu historians, records show that the present history of the world is now well over 7000 years.

Throughout this time there have been invaders who have come to different parts of India. The first known invaders were the Aryans, who arrived in north India around 1500 B.C. These Aryans fought and pushed the local dark-skinned people (Dravidians) southwards. After the Aryans others came, like Alexander the Great, and later the Kushans, Huns and much later the Muslin invaders; Turks, Arabs, Afghans and others. Later the Europeans came; Portuguese, Danish, Dutch, French and the English. In between the many invaders from foreign parts the Indians also established their own kingdoms and empires; fighting among themselves to expand their kingdoms boundaries.

A single kingdom had never ruled the whole of India.

These different kingdoms created different aspects of Indian history, hence the different religions, gods and heroes. Alongside the different empires there were also small kingdoms which ruled small parts of India. When the world famous Mogul Empire in the north of India collapsed, it fell into many small states. So that during the time we lived in Rajasthan, there were many such kingdoms, their rulers belonging to the Rajput caste; who still symbolize the warrior castes in India today.

Legend has it that when Columbus tried to get to India by sailing westwards, he presumed the earth was round, so he would eventually get to India if he sailed ever westwards! He ended up in America whose existence was not known at that time; Columbus thinking he'd arrived in India, called the natives of America 'Indians'.

The British control of India was a result of several factors; they ruled India via its provinces and Princely States. The Provinces were British territories completely under British control. The Princely States were in British India with a local ruler or king with titles such as Maharaja, Raja, Maharana, Rana, Nizam, Badshah and other titles, meaning king or ruler in different Indian languages.

As Europeans living in India during the many difficult years leading to India's Independence, the last few years we lived there were fraught with bad memories. After hundreds of years of living, working and laughing together, the people of India fought amongst themselves. Bloody battles ensued when the politicians decided it best to partition India; the Muslims to live in Pakistan and a small part of east India, and the Hindu's to live in the rest of India.

The killings that followed were horrendous, with train-loads of innocent people massacred as they tried to get to one or the other places designated for the different factions. Women were raped and murdered and small children were beaten to death. It was like living through a nightmare! The 'Quit India' movement daubed those very words on the houses of English people still living in India, although most of them were pacifists. Many Europeans had already left India, but my parents had yet to come to a decision about our future, and I was at boarding school at Deolali when my sister came to take me home!

We were leaving India for England. It was 1948, and I was seventeen at the time, and just about to sit for my final exams. Instead I had to bid a reluctant farewell to my school friends and travel back home to Ajmer. Along with the fear there was excitement too, about going to live in England; a place I felt I already knew from my fathers many descriptions.

But now we were actually going to live there!

Back home in Ajmer there was a great deal of bustle as all our possessions were to be sold; a lifetimes collection of personal items and furniture carefully chosen by my parents, most of it too heavy and cumbersome for use in England. As a temporary measure we would be staying at my aunts in Woking, Surrey, before buying a place of our own.

It was very hard deciding what to take and many of my things had to be given away. The servants whom we had known all our lives were being left behind.

It was funny getting our passports done and once again the durzi was summoned to make new clothes for the colder climes of Blighty. We were going to be sailing on a big P&O Liner called 'Strathmore', leaving from Bombay; the journey would last some seventeen or eighteen days.

As we were travelling first class, we were told we would require evening wear for attending the grand dinners in the evening, followed by dancing and cabaret acts later. So of course I just had to have lots of dresses; the poor durzi working flat out for several weeks with sewing my new frocks. I was very pleased with the way my designs had turned out.

My mother - whose parents were both dead - wasn't all that keen to be going to a cold country like England, but she knew my father longed to go back to his own country.

I couldn't believe it when the final day came!

We said our goodbyes, the tears falling thick and fast when we realised we might never see some of our neighbours and friends again. Our old ayah - who was ready to retire - gave me some pretty glass bangles to wear, the tears running down her brown weather-beaten cheeks. I kept promising that I would come back and see them all, and eventually father had to put his foot down.

"If we are going to get that boat we'd better catch this train," he said looking at his watch. We reluctantly got into the tongas, our new luggage piled high in one tonga alone; the four of us squeezing into the other, and we were soon heading for the station.

Our train passed the back of our old bungalow at Five Bungalows Road, where we used to live and then the countryside we'd grown up in. Then as the train gathered speed we left everything familiar far behind as we headed for our new life abroad.

In Bombay we stayed at a Hotel for the night, ready to board the ship next day. It was fun sightseeing and dining out in a restaurant and I don't think any of us got much sleep that night. Billy and I far too excited. We couldn't wait to get on that big liner that would be our home for the next few weeks.

Next morning we headed for the docks, and saw the big ship towering above us. It looked enormous! We couldn't believe we would actually be sailing in it! But as we climbed the gangway we knew this was for real.

White-uniformed stewards showed us to our cabins, and when they left Billy and I ran around examining everything. The small rooms reminding us of the train journeys with their tiny wash basins and bunk beds. And soon Billy and I were ready to go up on deck to 'explore'.

"You'll have to remember which deck we're on," mother warned, but we of course knew everything!

Leaving our parents having the inevitable pot of tea we practically ran off. It was our first time on a ship and there was so much to see. Making our way up to the top deck we found we could look down on the quayside and see people still arriving. There were so many people milling about; with bands playing in the bright sunshine, making it seem like Christmas. The poor Indian bandsmen sweated in their heavy uniforms as they played all the well-known tunes.

My brother and I knew which deck our cabin was on, but finding it again was impossible, so we were quite exhausted by the time one of the stewards finally showed us the way back.

Strolling along the decks later, the loud-speakers announced... "Would Mr Fisher and his family please go to 'A' deck?" We all looked at one another as we wondered what it was all about!

"What have you two been up to?" questioned father, certain that we'd been up to something on our 'snooping' quest. We looked blankly at him and shook our heads.

"We didn't touch anything, honest," we promised. There was nothing for it but to go up and see what we were wanted for. Climbing up the stairs we finally reached 'A' deck and approached one of the white-suited officers there.

"I believe I was wanted," father said to the man giving his name.

"Ah yes Mr Fisher," he said, shaking father's hand, "if you'd like to follow me." And as we followed him along the deck my brother and I held hands - hoping we really hadn't done anything.

There were dozens of people strolling about on 'A' deck, and some stopped to wonder at the group of uniformed men who were waiting there so patiently. Then as we skirted around them we suddenly realised they were the people who wanted to see us!

There was a whole delegation of my father's men; all dressed in khaki uniforms, their boots and belts polished to perfection and as we approached them the men stood stiffly to attention. One man who had obviously been chosen as their leader stepped forward, and saluted smartly. He explained that they had wanted to give my father a good send-off for all the kindness he'd shown them in the past. Then the man took one step backwards to where a very large basket of flowers stood. Carefully selecting the largest and best garland of flowers, he placed it reverently around my father's neck, saluting smartly. My mother got a smaller one and then I - a seventeen year old teenager squirming in embarrassment - received a garland too. I wanted the ground to open and swallow me!

After all there was I all of seventeen, trying to look sophisticated, and this was happening!

More and more people had stopped to look at what was going on and as the men stepped forward putting yet more garlands around our necks it must have seemed we were really quite important people. But all I wanted to do was run and hide!

Eventually after the garlanding ceremony, the men stood in a straight line before my father and saluted as one. My father standing stiffly to attention saluted them in return; then without the least bit of shame I saw those men and my father with tears rolling down their faces as they said their final farewells to one another.

I don't suppose I'll ever see anything like it for the rest of my life!

They had brought us fruit, candy and nuts for our voyage too, and as spontaneous clapping broke out from all the assembled people looking on, my father said a last farewell to those men who represented many of the others he'd met during his long stay in India.

Although he was pleased to be going 'home' his heart was breaking for the other country he'd come to love.

GLOSSARY OF INDIAN TERMS

A
adrak - *ginger*
aik - *one*
alloo - *potato*
almirah - *wardrobe*
angrezi - *English*
arrey - *oh/exclamation*
atcha - *o.k.*
ayah - *nurse-maid*
A.W.O.L - *absent without leave*

B
badmash/budmash - *bad man/rascal*
baksheesh - *gratuities*
bargh - *garden*
batman - *army helper*
beedies - *Indian cigarettes*
bhisti - *water carrier*
bookah - *hungry*
brinjalls - *aubergines*
Bronski Bullets - *nuggets of compressed coal dust*
bun-currow - *close it/them*
burra - *big*

C
chai - *tea*
chaprassi - *office servant*
chit/chitty - *note/letter/ promissory note*
chokra - *boy servant*
chota - *small*

chota-peg – *small measure of spirits*
chupplies – *slippers/sandals earthenware cups*
coolies – *hired labourers/ luggage handlers*

D
dekshi - *saucepan*
dhobi - *washer man*
dhood - *milk*
dhoti - *loin cloth*
dhurri - *rug*
djinns - *mischievous spirits*
durzi - *tailor*

G
godown - *store room/servants quarters*
gulal powder - *powdered dye*

H
hai - *yes*
hodhi - *brick container for water*
huzoor - *sir/honorary title*

J
jaffrey - *woven screen*
jarin - *tea cloth*
janter-manter - *nonsense*
Jemadhar - *Indian officer*
juldi - *quickly*
juldi-currow - *do it quickly*

K

khuss-khuss - *aromatic roots for water screens*
kithna-hai - *how much?*
kulfi - *ice-cream*
kurta - *long shirt*

L

lal-bargh - *red gardens*
lal-boochie - *red insect*
lathi - *5 foot stick with metal tip*
lusoon - *garlic*

M

maidhan - *open space/field*
mali - *gardener*
marlin - *woman vegetable seller*
mela - *fair/festival*
memsahib - *sahib's lady*
methar - *sweeper*
M.O. - *medical officer*
muckers - *mates*
mugals - *Mongols*
mutter-ka-fullee - *peas*

N

naga - *snake*
nai - *no*
nimbu-pani - *lime water*
nullahs - *gullies/deep ditches*
NCO - *non-commissioned officer*

O

oppo's - *mates/literally opposites*

P

paan - *betel leaf said to aid digestion*
pagli - *mad*
paisa/pice - *money of very little value*
pathan - *ethnic Afghan tribe*
poogas - *offerings*

R

rackhis - *wrist-bands*

S

saag - *greens for cooking*
sahib - *sir/master*
sari - *head and body covering*
seer - *kilo/aprox: 2lbs*
sev - *spicy, crispy fried snack*
shaithan - *Satan/devil*
shikari - *hunting expedition*

T

tamasha - *big show*
Tiffin box - *large food container*
tik-hai - *all right/O.K.*
thugee - *robber/murderer*
tonga - *horse-drawn two wheeled carriage*

W

wallah - *man/seller as in tonga-wallah*